Jeremiah Wesley Bray

A history of English critical terms

Jeremiah Wesley Bray

A history of English critical terms

ISBN/EAN: 9783744748681

Printed in Europe, USA, Canada, Australia, Japan

Cover: Foto ©ninafisch / pixelio.de

More available books at **www.hansebooks.com**

A HISTORY

OF

ENGLISH CRITICAL TERMS.

BY

J. W. BRAY, A.M.

PROFESSOR OF ENGLISH, JOHN B. STETSON UNIVERSITY.

BOSTON, U.S.A.:
D. C. HEATH AND COMPANY.
1898.

Copyright, 1898,
BY J. W. BRAY.

PREFACE.

THE purpose of the following work is to trace the changes of meaning which have taken place in the chief terms employed in English criticism. It is intended to be purely a study in criticism, and not to repeat information which can be obtained from an ordinary dictionary. The organizing idea of the work is found in the grouping of the terms in the Appendix. It is assumed that if the history of two or three of the most important terms of each group is given in full, the history of the synonymous and negative expressions will also have been given, at least as far as their critical and literary significance is concerned. Hence the secondary terms are given but scant notice, and their critical import is to be gathered mostly from the larger terms of their respective groups.

The history of the unimportant terms is thus given only in outline. Extensive tables were constructed showing the first use and frequency of occurrence at different times with regard to each critical term. These tables have been employed very largely in determining the relative influence of the different critical terms, and they furnish the basis for many statements, the authority for which it has not been possible to present in the printed text.

The present investigation grew out of class work in Criticism in the University of Chicago. It was found that the study of Criticism was vague and uncertain as long as the terms were left undefined, about which as central points the critical discussions usually turn. Prof. Wm. D. MacClintock suggested the present undertaking, and he has aided very materially in its prosecution. As completed, it represents more than three years of almost continuous labor.

About fourteen hundred terms have been mentioned or defined in historical perspective,— terms all of which have been employed in applied criticism as a direct means of estimating literary work. The history of the changes of meaning in such terms bears the same relation to Rhetoric as practice does to theory; and innumerable data are furnished in the present work for the historical study of Æsthetics. Applied Criticism, in fact, is the common meeting ground for rhetorical theory and the æsthetic instincts; the final test of the truthfulness and accuracy of the one, and of the genuineness and strength of the other. And this, which is true of Criticism in general, is especially true of those concentrated methods of criticism which find expression in the use of critical terms.

Among the best critics of late, there is a decided tendency toward a more careful and discriminative use of critical terms. This is only saying that the study of literature has, to a certain extent at least, become aware of its own methods and assumptions. No one critic has ever made use of half the critical vocabulary which is here presented. Wrong constructions of meaning have been given to terms, and controversies have been waged with no real ground for disagreement. Much needless confusion would be avoided by placing in clear relief the historical sequence of meanings which has taken place in the different terms; by remembering that any meaning once developed in a term tends to persist in some manner to the present; that though terms and words fade and pass away, principles abide and remain. And this represents the standpoint and purpose of the following work.

J. W. B.

INTRODUCTION.

I. What is a Critical Term?

BEFORE entering upon the history of the different critical terms, it will first be necessary to determine as accurately as possible what a critical term is, by what formal signs or characteristics it may be recognized, and what part it plays in the general process and methods of criticism. In order to do this, it may perhaps be best to begin with the most simple and typical use of a critical term, and then trace the modification of this simple type into the most complex, intricate, and uncertain forms that occur in actual criticism.

There are two elementary uses and forms of statement for critical terms. The most simple and typical form of statement occurs when the term is the unstudied expression of a spontaneous feeling,—a feeling which represents an æsthetic appreciation of some unified portion of literary work. The critic, let us suppose, has just read the literary production. His mind passes over it swiftly in review again and again. Certain features of the composition tend to rise into prominence more than others, — the language perhaps, the sentiment, the imagery, its truthfulness to actual life, — but these are quickly blended again into the general unified impression. The attention of the critic is wholly occupied with the literary work. It thoroughly arouses his sensibilities and feelings, which, by their inherent force, call for expression in language. Unconsciously as it were, the intense æsthetic feeling appropriates some word or phrase for its expression. A critical judgment is thus spontaneously formed. Some unified portion of literature is the subject, the appropriated word or phrase is the predicate of the critical judgment. The attention is centred upon the subject of the judgment; the predicate, or critical term, is, so far as relates to the immediate experience, evolved wholly out of the subject.

In the second elementary use of a critical term, the attention is divided between the predicate and subject of the critical judgment. The discriminating and selective powers of the mind are brought into full play in determining the word or phrase by which to characterize the literary work. The literary work may have been quite as fully appreciated by the critic as in the former type of judgment. But the æsthetic feeling which it aroused has passed for the most part into the memory. Continual effort is required to recall it into the focus of attention. One critical term after another is suggested by it, or is brought to it for comparison; and the one which is finally chosen, is usually felt to be more or less inadequate to indicate the original feeling in its fulness. A relation of some kind is asserted to exist between the subject and the predicate of the critical judgment, but they are not identified with each other. They represent two experiences intellectually joined, and not a single experience blended into a close emotional unity.

These two elementary uses of a critical term may be represented by the following forms of statement:

I. This poem is sublime.
II. This poem has sublimity.

The first may be called the æsthetic type of critical judgment, the second, the scientific type. Under one of these two general types, all uses whatever of critical terms may be classified.

In the scientific type of judgment, the predicate is not identified with the subject, is not taken up into it. A poem may have or contain a multitude of things which are of no literary significance whatever. One can never tell in this form of statement whether the predicate represents an essential or only an accidental trait of the literary work; whether the subject or literary work is characterized as a whole or only in some of its unimportant details. Hence the predicate can be regarded as a complete critical term only in so far as it conforms to the æsthetic type of a critical judgment, in so far as the characterizing word or phrase results immediately from the feeling aroused by some unified portion of literary work.

On the other hand, the scientific type of judgment is an essential prerequisite for the development of the æsthetic type. It continually presents possibilities for the wider and yet wider activity of the æsthetic feelings and sensibilities, — possibilities a few of which are appropriated and made use of, but many of which are not. The primitive æsthetic predicate is a mere exclamation of satisfaction and approval. It is the discriminating influence of the scientific method of judgment that causes this primitive critical term to become differentiated into all the subtle distinctions which critical terms now possess. The two types of critical judgment are thus complementary and indispensable to each other. The predicate of the scientific type possesses relative critical significance, but it is to the predicate of the æsthetic type of judgment that one must look for the most representative use of a critical term.

The great body of actual criticism, however, does not conform exactly to either of these types of judgment. Terms are scarcely ever, if at all, purely æsthetic in their significance, and the predicate of the scientific form of judgment is always more or less identified with the subject, and thus has, to that extent, the full force of a critical term. It is only within the present century that these two types of critical judgment have in theory been distinguished from each other, and have been assumed as the bases for distinct systems of criticism. The types given are ideal forms, by means of which it will now be necessary to explain the complex forms of actual criticism.

The simplest variation of the ideal forms arises from

the grammatical modification of the copula, from the different methods employed in connecting the subject with the predicate of the critical judgment. Of the æsthetic type of judgment, the chief grammatical variation consists in the omission of the copula, and the placing of the characterizing word or phrase as an immediate adjective modifier of the subject. *E. g.*: —

> Eloquent and stirring passages. T. ARNOLD, Man. of Eng. Lit., p. 248.

There are many grammatical variations of the scientific type of judgment. In all instances alike, however, a preposition intervenes between the subject and the predicate in such a manner as to make them be identified with each other only in part. *E. g.*: —

> The easy vigour *of* Horace. J. WARTON, II., p. 259.
> Shakespeare hath . . . deformed his best plays *with* prodigious incongruities. HURD, I., p. 69.
> There is great picturesque humour *in* the following lines. T. WARTON, H. E. P., p. 187.
> The Taming of the Shrew is . . . *full of* bustle, animation, and rapidity of action. HAZLITT, Shak., p. 219.

Such grammatical modifications of the types, however, do not really complicate the use nor render difficult the recognition of critical terms. They are little more than paraphrases which easily reduce to the simple types. But they do give evidence of the intimate relation which exists between the two types, and indicate how these types blend imperceptibly into each other.

The real complication in the use of critical terms arises from the influence of two tendencies, — from the tendency to analyze, and from the tendency to use figurative language. Analysis is characteristic of the scientific type of judgment, figurative language of the æsthetic type.

The analytic tendency manifests itself primarily in the subject of the critical judgment. The possible predicates, which have been discriminated and rejected, do not appear in the predicate of the completed judgment. In the subject, on the other hand, the literary work, or some portion of it, considered in its unity, furnishes a standard of reference by which the extent of the analysis can easily be determined. This differentiation of the subject may be roughly classed as of four general kinds.

One of the most common subjects of the critical judgment in actual criticism consists of the language or of some feature of the mechanical construction of the composition. This often represents the most extreme analytic tendency in criticism; though, on the other hand, many of the most purely æsthetic terms have taken their rise from this very source. *E. g.*: —

> Vida's versification is often *hard* and *spondaic*. HALLAM, Lit. Hist., I., p. 437.

Often, also, some characteristic of the literary production, some predicate of a former critical judgment, is assumed as an established fact, and is made the subject of a new judgment. This may occur with or without the connecting copula. *E. g.*: —

> *Simplicity* in Burns is never stale and unprofitable. LANDOR, IV., p. 54.
>
> Classically *correct*. WILSON, V., p. 357.

Frequently, as the exact opposite to the language and mechanical construction of the composition, the thought or sentiment expressed is made the subject of the critical judgment. This and the preceding class of subjects are intimately related to each other. *E. g.*:

> A certain intenseness in the *sentiment.* HAZLITT, Age of Elizabeth, p. 177.
> *Humour*, though not of the most delicate kind. CAMPBELL, p. 15.

The fourth class of analytic subjects represents an extremely slight analysis and abstraction of the æsthetic feeling. The subject is almost identical with the unified impression of the literary production. The unified impression, however, is not an immediate impression. It has passed into the memory and is represented by some such word as "air," "manner," "tone," "strain," or "style." *E. g.*:—

> Massinger's dialogues subside in the proper places to a refreshing conversational *tone.* LOWELL, Old Eng. Poets, p. 122.

All such division or abstraction of the subject reacts upon the predicate. It is always possible to apply many epithets to the special features or traits of a literary work which would not naturally be employed to characterize the literary work as a whole. In the scientific method of judgment, characterizing words and phrases are thus brought into the predicate which possess little critical significance, and in this method of judgment all predicated characteristics are incomplete critical terms to the extent that the subject is but a partial representation of literary work considered in its completeness and unity.

The modification of the ideal forms of statement from the tendency to use figurative language is seen in both the predicate and subject of the critical judgment. The modifying influence of figurative language in the predicate may be said to exert itself in four ways. By far the most usual method consists in the use of synonymous and heightened expressions in connection with critical terms already well established and familiar. The critical significance of the old term is brought into prominence by the unexpected newness of the reinforcing term. Often there is merely a fringe of novelty given to the familiar conception, often there is a decided extension of its meaning. The desire for the rhetorical variation of the well-known critical term has become a mania with a few recent critics, whose skill in accomplishing this result has rendered necessary the mention in the present volume of several hundred such figurative and sporadic critical terms. *E.g.*: —

> There is a *profusion* in Childe Harold which must appear mere *wastefulness* to more economical writers. JEFFREY, II., p. 456.
> There are indeed portions of the Faery Queen which are *not vital*, which are, so to speak, *excrementitious*. DOWDEN, Tr. and Studies, p. 287.

Often some conception which is familiar in ordinary life is transferred by a bold figure of speech into the predicate of a critical judgment, with little or no intervention or support from a critical term already well established. *E. g.*: —

> Jeremy Taylor's style is *prismatic*. It unfolds the colours of the rainbow. HAZLITT, Elizabethan Lit., p. 233.

Another source of figurative variation in the predicate arises from the transference into criticism of conceptions which have a more immediate æsthetic significance than those just mentioned. Any effect, however partial or accidental, which the literary work produces upon the mind of the reader is made the predicate of the critical judgment, and thus seems to refer directly to the literary work itself. This it can do only in so far as it has become well established as a critical term, as it has been employed again and again as a means of characterizing literary work, as the original figure of speech has died out of the term, and it has ceased to be thought of merely as a personal state of feeling. *E. g.*: —

> *Cloying* perhaps in the uniformity of its beauty. JEFFREY, III., p. 136.

Occasionally the figurative variation consists in bringing by analogy into criticism terms which in the arts related to literature are already well established. During the eighteenth century, the terms thus appropriated by literary criticism came chiefly from the art of painting, during the present century from the art of music. *E. g.*:—

> Mr. Philipps has two lines which seem to me what the French call very *picturesque*.
>> All hid in snow, in bright confusion lie,
>> And with one dazzling waste confuse the eye.
>
> POPE, VI., p. 178.

In the subject of the critical judgment, the figurative tendency assumes the form of a more or less direct personification. The author himself is substituted for his literary productions. This substitution is often merely formal, the name of the author being only an abbreviated and enlivened method of indicating his complete literary work. But the force of the figure soon makes itself manifest in the predicate. With the author as subject, instead of the literary production, the predicate also becomes more figurative and enlivened. Personal characteristics are predicated of the subject rather than literary characteristics. This substitution of the author for the literary work has been greatly increased by the psychological and realistic spirit of the present century. A complete explanation of the author's mental characteristics, it is assumed, will explain the literary work also. Moreover, an intensely realistic spirit is repelled by the original figure of speech in the statement that "This poem is sublime." The sublimity ascribed directly to the poem, it is recognized, is really derived from sources outside the poem, — most immediately, perhaps, from the mind of the author. In the criticism of the drama and the novel, the discussion of the "characters" leads to the same confusion between personal and literary characteristics, and thus renders the critical significance of the predicated qualities vague and uncertain. *E. g.*:

> His tone is manly and *gentlemanly*. WHIPPLE, Character and Char. Men, p. 89.
>
> Madame de Staël had more vehemence than truth, and more *heat* than light. (Quoted from Joubert.) M. ARNOLD, Cr. Es., 1st S., p. 270.

Thus in the typical forms of critical judgment, the predicate refers directly to the subject or literary work, from which its meaning is almost wholly derived. But in actual criticism, terms are continually brought into the predicate of the judgment, representing conceptions which are well known in ordinary life, but are not usually regarded as having any literary significance. The predicate of the judgment thus receives constant modification from influences that lie beyond the immediate province of literary art, — from the personal traits of the author; from effects produced in the mind of the reader; from conceptions familiar in ordinary life; and from terms brought over by analogy from the related arts.

These influences continually furnish material for the critical judgment and give to it its ultimate meaning. In a very large portion of actual criticism, no overt critical judgment is expressed. These surrounding influences of the literary work are dwelt upon and analyzed. The literary production is discussed in its relation to the author, to the reader, to the environment in general, and to other arts, but none of its definite characteristics are given. But behind all this personal reminiscence, paraphrase, and mere explanation, there is always assumed a critical judgment, which can often be detected and more or less definitely stated. Of these assumed critical judgments, which make no use of critical terms, the following examples may be given: —

I. Personal characteristics of the author. *E. g.*: —

Dryden had strong reason rather than quick sensibility. S. Johnson, VII., p. 339.

II. Effects upon the mind of the reader. *E. g.*: —

> Neither the inner recesses of thought nor the high places of art thrill to his appeal. ROSSETTI, Lives of F. P., p. 234.

III. The general environment of the literary work. *E. g.*: —

> Now the same soil that produced Bacon and Hooker produced Shakespeare. DOWDEN, Shak., etc., p. 23.

IV. Comparison of different art effects without any definite standard of comparison. *E. g.*: —

> The effect of Virgil's poetry is like that of some laborious mosaic of many years' putting together. CARLYLE, Hist. of Lit., p. 53.

It is evident that such statements are composed of explanations, analyses, and discussions preparatory to criticism, and can in no sense of the word be considered as criticism proper.

In real criticism, the critic as a critic must deal at first hand with the literary production considered as a literary production. He will explain and analyze, but this only as preliminary to the characterization of the literary work under discussion. The characterizing words and phrases are always critical terms. Words which are repeatedly employed in the characterization of literature, which are persistently placed as predicate of the typical critical judgment, acquire a meaning which is more or less peculiar to their use in criticism. Such only are really critical terms, and the number of such words is relatively very small. The history of the figurative and sporadic terms belongs to the general dictionary of the language rather than to the vocabulary of criticism. But in order to present not only the real, but also the possible critical vocabulary, these figurative terms have, in the following work, received a brief mention also.

II. General Historical Tendencies and Movements in Critical Terms.

There are certain broad lines of development or principles of differentiation, common to critical terms, which, to avoid constant repetition in the text, it will be necessary to state in the present connection. These principles are for the most part independent of each other. They are both logical and historical, and can perhaps be best represented by occasionally referring to the ideal form of judgment given in the preceding section.

It is a truism in logic that the predicate of one judgment is taken up into the subject of the next judgment. This augmentation or growth of content in the subject of judgment takes place in the history of critical terms, but the growth of content or meaning in the subject is less rapid than in the case of the individual judgment. Every term which persists as the predicate of a typical critical judgment, which has thus really come to be a critical term, not only tends to pass into the subject, but also to organize, to systematize other terms which may be used in the predicate. The well-established term will be used synonymously with other terms, or in contrast with them, or still more often they will be placed as subordinate to it. Often a strong organizing or schematizing influence is exerted over the more specific critical terms by some general expression which is itself very little employed as an active critical term. Such was the term "Gothic" previous to the middle of the eighteenth century, and such are the terms "romantic" and "classical" in the present century.

A general term or expression, in so far as it organizes and classifies the more specific terms of the predicate, tends to become an integral part of the subject, to enlarge or enrich the conception of literary composition itself, and perhaps to designate more or less distinctly a class or species or general division of literature. All classifying terms are also schematizing terms, but the opposite is not true to an equal extent. The term "Gothic," until the middle of the eighteenth century, though exerting a strong schematizing influence over the active and specific terms of criticism, was not regarded as in any sense representing an integral part of real literature. *E. g.*: —

> One may look upon Shakespeare's works in comparison of those that are more finished and regular, as upon an ancient majestic piece of *Gothic* architecture, compared with a neat modern building; the latter is more elegant and glaring, but the former is more *strong* and more *solemn*. POPE, X., p. 549.

All well-established critical terms tend in this manner to become classifying terms. This is true of the criticism of individual authors and of literature in general. Sublimity is an integral portion of our conception of Milton's works, and we look for more definite characterization. In the present century it is always assumed that any and every literary composition must in some manner be true to actual life. To portray the specific manner in which this truthfulness is manifested is the problem for criticism. Truth to real life is a part of our conception of literature itself.

All classifying terms, however, were not thus originally derived from the predicate of the critical judgment. Those terms which most persistently represent a class or species of literature, — such as dramatic, lyrical, and epic, — have without exception appeared in the subject first, have uniformly indicated at first the external circumstances under which literature was produced, or the mechanical forms which it assumed, and possessed no real literary significance whatever.

Whether thus mechanically derived, or whether taken up into the subject from the predicate, any classifying term, in so far as it becomes established firmly and beyond all question, possesses little or no immediate critical significance. Lyric poetry is simply lyrical, being neither worse nor better for the fact. But there are three influences which operate continually to bring these established classifying terms into touch with active critical terms. In the first place, the more firmly fixed the classifying word is, the greater is its schematizing influence over other critical terms. The poem is not merely lyrical, dramatic or classical, but it has "lyric sweetness," "dramatic vigor," or "classical purity of expression." In the second place, the different classes or species of literature are usually held by the critics in relatively higher or lower esteem, and this gives a certain amount of critical significance to the terms by which the different classes or species are designated. *E. g.*: —

> Tasso confesses himself too *lyrical*, beneath the dignity of heroic verse. DRYDEN, XIII., p. 15.
> Some kinds of poetry are in themselves lower kinds than others. The ballad kind is a lower kind. The didactic kind, still more, is a lower kind. M. ARNOLD, Cr. Es., 2d S., p. 139.

In the third place, however rigidly any class or species of literature may be defined in theory, there continually arises the practical need for deciding under what species or division new or unnoted features of literature are to be classified. In making this classification, the theoretical definition of the classifying term is usually modified and its critical significance brought more or less into the foreground of attention. In this manner the term "lyrical," representing at first any passionate or "pathetic" strain of song, — in opposition to epic and dramatic action, — has, from the great increase of subjective literature in the present century, undergone a complete transformation of meaning.

In determining the meaning of a critical term, it is necessary constantly to distinguish between theoretical and applied criticism. Terms are sometimes applied directly to literature, and sometimes they are merely theoretically defined and explained. Nor can the theory of a term at any given period of time be taken by any means as a sure index to its actual use in applied criticism. Even in the same author, theory and practice are often quite at variance with each other. *E. g.*: —

> The sum of all that is merely objective we will henceforth call *nature*, confining the term to its passive and material sense, as comprising all the phenomena by which its existence is made known to us. COLERIDGE, III., p. 335.
>
> The wonderful twilight of the mind! and mark Cervantes's courage in daring to present it, and trust to a distant posterity for an appreciation of its truth to *nature*. COLERIDGE, IV., p. 274.

Theoretical criticism represents the full analytic consciousness, which exists at any time, of the influences entering into the formation of the typical critical judgment. But in the typical judgment itself, this analytic consciousness is not immediately present so much as the æsthetic feeling for the literary work which forms the subject of the judgment. This æsthetic feeling, and the general conception of literature which accompanies it, ultimately controls and sets the limits to the analysis and theoretical discussion of critical terms and principles. Hence the direct application of a term to literature is the final criterion for its meaning at any given period of its history.

But, on the other hand, the theory of a term often reacts upon its actual application to literature in no uncertain manner. The interaction between theoretical and applied criticism is intimate and mutual, and may be said to take place in three ways: *First*, A critic's theory of a term may for the most part control his applied use of it; but no theory, in so far as it is mere theory, will be copied by other critics. Thus Leigh Hunt defined *passion* as a form of suffering, and Moulton defines it as a form of literary sympathy or appreciation. The latter critic follows up his definition by an extended application of the term to literature, but in the great body of critical usage the term is uniformly connected with the more active and impulsive part of our nature. *Second*, The theory of a term and its applied use are often made exactly, and at the same time conditionally, equivalent to each other, the theory of the term, based upon current usage, being stated definitely and explicitly as an immediate preliminary to its use in the characterization of literature. This method of criticism has been coming more and more into use since the middle of the eighteenth century. *E. g.*: —

> The French writers declare that the English writers are generally incorrect. If correctness implies an absence of petty faults, this perhaps may be granted; if it means a juster economy in fables, the notion is groundless and absurd. J. WARTON, 1., p. 196.

Third, The theory of a term is sometimes derived from an applied use of it which has since become obsolete. This corresponds to the retrospective stage of a term's history, and will be spoken of later.

The theory of a term may thus usually be regarded as an approximate statement of the meaning which the term possesses when actually applied to literature; but the theory must always be held in question by the facts upon which it is based. The living use of a term is the only real key to its meaning. It must be derived chiefly from the growing æsthetic sense of what literary art is, rather than from the more or less mechanical analysis of what literary art and criticism have been and might be.

A critical term may be theoretically defined in two general ways. Its meaning may be derived from the literary composition considered as a completed product, or it may be derived from the mental activities of the author or reader, which are brought into play in the production and appreciation of the literary composition. The definition and classification of all the known critical terms and principles with reference to the completed composition is ideal rhetoric; the same definition and classification with reference to the mind of the author or reader is ideal æsthetic. There has been a decided change in English criticism from the rhetorical to the æsthetic or psychological standpoint. This change has manifested itself in two ways: In the first place, there has been a gradual elimination of technical expressions from general criticism. Until within the eighteenth century, the chief terms employed in criticism represented for the most part principles of language, or the more or less mechanical features of a composition. Most of these terms were derived from ancient rhetoric, and their meaning was very largely determined by the rules which the rhetoricians themselves had laid down. By continually referring to certain fixed traits of a composition, the terms became isolated to a great extent from their ordinary use in speech, and there was often required for their comprehension an extensive technical knowledge of rhetoric and criticism. In 1700 there were some three hundred critical terms in general use, about half of which were of this technical nature, — such terms as *purity, correct-*

ness, proportion, decency, imitation, characters, manners. and *sentiments.*

But when literature is viewed as to its content rather than as to its form, its relations to actual life become too intimate to allow of such a technical isolation of meaning in critical terms. In English criticism, technical terms have constantly been paraphrased, explained, and illustrated by more popular expressions, by which they have been gradually superseded, or to which their meaning has been made gradually to conform. These popular expressions may be merely explanatory, figurative, and sporadic. But quite as often, they indicate a change of interest in criticism from the composition considered as a completed product to the mental powers by means of which the composition is called forth and appreciated. There have consequently appeared in modern criticism a multitude of psychological and æsthetic terms, whose meaning each person can determine in great measure for himself, by an introspective movement of his own mind. Of the fifteen hundred terms which constitute the present vocabulary of criticism, perhaps three fourths are distinctively of this psychological nature.

In the second place, the change from the rhetorical to the æsthetic or psychological standpoint is seen in the greatly increased emphasis which in criticism has come to be placed upon the progressive tendencies in literature. Any completed product, in so far as it is regarded merely as a completed product, as external, and disconnected with the mind producing it, is always thought capable of being reduced to fixed rules and methods. Rhetoric, whose primary concern consists in analyzing and classifying the characteristics of the completed composition, tends to set up rules which have all the rigid uniformity of a mechanical law rather than the progressive movement of a developing principle. Hence rhetorical terms and principles look to the past for their data, by the authority of which they would restrict future variation and development. Of such a conservative character were the great body of critical terms previous to the latter portion of the eighteenth century, — terms such as *taste*, *propriety*, *decorum*, *correctness*, *proportion*, and even *truth* and *nature*. *E. g.*: —

> Those rules of old discovered, not devised,
> Are nature still, but nature methodised.   POPE.

Since about the middle of the eighteenth century, this conservative critical vocabulary has been completely revolutionized. A few terms, such as "correctness," have become merely retrospective; others, such as "proportion," in being explained psychologically, have entirely changed their meaning; still others, such as "decorum," have become obsolete. The psychological terms and principles of modern criticism are essentially prospective in their outlook. The analytic terms and principles of psychology have received little mention in criticism; but the synthetic and propulsive mental energies are all represented, their significance being minutely developed, broadened, and strengthened.

Such are the terms *sensibility, feeling, passion, sentiment, wit, humor, fancy, imagination,* and a host of related expressions. This change from the rhetorical to the psychological standpoint is of the utmost importance in the general history of criticism. In a history of the critical vocabulary, there is merely required the statement of the fact of the change, and the general principle which produced it. The details, in so far as they appear, will be found in the history of the separate terms.

It is but restating the law of all development to say that in the history of criticism the meaning of the terms employed has shown a decided change from the indefinite to the definite. Four historical stages may be distinguished in the growth toward this definite use of critical terms.

I. Previous to the latter portion of the seventeenth century, terms were for the most part employed singly, and without explanation and illustration. Hence it is often difficult to ascertain their meaning with any degree of exactness. *E. g.*: —

How wonderful are the *pithey* poems of Cato. LODGE, p. 5.

II. From the latter portion of the seventeenth century until near the beginning of the present century, critical terms were usually employed synonymously, mutually supporting and explaining one another. That two or more terms are applied to the same passage of literature by a critic argues that they held in his mind some sort of relation to one another. But it is often by no means evident on the printed page what that relation was. Many such conglomerations of terms, in fact, must, for practical purposes of definition, be regarded as isolated expressions. Thus, for synonymous use: —

> *Bold* and *impassioned elevations* of tragedy.   T. WARTON, Hist. Eng. Poetry, p. 866.

III. From the latter portion of the eighteenth century until within the first few decades of the present century, critical terms were very generally contrasted and placed in opposition with one another. At first, this contrast between critical terms was little more than a rhetorical antithesis. The contrast between nature and art, genius and talent, was made with the tacit assumption that fundamentally nature and genius lay wholly beyond the province of literary art. But this assumption came to be questioned. One theory of literature was placed over against another theory, and almost the whole critical vocabulary was reorganized and drawn into the contention. The old antitheses between critical terms were deepened into essential opposition, and new antitheses were added to them. The imagination was contrasted with the fancy, wit with humor, the ideal with the real, and above and over all the subjective with the objective. *E. g.*: —

> Spenser . . . left no *Gothic* irregular tracery in the design of his great work, but gave a *classical* harmony of parts to its stupendous pile.   CAMPBELL, I., p. 97.

IV. During the present century, — and especially during the latter portion of it, — critical terms have been very generally explained in connection with their application to literature. This has already been spoken of in discussing the relations between theoretical and applied criticism. If the explanation of the term is accomplished merely by definition, the living strength of the term is often sacrificed to the desire for exactness; but if the explanation is accomplished by means of illustration, by comparing different passages of literature with one another, such a sacrifice need not occur. *E. g.*: —

> It has been said that Tennyson fails in *passion*, and when men say that, they mean the embodiment of love in verse. BROOKE, Tennyson, p. 201.

There is still another general historical tendency among critical terms which requires notice. It relates to the manner in which new terms are introduced into the vocabulary of criticism, grow into favor, and then tend to pass out of use and become obsolete. Critical principles are more permanent than critical terms, but critical principles are always in a process of change and development. A real critical principle must of necessity be a developing principle. Critical terms, on the other hand, the external signs or symbols of these principles, are more conservative. Thus, literature was formerly said to be an "imitation of nature." But when literature had come to be conceived of as an intuition of what was sometimes called the "spirit of nature," the term "imitation," unable fully to express the new conception, was, as a means of defining literature, gradually superseded by the term "imagination." Certain fundamental terms, such as "truth" and "nature," seem to have continued in use while their meaning has undergone a complete transformation. This persistence, however, is usually more apparent than real. "Truth" has been largely superseded by the term "realism," and "nature" has almost ceased to be a critical term in applied criticism.

Many terms, introduced into criticism merely for the purpose of reinforcing other terms and conceptions already well established, have been, so far as they attracted any attention at all, received into favor from the beginning. A few terms, also, such as "picturesque" and "musical," have been brought over into good standing at once from related arts. But most of the important critical terms now in use, were first employed with more or less disfavor. In regard to the favor with which they have been received, four stages may be distinguished in the history of the different critical terms.

I. In the first stage, the principle represented by the critical term is recognized as an active influence in literature, but this influence is thought to be more or less pernicious, and destructive to the integrity of literature as such. The term "Gothic," until the latter portion of the eighteenth century, was in this stage of development.

II. In the second stage, the term is not only seen to represent influential tendencies in current literature, but these tendencies are thought to be essential to literary art considered as literary art. The term is employed not only in explaining current literature, but also in interpreting the literature of the past. "Correctness" and "propriety" were so employed in the eighteenth century; "imagination," "humor," and "realism" in the present century.

III. In the third stage, the term represents a principle which is no longer active to any considerable extent in current literature. Enough appreciation of the principle still remains for it to be regarded as an integral portion of literary art. The term is thus essentially retrospective, and for an abbreviated form of statement may be spoken of as a retrospective term. The term "correct" is at present in this stage of its history.

IV. In the fourth stage, the term represents an influence once prominent in literature, which has since come to be regarded as wholly outside the limits of the real province of literary art. The more formal signification of the term "propriety" is at present in this final stage of its critical history.

III. Method of Dealing with the Separate Critical Terms.

The general conception of what critical terms are, which has now been given, and of the historical movements that take place among them, has determined the method employed in presenting the history of the different terms. Critical terms are regarded, not as having a significance, which is the result of mere accidental association, but as representing critical principles, which at a certain stage of their development require new methods of expression, and appropriate for their use certain words out of the vocabulary of the general language. Hence, corresponding to the stages of development in the critical principle, the history of the term which represents it will tend to separate itself into more or less definitely marked periods. The general characteristics of the term in each period of its history are given, — characteristics which are intended to define the term in relation to the principle it represents, as well as in relation to the more or less synonymous expressions which merely vary or reinforce the common meaning of the general principle. Occasionally some general term, during a single period of its history, has two or three different uses; but usually there is a characteristic use for every term at any given time or period of its history, to which all its special uses may be referred for explanation. It is this characteristic use of the term which in every instance is attempted to be defined or represented. Any use of a term once established tends to recur occasionally in a conventional manner throughout all the later stages of the term's development. These purely conventional uses of a term need not for historical purposes be taken into consideration. Negative terms, those which merely deny that a composition possesses a certain critical or literary principle, are treated as briefly as possible, since their meaning is included in that of the positive terms to which they are opposed.

With terms which have been very frequently employed in criticism, the references have been omitted, the space which they would have occupied — there were more than twenty-five thousand of them — being given to representative quotations. The marginal phrases, the text, and the quotations are intended to supplement one another in defining the general conception of a term at any period of its history. The marginal phrases are intended to suggest the essential relations existing between the different periods of the term's development; the text to give the essential relations between the special uses of the term in any one period of its history.

It was the design at first to present the history of the different terms in groups of synonyms, taking up the groups in the order of their greatest historical influence. But for ease of reference, it has been thought best to arrange the terms in alphabetical order, and place the historical grouping of synonyms in an appendix. (See Appendix.) The Roman numerals placed immediately after the terms indicate the group in the Appendix to which the terms respectively belong. The historical limit of the terms as given — *e. g.* "Milton to present" — is based upon their applied use in the main current of criticism. Mere theory, unless the illustration given is very prominent and significant, has not been regarded as giving active current usage to a term; and the historical limits to many of the terms would no doubt be much changed by a study of minor critics, which, from the necessary limits of the present investigation, has not been permitted.

BIBLIOGRAPHY.

Nearly all the works of criticism in the Library of the University of Chicago, in the Chicago City Library, and in the Newberry Library were read and consulted. A few rare books were obtained from private sources. The following list contains those works to which most frequent reference is made. References in the book to other works and editions than those mentioned below are given in full in connection with the separate quotations.

A. Addison: Bohn's edition, 6 vols., London, 1891. M. Arnold: Works, Macmillan & Co., 1883-1891. T. Arnold: Man. of Eng. Lit., London, 1888. Ascham: 3 vols., London, 1864.

B. Bacon: Complete Works, Spedding's edition, London, 1857. Bagehot: Literary Studies, 2 vols., London, 1891. Beers: 2 vols., New York, 1886 and 1891. Bentley: Complete Works, 3 vols., London, 1836-38. Blair: Rhetoric and Belles Lettres, University edition, Philadelphia. Brooke: 3 vols., New York and London, 1892-94. E. Browning: Prose, 2 vols., London, 1877. Bryant: Prose, New York, 1889. Burke: Bohn, 5 vols., London, 1881. Byron: Life and Letters, Murray, London, 1892.

C. Camden: Remains Concerning Britain, London, 1870. Campbell: Murray's edition, London, 1848. Campion: Works, Bullen, London, 1889. Carlyle: Crit. and Mis. Essays, 7 vols., London, 1888-91. Channing: Remarks, etc., on Milton, London, 1845. Coleridge: Complete Works, 7 vols., Shedd, New York, 1884; Letters, Boston and New York, 1895. Collier: Murray, London, 1831. Courthope: Lib. Movement in Eng. Lit., London, 1885.

D. Daniel: Complete Works, 4 vols., Grosart, 1885. Dekker: Huth Library, 5 vols., 1884. De Quincey: Masson's edition, Edinburgh, 1889. Dowden: Works, London, 1888-89. Dryden: Scott and Saintsbury edition, 18 vols.

E. George Eliot: Essays, Edinburgh and London, 1885. Emerson: Works, Houghton, Mifflin & Co., Boston, 1891-92.

G. Gascoigne: Arber's Reprints, Birmingham, 1869. Gibbon: Murray, 5 vols., 1814. Goldsmith: Bohn, London, 1886. Gosse: 5 vols., London, 1882-91; A Study of the Writings of Bjornson, New York, 1895. Gosson: Arber's Reprints, Birmingham, 1868. Gray: Gosse's edition, 4 vols., New York, 1890.

H. Hallam: Lit. Hist., 4 vols., London, 1882. Harvey: Grosart, London, 1884. Haslewood: The Arte of English Poesie, London, 1815. Hazlitt: Works, W. C. Hazlitt's edition, London, 1886. Hobbes: Complete Works, Molesworth, London, 1811. Howells: Crit. and Fiction, New York, 1891. D. Hume: Essays, 2 vols., Green and Grose, London, 1889. Hunt: Prose, London, 1891. Hurd: Complete Works, London, 1811.

J. H. James: Partial Portraits, London, 1888. K. James: Arber's Reprints, Birmingham, 1869. Jeffrey: Longmann et al., editors, 1846. S. Johnson: Complete Works, 11 vols., London, 1825. B. Jonson: Timber, Schelling's edition, Boston, 1892; Complete Works, 3 vols., London, 1889.

K. Keats: Letters, New York, 1891; Life and Letters, London, 1889.

L. Lamb: Works, New York, 1887-90. Landor: Life and Works, London, 1876. Lodge: Collier, 1851. Lowell: Works, Houghton, Mifflin & Co., Boston and New York, 1892.

M. Macaulay: Mis. Works, 4 vols., Trevelyan edition, New York. Mathews: Literary Studies. Milton: Prose, London, 1890. Minto: Man. of Eng. Prose Lit., Char. of Eng. Poets, Boston, 1891. J. Morley: Works, Macmillan & Co., London, 1891. Moulton: Shakespeare as a Dramatic Artist, Oxford, 1888.

N. Newman: Essay on Aristotle's Poetics, Boston, 1891.

P. Pater: Appreciations, etc., London, 1890. Poe: Works, 4 vols., New York. Pope: Courthope, etc., 10 vols., London, 1871-86. Puttenham: Arber Reprints, Birmingham, 1869.

R. Robertson: Essays toward a Critical Method, London, 1889. Rossetti: Lives of Famous Poets, London, 1878. Preface to Blake's Poetical Works, London, 1891. Ruskin: Works, New York, 1891. Rymer: 'Tragedies, Parts I. and II., London, 1692-93.

S. Saintsbury: Specimens of English Prose Style, London, 1885; Hist. of Eng. Lit., vol. ii., Macmillan, London; Essays in Eng.

Lit., 1780–1860, New York, 1891; A Short Hist. of Fr. Lit., Oxford, 1892; A Hist. of 19th Century Lit., New York, 1896. Scott: Editor of Dryden, Edinburgh, 1882; Editor of Swift, London, 1883. Shaftesbury: Complete Works, 3 vols., 1757. Shelley: Complete Works, 3 vols., Forman, London, 1880. Sherman: Analytics of Lit., Boston, 1893. Sidney: Cook, Boston, 1890. Stedman: Victorian Poets, Boston, 1891; The Nature and El. of Poetry, do., 1893. Stephen: Hrs. in a Lib., 3 vols., London, 1874; Lives of Pope, Johnson, and Swift in Morley Series, Harpers, New York. Stephenson: Familiar Studies of Men and Books, New York, 1895. Swift: Scott, 19 vols., London, 1883. Swinburne: Works, London, 1875–89. J. A. Symonds: Es., Spec. and Suggestive, London, 1893.

T. Thackeray: 2 vols., Harper's Half Hour Series, New York.

W. Walton: Lives, London, 1888. J. Warton: Essay on Pope, 2 vols., London, 1806. T. Warton: Hist. of Eng. Poetry, Ward, etc., London, Reprint of 1778–81. Webbe: Arber Reprints, Birmingham, 1870. Whetstone: Shakespeare Library, Vol. VI., London, 1875. Whipple: Works, Boston, 1891. J. Wilson: Essays, Critical and Imaginative, Blackwood & Sons, London and Edinburgh. T. Wilson: The Arte of Rhetorique, Printed by R. Grafton, 1553. Wordsworth: Prose, Grosart, 3 vols., London, 1876.

A HISTORY

OF

ENGLISH CRITICAL TERMS.

Ability, Group V. *b*: Jeff., Swin., Gosse.
    Wilson's drama (1690) was full of ability.   GOSSE, Hist. of Eng., Lit., p. 40.
Abortive (V.) *b*: Dramatic abortions . . . misbegotten by dullness upon vanity (of Byron). SWINBURNE, Mis., p. 81.
Abrupt (XIII.): Harvey to present.

May be a praiseworthy quality of composition, but usually is not so.

    Samson Agonistes opens with a graceful abruptness.   S. JOHNSON, Vol. III. p. 158.
    Let there be nothing harsh or abrupt in the conclusion of the sentence on which the mind pauses and rests. BLAIR, Rhet., p. 140.   (Quoted from Quintilian.)
Absolute (XXII.) *a*: Swinburne, Studies, p. 165.
Abstract, Abstracted (VIII.): Jef. to present.
    Keats' poetry is . . . too dreamy and abstracted to excite the strongest interest. JEFFREY, II., p. 376.
    In Rossetti . . . a forced and almost grotesque materializing of abstractions. PATER, Ap., p. 232.
Abstinent (XIX.): Purity and abstinence of style (Wordsworth). LOWELL, Prose IV., p. 415.

Abstruse (III.): Minto to present. Gosse, From Shakespeare to Pope, p. 125.
Absurd (XX.): Sidney to present; in considerable use.
The absurd naïvety of Sancho Pancho. D. HUME, I., p. 240.
This extravagant and absurd diction. WORDSWORTH, II., p. 103.
Abundance (XI.) *b*: Dekker to present.
Chaste abundance . . . of Goethe. CARLYLE, I., p. 230.
The stately and gorgeous abundance of the vocabulary with which the Hellenizing and Latinizing innovations of the Pleiade enriched the French language. SAINTSBURY, Hist. Fr. Lit., p. 211.
Academic (XX.): The Idylls of the King . . . are a little too academic. BROOKE, Tennyson, p. 268.
Blending of the academic and classical manner with the romantic and discursive (of Hooker). SAINTSBURY, Hist. Eng. Lit., II., p. 44.
Accomplished (V.) *b*: Rossetti to present.
Accomplished and dextrous rhythm . . . of Swin. SAINTSBURY, Es. in Eng. Lit., p. 394.
ACCURATE (VIII.): B. Jonson to present; in considerable use.

Previous to the present century, the term "accurate" usually referred to the language of a composition, indicating a careful choice of words and exactness of method in their arrangement.

As exactness of expression.

> Our composition must be more accurate in the beginning and end than in the midst, and in the end more than in the beginning. B. JONSON, Timber, p. 62.
> No matter how slow the style be at first, so it be laboured and accurate. ID., p. 54.
> Accuracy is seen in the expression. DRYDEN, XII., p. 284.

During the present century, the term has almost uniformly represented a faithful and perhaps detailed description of actual facts and events.

As truthfulness to fact.

Truth and accuracy. HAZLITT, El. Lit., p. 7.

The accuracy on which Pope prided himself . . . was not accuracy of thought so much as of expression. LOWELL, IV., p. 37.

A figure may be ideal and yet accurate. SWINBURNE, Es. and St., p. 220.

Scientifically accurate in his statement of the fact. DOWDEN, Shak., etc., p. 247.

Acerbity (XIV.): Cole., Macaulay.
Acrimony (XIV.): Jeffrey.
ACTION (XVIII.): Whetstone to present.

The word "action," though occurring frequently in criticism, has very seldom been employed as an actual critical term. Until the middle of the eighteenth century, the term usually referred to historic deeds, to external events, to heroic adventures, celebrated chiefly in song and in Epic story. *As Epic movement.*

What . . . the poet . . . imitates is action. ARISTOTLE, Poet., p. 31.

In the Iliad, which was written when Homer's genius was in its prime, the whole structure of the poem is founded on action and struggle. LONGINUS, pp. 20, 21.

The Epic asks a magnitude from other poems, since what is place in the one is action in the other. B. JONSON, Timber, p. 83.

The spectators are always pleased to see action, and are not often so ill-natured to pry into and examine whether it be proper. RYMER, 2d Pt., p. 3.

The relations between action and passion were always regarded as being very intimate. During the latter half of the eighteenth century, this intimacy of relation became greatly increased. By the beginning of the present century, action had become *As Dramatic movement.*

subordinated to passion, or at most action was made to represent more or less directly the flow of mental imagery, the sequence of thought, the suspense, the emotion aroused by the description of an event, rather than the mere event itself, considered as an external movement, a fact of history.

> Whence it comes to pass that the action, having an essential dignity, is always interesting, and by the simplest management of the poet becomes in a supreme degree pathetic. HURD, II. p. 34.
> Cato wants action and pathos, the two hinges on which a just tragedy ought to turn. J. WARTON, p. 257.
> The feeling . . . in Lyrical Ballads . . . gives importance to the action and situation, and not the action and situation to the feeling. WORDSWORTH, II., p. 183.
> Action . . . the eternal object of poetry. M. ARNOLD, Mix. Es., p. 489, etc.

Actual (VIII.) : Swinburne.

Acute: (XX.) *b*; Milton to present.
> Acuteness of remark, or depth of reflection. MILTON, III. p. 498.

Acumen (XX.) *b*: Acumen of thought. T. ARNOLD, Man., etc., p. 459.

Adapted (IV.): S. Johnson to present.
> Thoughts and words elegantly adapted to the subject. DRYDEN, V., p. 124.

Admirable (XXII.) *a*: Jef., Swin. Dowden, Trans. & St., p. 229.

Adolescent (XV.): The beauty . . . of Keats' poems . . . have an adolescent and frequently a morbid tone. ROSSETTI, Life and Letters, p. 208.

Adorable (XXII.) *a*: Swinburne, Mis., pp. 46, 221, etc.

ADORNED (V.): Webbe to present. Ornamented; colored.

The term refers to the result rather than to the process of ornamentation. The result may be brought about either by elaborate design or by spontaneous processes.

> The great art of poets is . . . the adorning and beautifying of truth. DRYDEN, XV., p. 408.
> The object of the poetry of the imagination is to raise or adorn one idea by another more striking or more beautiful. HAZLITT, Eng. Com. Writers, p. 64.

Adroit (V.) *b*: Hallam to present.
> Adroitly extravagant. SWINBURNE, Mis., p. 69.

Adventurous (XIX.): Hazlitt to present.
> Romantic and adventurous incidents. STEPHEN, Hrs. in a Lib., pp. 56, 57.

Aerial (XXII.) *b*: Pure, lucid, aerial. SWINBURNE, Es. & St., p. 139.

ÆSTHETIC (XXII.) *b*: Much used, but almost wholly in theory.
> The writings of the "romantic school," of which the æsthetic poetry is an afterthought . . . mark a transition from a lower to a higher degree of passion in literature. PATER, Ap., p. 214.

AFFECTATION (VII.): **AFFECTED**: T. Wilson to present.

Much in use, but has not, perhaps, changed its meaning. In theory, it indicates the assumption on the part of the author of a style or method of expression which is unnatural, not spontaneous. As actually applied to literature, it indicates a style or method of expression which offends the taste of the critic. In early English criticism, the diction and language employed gave most offence; later, the general tone and spirit of the composition.

> Spenser, in affecting the ancients, writ no language. B. JONSON, Timber, p. 57.
> Shakespeare's whole style is so pestered with figurative expressions, that it is as affected as it is obscure. DRYDEN, VI., p. 255.

Wordsworth ... is affected. JEFFREY, II., p. 523.

The essence of affectation is that it be assumed; the character is, as it were, forcibly crushed into some foreign mould, in the hope of being thereby reshaped and beautified. CARLYLE, I., p. 11.

Longfellow oftener runs into affectation through his endeavors at simplicity than through any other cause. POE, II., p. xviii.

Affecting (XVII.): Jef. to present. 1st. As the "affected." 2d. As the touching, pathetic.

Affinity (XXII.) *b*: Hazlitt, Shak., p. 7.

Affluent (XI.) *b*: Whip. to present.

Those poems ... which are apparently the most affluent of imagery, are not always those which most kindle the reader's imagination. BRYANT, Prose, I., p. 9.

Aggressive (XII.), cf. (XIV.): Ros. M. Arnold, Cr. Es., 1st S., p. 66.

Agreeable (XXII.) *b*: Most pathetic and most interesting, and by consequence the most agreeable. D. HUME, I., p. 264.

Airy (XXII.) *b*: S. Johnson to present.

Airy, rapid, picturesque. JEFFREY, II., p. 46.

Airiness of fancy. LOWELL, IV., p. 267.

Airy and pretty. T. ARNOLD, Man. etc., p. 272.

Alacrity (V.) *b*: An alacrity of language. LOWELL, Prose, IV., p. 304.

Alembicated: Inequality and alembicated character of the poetry in vogue. GOSSE, From Shak. to Pope, p. 33.

ALLEGORIC (XXI.).

Primarily a classifying term. Symbolism of moral traits by means of fables. More in favor in early English criticism than at present.

A continuous allegory or dark conceit. SPENSER, Introduction to Faery Queen.

Poetry, composed of allegory, fables, and imitations, does not deal in falsehoods. 1591. HARRINGTON, in Haslewood's Arte of Poetry, p. 127.

Stale allegorical imagery. SAINTSBURY, Hist. Fr. Lit., p. 104.

Alliterative (X.): Hallam to present. Swinburne, Es. & St., p. 265.
Allusive (XVI.): Saints. to present.
    Three kinds of poetry: Narrative; Representative; Allusive,— to express some special purpose or conceit. BACON, IV., p. 402.
    Fertility of allusion . . . in Butler. BRYANT, I., p. 49.
    Dryden . . . taught the poets to be explicit where they had been vexatiously allusive. GOSSE, Hist. Eng. Lit., III., p. 26.
Ambiguous (III.): T. Wilson to present. Puttenham, p. 267.
Ambitious (XII.): Dryden to present. Jeffrey, II., p. 229.
Ambling (X.): Hazlitt to present.
    Graceful ambling . . . of Addison. WHIPPLE, Es. & Reviews, p. 60.
Amenity (XIV.): Blair. Gosse, Hist. Eng. Lit., p. 19.
Amorphous (II.): Sidney's Arcadia is dreadfully amorphous and invertebrate. GOSSE, From Shak. etc., p. 22.
Ample (XI.) *b*: B. Jonson to present. Swin., Es. & St., p. 69.
Amplification, **Amplified** (XIX.) *c*: T. Wilson to present.

Used for the most part previous to the present century.

    Amplifying and beautifying. T. WILSON, Rhet., p. 25.
Amplitude (XI.) *b*: Landor to present.
    Sonorous amplitude of Milton's style. LOWELL, IV., p. 84.
Amusing (XVII.): Jef. to present.
    More amusing than accountable. HUNT, Wit and Humour, p. 10.
Anachronism (IV.), cf. (VIII.): J. Warton to present. J. Warton, II., p. 16.
ANALYTIC (XX.) *b*: Stedman to present.

Analysis as such, the mere tendency to discriminate and to separate anything into its elements, has never been regarded with much favor in criticism. To possess literary value, analysis must in some manner be combined with synthesis.

    Wit is negative, analytical, destructive; Humor is creative. WHIPPLE, Lit. & Life, p. 91.

Possessing a sense of proportion, based upon the highest analytic and synthetic powers. STEDMAN, Vic. Poets, p. 199.

Scott was often tediously analytic where the modern novelist is dramatic. HOWELLS, Crit. & Fiction, p. 21.

Aniline (V.): Saintsbury, Eng. Pr. Style, p. xvii.

Animated (XII.): Mil., J. Warton to present. Much in use.

An infinite variety of tropes, or turns of expression . . . which serve to animate the whole. GOLDSMITH, I., p. 357.

The animation, fire, and rapidity which Homer throws into his battles. BLAIR, Rhet., p. 40.

Anticlimax (XII.): Stephen to present.

The Lotus Eaters . . . closes in a feeble anticlimax. BROOKE, Ten., p. 124.

Antiphonal (X.): Swinburne, Es. & St., p. 200.

Antiquated (IV.): Goldsmith to present.

Antiquated and colloquial. JEFFREY, I., p. 416.

Antithetical (II.): Scott to present.

Snapping antitheses of Macaulay. SAINTS., Eng. Pr. St., p. xxxi.

Appropriate (IV.): Collier to present. POE, II., p. 163.

Apt (IV.): Ascham to present.

The unaptness of our tongues and the difficulty of imitation disheartens us. CAMPION, p. 233.

Not only what is great, strange, or beautiful, but anything that is disagreeable, when looked upon, pleases us in an apt description. ADDISON, III., p. 418.

Arabesque (II.): Byron to present.

Richter's manner of writing is singular; nay, in fact, a wild complicated arabesque. CARLYLE, I., p. 16.

Archaic, Archaisms (I.): Landor to present.

Antiquated expressions, which, from a certain unexpectedness and quaintness, may possess literary merit.

A grave and sparkling admixture of archaisms in the ornaments and occasional phraseology . . . of Southey's prose. HAZLITT, Sp. of Age, p. 145.

A permissible archaism is a word or phrase that has been supplanted by something less apt, but has not become unintelligible. LOWELL, IV., p. 217.

The natural effect of archaisms on pathetic passages is to make them sweeter and simpler, by making them more childlike. Minto, Char. of Eng. Poets, p. 26.

Architectonics (XXIII.): M. Arnold.
Archness (XVII.): Campbell to present.
Arctic (XV.): Hunt.
Ardent (XV.): Scott to present.
Ardour (XV.): Masculine ardour . . . of Milton. Dowden, Tr. & St., p. 270.
Arid (XVI.): Hallam.
ART (XXII.) *b*.

The history of the term "art" is to be connected with that of the term "artistic," — the two together representing the development of a single critical principle. The term "art" was chiefly used previous to the present century, "artistic" during this century. "Art" as a critical term has almost invariably been placed in antithesis to "nature," and hence its meaning is in large part determined by the use of the term to which it has been opposed. It has perhaps been used in two slightly different ways.

When "nature" represented subjective impulses and instincts, the term did not indicate the entire mental process which takes place in the production of literature. "Art" denoted whatever in the composition results from skill, from conscious device and design, from the employment of rules and method. *As device and design.*

> · If a thing admits of being brought into being without art or preparation, *a fortiori*, it will admit of it by the help of art and attention. Aristotle, Rhet., p. 163.
>
> In Sallust's writing is more art than nature, and more labor than art. 1568. Ascham, III., p. 264.

The courtier following that which by practice he findeth fittest to nature, therein though he know it not, doth according to art, though not by art. 1583. SIDNEY, p. 54.
Art is only a help and remembrance to nature. 1585. K. JAMES, p. 66.
Nature engendereth, art frameth. 1593. HARVEY, I., p. 263.
Art, when it is once matured to habit, vanishes from observation. 1751. S. JOHNSON, III., p. 80.
Some had the art without the power; others had flashes of the power without the art. SAINTSBURY, Hist. E. L., p. 53.

When "nature" was regarded as external and objective, "art" indicated the whole mental process necessary for giving to this external nature a literary representation. "Art" thus included not only skill and design, but also in a vague way the more primal and instinctive literary activities of the mind.

As selective skill, and power.

Art and nature compared (summary).
1. Art an exact imitator of nature, *e. g.* Painting.
2. Art covers defects of nature.
3. Art heightens the beauties of nature.
4. Art develops forms wholly beyond nature. 1585.
PUTTENHAM, pp. 308–312.
We should be admiring some glorious representation of nature, and are stopped on a sudden to observe the writer's art. 1751. HURD, I., p. 364.
Artful (V.) *b*: Dryden to present.

That which in composition gives evidence of conscious design and device. In better repute during the eighteenth century than during the present century.

The plot . . . of Measure for Measure . . . is rather intricate than artful. S. JOHNSON, V., p. 158.
Artful but not artistic. WHIPPLE, Age of El., p. 118.

Artifice (V.): Hume to present. Device for producing artful effects.
> The simple manner . . . conceals the artifice as much as possible; endeavoring only to express the effect of art, under the appearance of the greatest ease and negligence. SHAFTESBURY, I., p. 202.

Artificial (VII.): Ascham to present. Much in use.

I. Until the latter portion of the eighteenth century, the "artificial" occasionally represented the "artful."
> In Gorboduc . . . there is both many days and many places inartificially imagined. SIDNEY, p. 48.

II. Usually the term indicates the unnatural, that which is at once artful and labored.
> Those artificial assemblages of pleasing objects, which are not to be found in nature. J. WARTON, I., pp. 3, 4.

ARTISTIC (XXII.) *b*. (See **ART**.)

The term "artistic" represents a blending of the old antithesis between art and nature into an æsthetic unity,—a unity which refers not only to the active process of composing, but also to the effect of the composition on the mind of the reader. As denoting the active process of composing, the artistic necessitates the exercise both of acquired skill and of the spontaneous powers of the mind,—of feeling, of passion, of imagination. As referring to the appreciation of literature, the artistic includes both cultivated taste and native sensibility. The artistic represents such a refinement of the crude facts and materials of literature as to give no offence to the most cultivated taste, and at the same time such an accurate and vivid portrayal of these facts as to stimulate the most healthful and vigorous imagination. The term is thus a complete expression at any given time for the progressive æsthetic sense which accompanies literary development.

> If by saying that a poem is artistical we mean that its form corresponds with its spirit, that it is fashioned into the likeness of the thought or emotion it is intended to convey, then "The Buccaneer" and "Thanatopsis" are as artistical as the "Voices of the Night." . . . The best artist is he who accommodates his diction to his subject, and in this sense Longfellow is an artist. 1844. WHIPPLE, Es. and Reviews, p. 59.
> Artful but not artistic. 1859. WHIP., Lit. of Age of E., p. 108.
> Nothing but the highest artistic sense can prevent humor from degenerating into the grotesque. 1866. LOWELL, II., p. 90.
> In works of art or pure literature, the style is even more important than the thought, for the reason that the style is the artistic part, the only thing in which the writer can show originality. MATHEWS, Lit. St., p. 9.
> And when one's curiosity is in excess, when it overbalances the desire of beauty, then one is liable to value in works of art what is inartistic in them. 1886. PATER, Ap., p. 248.
> Some sonnets of Mrs. Browning lack that fine artistic self-control, the highest obedience to the law of beauty, which should be as stringent as the self-control of asceticism, and is so much more fruitful. 1887. DOWDEN, Tr. & St., p. 229.
> That fine effluence of the whole artistic nature which can hardly be analyzed and which we term style. DOWDEN, St. in L., p. 192.

Artless (VII.): Campbell to present.
> The term artlessness may be applied to Heywood in two very opposite senses: as truth to life and natural feeling; as being without art. CAMPBELL, I., p. 219.

Asiatic (XIX.): Milton to present.
> The exuberant richness of Asiatic phraseology. MILTON, III., p. 204.
> A feeble, diffuse, showy, Asiatic redundancy. HAZLITT, Sp. of A., p. 204.

Assonant (X.): Assonant, harmonious. STEDMAN, Vic. Poets, p. 46.

A HISTORY OF ENGLISH CRITICAL TERMS. 45

Attractive (XXII.) *b*: Wordsworth to present. Mathews, Lit. Studies, p. 29.
Audacity (XII.): Ruskin to present. Swinburne, Es. & St., p. 86.
August (XI.): Milton to present. Swinburne, Es. & St., p. 65.
Austere (XV.): Hume to present. Swinburne, Mis., p. 142.
Authentic: (VIII.); Authentic, honest, and direct terms. JEFFREY, I., p. 211.
Autumnal: Gosse, From Shak., etc., p. 178.
Awkward (XIX.): Dryden to present.
  Simplicity may be rustic and awkward, of which there are innumerable examples in Wordsworth's volumes. LANDOR, IV., p. 61.
Babyish (XI.): Babyish interjections. JEFFREY, II., p. 175.
Balance (II.): T. Newton to present.

  Equipoise of phrase, thought, and feeling.

  Precise balance. T. NEWTON, Spen. Society, vol. 43, p. 2.
  I would trace the origin of meter to the balance in the mind effected by that spontaneous effort which strives to hold in check the workings of passion. COLERIDGE, III., p. 415.
  The imagination . . . the faculty that shapes, gives unity of design, and balanced gravitation of parts. LOWELL, III., p. 30.
  The needful qualities for a fit prose are regularity, uniformity, precision, balance.
  Tennyson's poetry exhibits a well-balanced moral nature. DOWDEN, St. in Lit., p. 113.
Bald (XVI.), cf. (V.): Milton to present.
  Wordsworth . . . a baldness which is full of grandeur. M. ARNOLD, Cr. Es., 2d S., p. 159.
  Locke's style . . . is bald, dull, plebeian. SAINTS., Eng. Pr. St., p. xxiv.
Balderdash (XXII.) *b*: Frantic balderdash. SAINTS., Hist. Fr. Lit., p. 25.
Barbarism (I.): Webbe to present.
  The craving for instant effect in style . . . brings forward many disgusting Germanisms and other barbarisms. DE QUINCEY, XI., p. 422.
Barbarous (IV.): Ascham to present.

  That which very much offends taste and propriety.

Barbarity and Gothicism. SHAFTESBURY, I., p. 174.
We are apt to call barbarous whatever departs widely from our own taste and apprehension. HUME, I., p. 266.
A tasteless and barbarous turn of phrase, in which all feeling of propriety and elegance was lost. HALLAM, Lit. Hist., II., p. 23.

Bare (V.): Scott to present. Swinburne, Es. & St., p. 126.

Barren (XVI.): Puttenham to present.
The remedy for exuberance is easy; barrenness is incurable by any labor. QUINTILIAN, II., p. 106.
Dry, hard, and barren of effect. HAZLITT, Age of El., p. 207.

Barytone (X.): M. Arnold.
Virile barytone quality. STEDMAN, Vic. Poets, III.

Base (V.): Ascham, Puttenham.
Thus rudely turned into base English. ASCHAM, III., p. 197.

Bastard (VII.): M. Arnold to present.
Bastard Epic style . . . of Scott. M. ARNOLD, Celtic Lit., etc., p. 195.

Bathos (XI.): Scott to present.
Mistaking vulgarity for simplicity, turned into bathos what they found sublime. CAMPBELL, I., p. 49.

Bawdry (XIV.): Burlesque or bawdry . . . of Breton. SAINTSBURY, Hist. of Eng. Lit., p. 239.

BEAUTY (XXII.) *b*.

The history of the term "beauty" may be divided into three general periods. Previous to the eighteenth century, the beautiful was uniformly regarded as a result of a certain rearranging and polishing of a truth that was thought to be external and unchangeable. This rearranging and polishing was attained by conscious ingenuity. Hence the conception of the beautiful in early criticism is usually expressed by means of an active verb, which designates the skill of the author in manipulating his material. The beautiful thus, for the most part at

As ornamentation and artifice.

least, was capable of being reduced to rule and method. It was a product of invention, and was copied or imitated from author to author.

> Beauty lies in compass and order. ARISTOTLE, Poetics, p. 25.
> Amplifying and beautifying. 1553. TH. WILSON, Rhet., p. 25.
> Only man and no beast hath that gift to discern beauty. 1583. SIDNEY, Poet., p. 37.
> Figures which beautify language. 1585. PUTTENHAM, p. 206.
> Beautify the same with brave devices. 1586. WEBBE, p. 36.
> Periods are beautiful when they are not too long. (Pub.) 1641. B. JONSON, Timber, p. 62.
> If the parts are managed so regularly, that the beauty of the whole be kept entire. 1668. DRYDEN, XV., p. 335.
> His genius is able to make beautiful what he pleases. 1674. DRYDEN, V., p. 112.
> It is better to trespass on a rule than leave out a beauty. 1692. DRYDEN, VIII., p. 221.
> Persius borrows most of his beauties from Horace. 1693. DRYDEN, XIII., p. 73.
> The least proportion or beauty of tragedy. 1678. RYMER, 1st Pt., p. 41.

During the eighteenth century, the beautiful was regarded not so much as something which could be consciously constructed as something which was merely to be apprehended. The beautiful was apprehended by means of taste or "delicacy of imagination." Both taste and the sense of the beautiful varied with increasing knowledge (see Taste). In the latter part of the century, when taste came to be founded more on sensibility and less on culture, the beautiful likewise was thought to have less intimate relations with proportion and the understanding than with the more spontaneous activities of

As the extremely pleasant and agreeable.

the mind. But whether associated with understanding or with feeling, the final test of the beautiful was the amount of immediate pleasure that was produced in the mind of the reader. The critics usually found this greatest pleasure in the "proprieties," occasionally, however, in an impropriety.

> Any writer who shall treat on this subject after me may find several beauties in Milton which I have not taken notice of. 1711. ADDISON, III., pp. 223-24.
> I have endeavored to show how some passages are beautiful by being sublime, others by being soft; others by being natural. 1711. ID. p. 283.
> It is impossible to continue in the practice of contemplating any order of beauty, without being frequently obliged to form comparisons between the several species and degrees of excellence, and estimating their proportions to each other. 1742. HUME, I., p. 275.
> It seldom or never happens that a man of sense, who has experience in any art, cannot judge of its beauty. 1742. ID., I., p. 278.
> It is in many cases apparent that beauty is merely relative . . . that we transfer the epithet as our knowledge increases, and appropriate it to higher excellence, when higher excellence comes within our view. 1751. S. JOHNSON, II., p. 431.
> It has been the lot of many great names not to have been able to express themselves with beauty and propriety in the fetters of verse. 1756. J. WARTON, I., pp. 265-66.
> The qualities of beauty are all sensible qualities: I. Small. II. Smooth. III. Variety in the direction of the parts. IV. Parts not angular but melted as it were into each other. V. Delicate frame without any remarkable appearance of strength. VI. Colors clear and bright but not strong or glaring. VII. If any glaring color to have it diversified with others. 1756. BURKE, I., p. 136.
> Proportion is a creature of the understanding . . . but beauty demands no assistance from our reasoning. 1756. ID., p. 114.

> What is false taste but a want of perception to discern propriety and distinguish beauty? 1761. GOLDSMITH, I., p. 324.
>
> For the sake of showing how beautiful even improprieties may become in the hands of a good writer. S. JOHNSON, V., p. 263.

During the present century, in so far as the beautiful has been founded upon taste, taste itself has been supposed to consist chiefly of native sensibility. *As æsthetic feeling.* This makes the sense of the beautiful tend to pass over from an appreciation of many beauties by means of taste, to the appreciation of a single beauty by means of certain fundamental and progressive forms of feeling. These forms of feeling, whether designated as imaginative or as the "artistic sense," are, as it were, the connecting link between pure æsthetic feeling and the more active artistic processes which give expression to this æsthetic feeling. The beautiful is thus the most full and direct expression possible for pure æsthetic feeling. The progressive nature of this æsthetic feeling itself, however, as evidenced in modern realism, keeps the question continually open as to whether or not the sense of the beautiful and the limits of literary art are at any given time exactly coextensive and identical with each other.

> Greek art is beautiful . . . but Gothic art is sublime. 1810. COLERIDGE, IV., p. 235.
>
> No great work should have many beauties: if it were perfect, it would have but one; . . . that but faintly perceptible, except on a view of the whole. 1817. JEFFREY, II., p. 472.
>
> What the imagination seizes as beauty must be truth, — whether it existed before or not, — for I have the same idea of all our passions as of love: they are all, in their sublime, creative of essential beauty. 1817. KEATS, Letters, pp. 41, 42.

It may be interesting to you to pick out some lines from Hyperion, and put a mark × to the false beauty proceeding from art, and an || to the true voice of feeling. 1819. ID, p. 321.

The ideal is that which answers to the preconceived, and appetite in the mind for love and beauty. 1819. HAZLITT, Table Talk, p. 448.

Poetic beauty in its pure essence . . . is not derived from anything external, or of merely intellectual origin; not from association . . . nor from imitation, of similarity in dissimilarity, of excitement by contrast, or of seeing difficulties overcome. Underived from these it gives to them their principal charm. It dwells and is born in the inmost spirit of man. . . . 1827. CARLYLE, I., p. 47.

Fiction has no business to exist unless it is more beautiful than reality. Certainly the monstrosities of fiction may be found in the bookseller's shops . . . but they have no place in literature, because in literature the one aim of art is the beautiful. Quoted from Joubert. M. ARNOLD, Cr. Es. 1st S., p. 292.

Pope had a sense of the neat rather than of the beautiful. LOWELL, Prose Works, IV., p. 48.

The world of the imagination is not the world of abstraction and nonentity, as some conceive, but a world formed out of chaos by a sense of the beauty that is in man and the earth on which he dwells. 1885. ID., VI., p. 94.

And further, all beauty is in the long run only *finesse* of truth. 1886. PATER, Appreciations, p. 6.

Becoming (IV.), cf. (XXII.) *b* : Puttenham, Landor.

Such a play on words would be unbecoming. LANDOR, IV., p. 438.

Biting (XIV.) : T. Newton, Whipple, El., Lit., p. 98.

Bitter (XIV.) : Jeffrey to present.

Richter's satire . . . is never bitter, scornful, or malignant. DE QUINCEY, XI. p. 271.

Bizarre (IX.) : Hume to present.

Bizarre mixture of the serious and comic styles. HUME, I., p. 270.

Bizarre and extraordinary. JEFFREY, II., p. 116.

Bizarre or unnatural. WHIPPLE, Lit. of Age of El., p. 232.

Blithe (XVIII.) : Stedman, Pater, p. 56.

Blithe, unstudied utterance. STEDMAN, Vic. Poets, p. 73.

Blundering (XIX.), cf. (II.) and (XVIII.) : Swinburne, Mis., p. 76.
Blunt (V.): Ascham to present.
  When they wrote, their head was solitary, dull, and calm; and so their style was blunt and their writing cold. Ascham, III., p. 210.
Bluster (XIX.), cf. (XII.): Whip. to present.
  Bluster or bombast. Whipple, Es. & Rev., II., p. 49.
Body (XIII.) *b*: Swinburne, Mis., p. 9.
Boisterous (XIX.) *c*; cf. (XII.): Saintsbury.
Bold (XII.): Dryden to present.
  Bold and rhetorical style. D. Hume, I., p. 168.
Bombastic (XIX.): Puttenham to present.
  Pure simple bombast . . . arises from putting figurative expression to an improper use. Hurd, I., p. 103.
  Marlowe . . . constantly pushes grandiosity to the verge of bombast. Lowell, O. E. D., p. 36.
  The rhetorical sublimity of their diction comes most perilously near the verge of bombast. Swinburne, A St. of B. Jonson, p. 58.
Bon-mot (XVII.) : Watson was possessed of a most copious collection of bon-mots, facetious stories, and humorous compositions of every kind. Wakefield, in Literaria Centuria, Vol. I., p. 20.
Bookish (VII.) : Whip. to present.
  The dialogue . . . in Mosses from an Old Manse . . . is bookish. Whipple, Char. & Char. Men, p. 226.
Brave (XXII.) *a*: Beautify the same with brave devices. Webbe, p. 36.
Brazen (XIX.): Dryden's brazen rant. Gosse, Hist. Eng. Lit., III., p. 43.
Breadth (XIII.) *b*: Campbell to present.
  Breadth and comprehensiveness. Dowden, Shak., pp. 166-67.
Brevity (XIX.): Gascoigne to present.
  What is quickly said the mind readily receives and faithfully retains. Horace, Art of Poesy, p. 214.
  There is a briefness of the parts sometimes that makes the whole long. . . . Seneca may be impeached of this. B. Jonson, Timber, p. 70.

Bright (V.): Swin. to present.
    The sweet pastoral strain, so bright, so tender. DOWDEN, Shak., p. 81.

Brilliant (V.): Hume to present.
    An over brilliant style obscures character and sentiment. ARISTOTLE, Poetics, p. 81.
    The brilliant felicity of occasional images. DE QUINCEY, XI., p. 337.

Brisk (XVIII.): Dryden to present. Swinburne, A St. of B. Jonson, p. 83.

Brocaded (V.): Gosse, Hist. of Eng. Lit., pp. 391–92.

Broken (XIII.): Dekker to present.
    A broken language . . . monosyllabic. DEKKER, III., p. 188.

Brooding (XX.) *b*: Swinburne, Mis., p. 230.

Brutish (XXII.) *b*: This brutish poetry. WEBBE, p. 31.

Bucolic (XXI.): Shelley to present.
    The bucolic and erotic delicacy in written poetry is correlative with that softness in statuary, music, and the kindred arts . . . which distinguished the later Grecian epoch. SHELLEY, VII., pp. 118, 119.
    Flexible, bucolic hexameter. STEDMAN, Vic. Poets, p. 226.

Buffoonery (XVII.): Put. to present.
    Ford's cold and dry manner makes his buffoonery at once rancid and insipid. SWINBURNE, Es. & St., p. 290.

Buoyancy (XVIII.): Whip. Swinburne, Es. & St., p. 291.

Burlesque (XVII.): Rymer to present.
    The French had the like vicious appetite, and immoderate passion for *vers burlesque*. RYMER, 2d Pt., p. 10.
    Burlesque consists in a disproportion between the style and the sentiments, or between the adventitious sentiments and the fundamental subject. S. JOHNSON, VII., p. 155.

Cacophonous (X.): Lowell to present.
    Such cacophonous superlatives as "virtuousest," "viciousest," etc. LOWELL, Latest Lit. Essays, p. 105.

Cadence (X.): Keats to present.

Long applied in theory to metrical form; came to refer to the mental rhythm and perhaps to a form of feeling; and thus acquired direct critical significance.

The cadence of one line must be a rule to that of the next. DRYDEN, XII., p. 301.
A certain musical cadence, or what we call rhythm. HURD, II., p. 6.
A cadence and symphony of suffering. SWINBURNE, Es. & St., p. 11.

Calm (XIX.): Hume to present.
Composed, calm, and unconscious way. JEFFREY, I., p. 225.

Candor (XIV.): Gold. to present. Jeffrey, I., p. 27.

Canorous (X.): Lowell.
The Latin has given us most of our canorous words, only they must not be confounded with merely sonorous ones. LOWELL, Pr. III., p. 184.

Cant (VII.): Dekker to present.
If there be not something very like cant in Mr. Carlyle's later writings, then cant is not the repetition of a creed after it has become a phrase. LOWELL, II., p. 97.

Capacity (V.) *b*: Swinburne, Es. & St., p. 312.

Capricious (XIX.): T. Warton.
Irregular and capricious. JEFFREY, II., p. 235.

Careful (XIX.): Ros. Swinburne, Mis., p. 44.

Careless (XIX.) or (II.): Jef. to present. Jeffrey, II., p. 49.

Caricature (VIII.): Scott to present.
This exaggeration . . . is not caricature, for caricature never gives the impression of reality. WHIPPLE, Success, etc., p. 258.

Catholic (XIV.): Hallam to present.
Catholic poetry . . . that which is good in all ages and countries. HALLAM, III., p. 228.

Caution (XIX.): Jef., Swin.
Caution, timidity, and flatness . . . of Addison. JEFFREY, I., p. 45.

Changeful (II.): Swinburne, Es. & St., p. 68.

Chaotic (II.): Lowell to present.
The chaotic never pleases long. LOWELL, Prose, III., p. 65.
Dark and chaotic . . . Blake. ROSSETTI, Pref. to Blake, p. cxiii.

CHARACTER (VI.).

Until the latter portion of the eighteenth century, "characters" as employed in criticism denoted certain general traits, certain generic qualities of motive and disposition,— the word being usually found in the plural form, and referring to the personnel of a drama. These general dramatic types of character were to a great extent an inheritance from literary precedent and custom. Certain mental characteristics had been abstracted, personified, and put into action. More definite characterization was wholly subordinated to plot complication. "Character," thus indicating a given native bent of disposition, was both more inclusive in its meaning than the word "manners," and more fundamental, more nearly related to the sources of motive and of conduct.

As general types of dramatis personæ.

> Character,— that whereby we say the actors are of one kind or another. ARISTOTLE, Poetics, p. 21.
>
> Character,— is whatever shows choice. ID., p. 23.
>
> Beginners in composition succeed sooner in style and character than in arrangement of incident. . . . The plot then is the basis, and, as it were, the soul of tragedy, character coming next. ID., p. 23.
>
> From the manners, the characters of persons are derived; for indeed the characters are no other than the inclinations, as they appear in the several persons of the poem; a character being thus defined,— that which distinguishes one man from another. 1679. DRYDEN, VI., p. 269.
>
> The several manners which I have given to the *persons* of this drama . . . are all perfectly distinguished from each other. 1694. ID., VIII., p. 374.
>
> The manners flow from the characters. ID., XV., p. 388.
>
> The fable is properly the poet's part, since —
>   The characters are taken from Moral Philosophy,
>   The thoughts or sense from Rhetoric,
>   The expression from Grammar. RYMER, 2d Pt., pp. 86, 87.

Since within the eighteenth century, there has been a constant growth in the conception of character toward specification, and the fullest portrayal possible of motives and disposition. Character has come to represent personality,—that which distinguishes one man from other men as in actual life, not that which distinguishes certain general types of literary representation. *As personality.*

> Nothing affects the heart like that which is purely from itself, and of its own nature; such as the beauty of sentiments, the grace of actions, the turn of characters, and the proportions and features of a human mind. SHAFTESBURY, I., p. 105.
> Cato ... wants character, although that be not so essentially necessary to a tragedy as action. 1756. J. WARTON, p. 257.
> There is ... a little degradation of character for a more dramatic turn of plot. 1830. WORDSWORTH, III., p. 303.
> In Shakespeare ... the interest in the plot is always ... on account of the characters, not *vice versa*, as in almost all other writers. 1810. COLERIDGE, IV., p. 62.
> Character of two kinds ... Generic, representative, symbolical, instructive; or specific, interesting. 1817. ID., III., p. 561.
> Cervantes is the father of the modern novel, in so far as it has become a study and delineation of character instead of being a narrative seeking to interest by situation and incident. 1885. LOWELL, VI., p. 135.

Charm (XXII.) *b*: Jeffrey to present.
> A noble union of truth and charm. SWINBURNE, Es. & St., p. 76.

CHASTE (I.) or (XIX.) *b*; **CHASTITY**.

Correctness in the use of language, and moderation in figures of speech or mental imagery; a careful and restrained method of expression, the result of delicate sensibility and pure taste.

> Sentiments chaste but not cold. ADDISON, I., p. 254.
> Chaste and correct. J. WARTON, I., p. 258.

The chaste elegance of the following description . . . will gratify the lover of classical purity. T. WARTON, p. 863.

Critics have a habit of calling certain sorts of work "chaste"; not as indicating any quality of moral continence, but as implying the correctest and purest taste, unmixed with any license or audacity. ROSSETTI, Lives of Poets, p. 262.

Chastised (XIX.) *b*: Chastised gravity of the sentiments. JEFFREY, I., p. 393.

Cheerful (XIV.): Swinburne, Mis., p. 30.

Childish (XI.): Childish and preposterous. JEFFREY, I., p. 212.

Chiselled (V.): Ruskin to present.

The Dunciad is the most absolutely chiselled and monumental work "exacted" in our country. RUSKIN, Lectures on Art, pp. 86, 87.

Choral (XXI.): Choral accompaniments to the performance. JEFFREY, II., p. 129.

Chosen (IV.): Brooke, Tennyson, p. 251.

Circuitous (XVIII.): Hazlitt, Whipple.

Circumstantial (VIII.): *b* J. Warton to present.

Circumstantial richness of description. MINTO, Char. of Eng. Poets, p. 327.

Clang (X.): Swinburne. High-ringing clang. BROOKE, Tennyson, p. 130.

Clangour (X.): Clangour of sound. SAINTSBURY, Hist. of Fr. Lit., p. 213.

Clarion-versed (X.): Brooke, Tennyson, p. 308.

Clarity (III.): Swinburne. Clarity of statement and reflection. GOSSE, Seventeenth Cent. St., p. 298.

Clashing (X.): Rugged, clanging, clashing lines. BROOKE, Ten., p. 274.

CLASSICAL (XIX.) *b*.

As the classic.

The term "classical" appeared in English criticism about the middle of the eighteenth century. Though there are no definitely marked periods in its history, five more or less distinct shades of meaning may perhaps be distinguished in the use of the term. Occasionally the term merely represents the literature of Greece and Rome, whatever was then and there written and has in any manner been transmitted to us. In this sense of the term, the "classical" is found opposed to the "Gothic," but the opposition between the terms is not essential or philosophical, — they are not really exclusive of each other.

> Cambuscan is a composition, which at the same time abundantly demonstrates that the manners of romance are better calculated to answer the purposes of pure poetry, to captivate the imagination, and to produce surprise, than the fictions of classical antiquity. 1778. T. WARTON, H. E. P., p. 287.
> This fatal result of an enthusiasm for classical literature was hastened and heightened by the misdirection of the powers of art. The imagination of the age was actively set to realize these objects of Pagan belief. 1846. RUSKIN, St. of V., II., p. 133.

Very frequently in actual criticism the term "classical" has been used to represent those literary principles or qualities which are thought to be characteristic of the literary compositions of the ancient classics, — of those ancient authors who are firmly established in public esteem.

As the characteristics of the ancient classics.

> Classical purity. 1756. J. WARTON, I., p. 185.
> A writer so pure, sensible, and classical as Boileau. ID., II., p. 393.
> Surrey for his justness of thought, correctness of style, and purity of expression, may justly be pronounced the first English classical poet. 1778. T. WARTON, Hist. E. P., p. 645.
> Elegant and classical. BLAIR, Rhet., p. 446.
> Classical harmony of parts. 1819. CAMPBELL, I., p. 97.
> The great difference, then, which we find between the classical and romantic style, between ancient and modern poetry, is, that the one more frequently describes things as they are interesting in

themselves, the other for the sake of the associations of ideas connected with them; that the one dwells more on the immediate impressions of objects on the senses, the other on the ideas which they suggest to the imagination. The one is the poetry of form, the other of effect. 1820. HAZLITT, Ag. of El., p. 246.

Milton's place is fixed as the most classical of our poets. 1872. LOWELL, IV., p. 80.

Classic elegance, polish, and correctness. 1884. T. ARNOLD, Man. of E. L., p. 306.

Occasionally the "classical" denotes the characteristic qualities of all literary classics, whether of ancient or of modern times, — of all authors who from their permanent influence are thought to embody the more essential principles of literary art.

As the characteristics of all classics.

> The problem is to express new and profound ideas in a perfectly sound and classical style. He is the true classic in every age who does that. 1865. M. ARNOLD, Cr. Es., 1st S., p. 65.
>
> To get rid of provinciality is a certain stage of culture; a stage the positive result of which we must not make of too much importance, but which is nevertheless indispensable, for it brings us on to the platform where alone the best and highest intellectual work can be said fairly to begin. Work done after men have reached this platform is classical; and that is the only work which in the long run can stand. 1865. ID., p. 61.
>
> Classical lucidity, measure, propriety, sobriety, temperance, soul, simplicity, delicacy, truth, grace, sureness. ID, pp. 65-76.
>
> Out of an atmosphere of all-pervading oddity and quaintness arises a work really ample and grand, nay, classical, by virtue of the effectiveness with which it fixes a type in literature; as indeed, at its best, romantic literature in every period attains classical quality, giving true measure of those well-worn critical distinctions. 1886. PATER, Appreciations, p. 161.
>
> In whatever style an artist works, the style will be classical, provided the work itself be good, sincere, and representative of sterling thought. J. A. SYMONDS, Es., Sp. & Sug., p. 225.

Frequently in theoretical discussion, during the present century, and occasionally in applied criticism, the "classical" and the "romantic" have been placed in an antithesis with each other, *As the non-romantic.* which is intended to be real and philosophical, each term being mutually complementary and exclusive of the other one. However, the historical and the philosophical antitheses between the two terms are constantly confused with each other, and the real distinctions between the terms are only approximately drawn. The "classical" requires a more temperate use of energy, of passion, of imagination, of all the mental activities that are brought into play in literary idealization than the "romantic." At its best the "classical" represents self-restraint of the literary and idealizing energies; at its worst, a restraint imposed by custom and precedent.

> The characteristic of the classical literature is the simplicity with which the imagination appears in it; that of modern literature is the profusion with which the most various adornments of the accessory fancy are thrown and lavished upon it. 1856. BAGEHOT, Lit. St., I., p. 118.
>
> There is one play, and only one, of his epoch that is not classic and is not romantic, but speaks independently the truest and best mind of the eighteenth century itself in its own form and language. That play is Nathan the Wise. 1878. J. MORLEY, Diderot, I., p. 347.
>
> Qualities of measure, purity, temperance, of which it is the especial function of classical art and literature, whatever meaning, narrower or wider, we attach to the term, to take care. 1886. PATER, Ap., p. 247.
>
> The charm, therefore, of what is classical, in art or literature, is that of the well-known tale, to which we can, nevertheless, listen over and over again, because it is so well told. ID., p. 247.

Occasionally, when placed in opposition to the "romantic," the "classical" has been made to signify the well-worn, the conventional, the pedantic.

As the conventional.

> Classical and artificial. 1825. HAZLITT, Sp. of Age, p. 154.
> Irish oratory . . . is romantic, Scotch oratory . . . classical. The one may be disciplined and its excesses sobered down into reason; but the dry and rigid formality of the other can never burst the shell or husk of oratory. ID., pp. 256, 257.
> Classicism, then, means for Stendhal, for that younger enthusiastic band of French writers whose unconscious method he formulated into principles, the reign of what is pedantic, conventional, and narrowly academical in art; for him, all good art is romantic. 1890. PATER, Ap., p. 262.

Clean (I.): Puttenham to present.

I. Until the present century, the term "clean" denoted purity of language, or chastity of language and thought.

> More curiously than cleanly. PUTTENHAM, p. 28.
> The language . . . of Waller's poem on the Navy . . . is clean and majestic. RYMER, 2d Pt., p. 79.

II. During the present century, the term has represented moral purity.

> Vulgarity of its flat and stale uncleanliness. SWINBURNE, Mis., p. 86.

Clear-cut (III.): Swinburne, Mis., p. 51.
CLEARNESS (III.).

The term "clearness," representing a general effect which the composition produces on the mind of the reader,—the ready and vivid comprehension of the thought expressed,—has naturally varied in meaning according as criticism has been especially occupied now with one part of the

From grammatical construction.

composition and now with another. In early English criticism, and occasionally even to the present time, "clearness" was thought to result chiefly from an apt choice of single words, and from exactness in the grammatical construction of the composition.

> Raleigh ... is full of proper, clear, and courtly graces of speech. 1610. BOLTON, Hypercritica, p. 249.
>
> Lydgate's manner is naturally verbose and diffuse. This circumstance contributed in no small degree to give a clearness and a fluency to his phraseology. 1778. T. WARTON, Hist. E. P., p. 353.

During the greater part of the seventeenth and eighteenth centuries, "clearness" was thought to be attained chiefly by the methodic arrangement of the language and of the thought of a composition. It was questioned, however, whether this was always the more poetical or effective method of statement. *From logical construction.*

> In a style that expressed such a grave and so humble a majesty with such clear demonstration of reason. 1670. WALTON, Lives, p. 184.
>
> It is one thing to make an idea clear, and another to make it affecting to the imagination. 1756. BURKE, Vol. I., pp. 90, 91.
>
> A clear idea is another name for a little idea. ID., p. 93.
>
> Dryden expresses with clearness what he thinks with vigor. 1781. S. JOHNSON, VII., p. 307.

During the present century, "clearness" sometimes has distinct reference to mental imagery, and to the process of the mind by which it is called into existence. *From mental imagery.*

> Artistic ability is co-ordinate with the clearness and staying power of the imagination. 1875. STEDMAN, Nat. of Poetry, p. 233.

More frequently the term has been employed to indicate the agreement of the literary statements with the facts which they are supposed to represent. The apparently clear statement is often found to be most obscure and incomprehensible when the premises and assumptions are examined in the light of the facts of actual experience. There is said to be a superficial or apparent clearness, and a fundamental or real clearness.

From correspondence to fact.

> In every department of eloquence, and particularly in poetry, we look for depth and clearness; a clearness that shows depth. 1824. LANDOR, II., p. 415.
> In Macaulay's History of England . . . everything is plain; all is clear; nothing is doubtful. Instead of probability being, as the great thinker expressed it, the very guide of life, it has become a rare exception, an uncommon phenomenon. You rarely come across anything which is not decided. . . . This is hardly the style for history. . . . History is a vestige of vestiges; few facts leave any trace of themselves, any witness of their occurrence. 1856. BAGEHOT, II., p. 256.
> Clearness is so eminently one of the characteristics of truth that often it even passes for truth itself. 1865. M. ARNOLD, Cr. Es., 1st S., pp. 283, 284.
> Macaulay's writing passes for being admirably clear, and so externally it is; but often it is really obscure, if one takes 'his deliverances seriously, and seeks to find in them a definite meaning . . . a distinct substantial meaning. ID., Mixed E., p. 181.

Clench (XVII.): Withers, Dry., Johnson.

A play upon words; a pun.

> Clinches, anagrammatical fancies, or such like verbal or literal conceits. WITHERS, in Spenser Society Series, vol. 26, Pt. I., pp. 15, 16.
> Shakespeare . . . is many times flat and insipid; his comic wit degenerating into clenches. S. JOHNSON, V., p. 153.

Clever (V.) *b*: Jef. to present.
   Clever and original writer. Gosse, Hist. Eng. Lit., III., p. 67.
Clinquant (V.): Saintsbury, Eng. Prose Style, p. xix.
Cloudy (III.): Swin. to present.
   Cloudy vagueness. Saintsbury, Es. in Eng. Lit., p. 413.
Cloying (XXII.) *b*: Jeffrey to present.
   Cloying perhaps in the uniformity of its beauty. Jeffrey, III., p. 136.
   Cloying sentimentalism. Lowell, Prose, II., p. 145.
Clumsy (II.): T. Warton to present.
   Cumbrous and clumsy. Wilson, VIII., p. 44.
   German clumsiness. Howells, Crit. and Fiction, p. 22.
Clownish (XIX.): Webbe.
Club-footed (XVIII.): Walton's lyrics are mechanical and club-footed. Lowell, Latest Lit. Es., p. 70.
Coarse (V.): Webbe to present.

Lack of refinement; strength rather than delicacy of feeling.

   Chaucer's style may seem blunt and coarse. Webbe, p. 32.
   This very coarseness of fibre, added to Vanbrugh's great sincerity as a writer, gives his best scenes a wonderful air of reality. Gosse, Hist. Eng. Lit., III., p. 68.
Cogency (XXII.) *b*: J. Warton, Blair.
COHERENCE (XIII.): Dryden to present.

The term has at times been employed to indicate a continuity of sound, of ideas, and of plot incidents; but usually it refers to the composition as a whole.

   A compactness and coherence of language. Cicero, Orators, p. 383.
   In the best conducted fiction, some mark of improbability and incoherency will still appear. J. Warton, I., p. 250.
Cold (XV.): Ascham to present.

Either a deficiency or extravagance of emotion.

   Cold ... without imagination or sensibility. Hallam, IV., p. 305.

Cold-blooded (XV.): Jef. to present.
  Cold-blooded ribaldry. JEFFREY, II., p. 125.
Colloquial (I.): J. Warton to present.
  A free and colloquial air. J. WARTON, II., p. 9.
COLOR (V.) *a*.

The history of the term "color" may be divided into two periods. Until within the eighteenth century, As figurative language. "color" usually referred to the figurative use of single words; occasionally to more extended figures of speech.

>Just colours, good rhyme, etc. 1585. K. JAMES, p. 57.
>Virgil maketh a brave coloured complaint of unsteadfast friendship. 1586. WEBBE, p. 53.
>Now the words are the colouring of the work, which in the order of nature is last to be considered. . . . Words indeed, like glaring colours, are the first beauties that arise and strike the sight; but if the draught be false or lame, the figures ill-disposed, the manners obscure or inconsistent, or the thoughts unnatural, then the finest colours are but daubing, and the piece is a beautiful monster at the best. 1699. DRYDEN, XI., p. 216.

During the present century, the term "color" has steadily increased in use, and it has been employed in As vivid imagery. three more or less distinct ways. Frequently it signifies word painting,—the vivid portrayal of single images, which, like a picture, seem filled with all the colors of the actual scenes represented, and thus literally give color to the composition itself. This use of the term was prefigured during the eighteenth century in the discussion of the pictorial effect of the imagination.

A HISTORY OF ENGLISH CRITICAL TERMS. 65

The poets who are always addressing themselves to the imagination, borrow more of their epithets from colours than from any other topic. 1712. ADDISON, III., p. 400.
Colouring of the imagination. HUME, I., p. 278.
Poetry is a species of painting. . . . The poet, instead of simply relating the incident, strikes off a glowing picture of the scene, and exhibits in the most lively colours to the eye of the imagination. 1761. GOLDSMITH, I., p. 354.
The contrast was remarkable between the uncolored style of his general diction and the brilliant felicity of occasional images, embroidered upon the sober ground of his text. 1845. DE QUINCEY, XI., p. 337.
Richness, color, warmth. M. ARNOLD, Mixed Es., p. 218.
All Chaucer's works are full of bright colour, fresh feeling. 1874. MINTO, Char. of E. P., p. 29.

More usually "color" represents a general brilliancy of thought and imagery in a composition,— imagery which is associative and illustrative rather than concentrated into single glowing pictures. *As brilliancy of style.*

Where one idea gives a tone and colour to others. 1818. HAZLITT, Eng. Poets, p. 16.
The colours (in Gibbon's "Decline, etc.") are gorgeous like those of the setting sun; and such were wanted. 1826. LANDOR, IV., p. 95.
Cowley's want of colour . . . recommended him to the classic poets. 1888. GOSSE, Hist. Eng. Lit., III., p. 6.

Occasionally the term denotes an imaginative overstatement of fact. *As exaggeration.*

Colours of poetical ingenuity. HAZLITT, Eliz. Lit., p. 110.
A poetical colouring of facts. WILSON, V., p. 388.

COMEDY (XXI.).

I. Previous to the present century, "comedy" was the representation of manners, customs, and incidentally of character, the plot having an agreeable outcome.

> Some have made it a question whether comedy be poetry at all, for there is no inspiration and vigour either in the diction or the subjects. HORACE, p. 115.
>
> Comedy is no more at present than a well-framed tale handsomely told as an agreeable vehicle for counsel or reproof. Farquhar's "Love and Business," 1702. GOSSE, H. E. Lit., p. 72.
>
> And my idea of comedy requires only that the pathos be kept in subordination to the manners. 1751. HURD, II., p. 95.
>
> To please our curiosity and perhaps our malignity by a faithful representation of manners is the purpose of comedy. To excite laughter is the sole . . . aim of farce. 1762. GIBBON, IV., p. 134.
>
> Comedy was used all through the Elizabethan age in a loose sense, which would embrace anything between a tragi-comedy and a farce. Thus the Merchant of Venice is reckoned among the comedies of Shakespeare. T. ARNOLD, Man. of Eng. Lit., p. 493.

II. During the present century, "comedy" is the representation of manners, and perhaps of character, so as to appear ridiculous,— the corrective or reforming influence being subordinated to this.

> It is . . . the criticism which the stage exercises upon public manners that is fatal to comedy, by rendering the subject matter of it tame, correct, and spiritless. HAZLITT, The Round Table, p. 14.
>
> Comedy, as the reflex of social life, will shift in correspondence to the shifting movements of civilization. DE QUINCEY, X., p. 342.

Comely (XXII.) *b*: Gas., Put., Webbe.
COMIC-AL (XVII.).

A comprehensive expression for the laughable or humorous, and more direct in its application than the noun "comedy." Indicative of acuteness and subtlety; often, during the present century, of sympathy also.

A ramble of comical wit . . . in Othello. RYMER, 2d Pt., p. 146.
A certain tincture of the pitiable makes comic distress more irresistible. CAMPBELL, Vol. I., p. 71.
Commérage: The commérage of the letters of Walpole. SAINTSBURY, Eng. Pr. St., p. xxvi.
Common (IX.): J. War. to present. Swinburne, Es. & St., p. 12.
COMMONPLACE (IX.): Dryden to present.

I. Until within the eighteenth century, the word "commonplace" was often employed in a technical sense to denote certain universally admitted facts or truths, which could be made the basis for argument, or the means for setting forth a moral lesson.

> To dwell in Epitomes and books of common places . . . maketh so many seeming and sunburnt ministers as we have. ASCHAM, III., p. 201.
>
> Christ could as well have given the moral commonplace . . . of disobedience and mercy, as that heavenly discourse of the lost child and the gracious father . . . but that his through-searching wisdom knew . . . that it would more constantly . . . inhabit both the memory and judgment. SIDNEY, pp. 17, 18.

II. More recently the term has represented that which is common, trite, and well known. Often this has been regarded as the foundation of literary truth; its more clear and vivid apprehension marking the culmination of literary art.

> To restore a commonplace truth to its first uncommon lustre, you need only translate it into action. But to do this, you must have reflected on its truth. COLERIDGE, I., p. 117.
>
> The eternal grandeur of commonplace and all-time truths, which are the staple of all poetry. WILSON, VI., p. 117.
>
> Exaltation of the commonplace through the scientific spirit in realism. HOWELLS, Crit. and Fiction, p. 16.

III. More often, however, the commonplace, as such, has not been considered as fit material for literature; it represents the unrefined, the unimpassioned, the stale, the insipid.

> Thompson abounds in sentimental commonplaces. WORDSWORTH, II., p. 119.
> Nothing can be farther from the stale commonplace and cuckooism of sentiment than the philanthropic eloquence of Cowper. CAMPBELL, I., p. 428.
> The love scenes are . . . gross and commonplace. HAZLITT, Age of El., p. 113.
> To take the passion out of a novel is something like taking the sunlight out of a landscape; and to condemn all the heroes to be utterly commonplace is to remove the centre of interest in a manner detrimental to the best interests of the story. STEPHEN, Hrs. in a Library, I., p. 239.

Compact (XIII.): J. War. to present.
Compass (XIII.): De Quin. to present.
Competence (XXII.): Swinburne, Es. & St., p. 137.
Complete (XIII.): Wilson, VI., p. 134.
Complex (III.): De Quin. to present. De Quincey, X., p. 149.
Complication (II.): Of plot, and resolution. MOULTON, Shak., etc., p. 664.
Composed (XIX.) *b*: Jef. to present.
> Composed, calm, and unconscious way. JEFFREY, I., p. 225.

Composite (XIII.): Haz., Saints.
> Sir James Macintosh may claim the foremost rank among those who pride themselves on artificial ornaments and acquired learning, or who write what may be termed a composite style. HAZLITT, Sp. of Age, p. 178.

Comprehensive (XIII.): J. War. to present.
> Comprehensiveness . . . of Shakespeare's Historical plays. DOWDEN, Shak., etc., p. 167.

Compression (XIX.): Lan. to present.
> Compressed manner. M. ARNOLD, Celtic Lit., etc., p. 207.

CONCEIT (XXIII.).

Until the beginning of the eighteenth century, "conceit," as used in criticism, denoted in general the power of the mind to combine and recombine the elements given in experience, especially when the combinations from their novelty or beauty gave rise to æsthetic pleasure. Novelty, however, in such combinations usually dominated the sense of beauty, and hence conceits during this period ceased to be synonymous with thought in general, or with imaginative thought, and came to be closely related in meaning to a witticism, or to mere fancy. "Conceit" during this period was very seldom employed as an active critical term. *As conception.*

> Conceit of wit. 1580. HARVEY, p. 48.
>
> That high-flying liberty of conceit proper to the poet. 1583. SIDNEY, pp. 5, 6.
>
> We must prescribe to no writers (much less to poets) in what sort they should utter their conceits. 1586. WEBBE.
>
> The number is voluble and fit to express any amorous conceit. CAMPION, p. 254.
>
> This letter was writ in such excellent Latin, was so full of conceits, and all the expressions so suited to the genius of the king, etc. 1678. WALTON, Lives, p. 235.
>
> When he aimed at wit in the stricter sense, that is, sharpness of conceit. 1670. DRYDEN, IV., p. 237.
>
> A miserable conceit tickling you to laugh. 1699. ID., VIII., p. 374.

During the eighteenth and the present century, "conceit" has indicated strange combinations of ideas or of images, which seem to be made for the sake of the strangeness, and which have no essential relations with each other either from the æsthetic *As far-fetched comparisons.*

or practical point of view. Usually a conceit consists of a too great elaboration of a real analogy,—an elaboration so great, in fact, that the real analogy is wholly lost sight of in view of the elaboration. During these two centuries, "conceit" has been in general a term of condemnation, though often some adjective prefixed, such as "forced" or "far-fetched," is necessary in order to give to it this negative force.

> If defective, or unsound in the least part, the methodical style must of necessity lead us to the grossest absurdities, and stillest pedantry and conceit. SHAFTESBURY, I., p. 202.
>
> Conceit is to nature what paint is to beauty; it is not only needless, but impairs what it would improve. 1706. POPE, VI., p. 51.
>
> > Some to conceit alone their taste confine,
> > And glittering thoughts strike out at every line.
> >   1711. ID., II., p. 50.
>
> Puerile and far-fetched conceit. 1756. J. WARTON, I., p. 8.
>
> Forced conceits, . . . violent metaphors, . . . swelling epithets. ID., II., p. 21.
>
> Puns and conceits. T. WARTON, II. E. P., p. 647.
>
> With men like Earle, Donne, Fuller, Butler, Marvell, and even Quarles, conceit means wit; they would carve the merest cherry-stone of thought in the quaintest and delicatest fashion. But with duller and more painful writers, such as Gascoigne, . . . where they insisted on being fine, their wit is conceit. 1858-64. LOWELL, Lit. Es., I., p. 303.
>
> Now when this kind of thing is done in earnest, the result is one of those ill distributed syllogisms which in rhetoric are called conceits. 1868. ID., III., p. 53.
>
> The novel is not only in itself . . . unfriendly to the pompous style, but it happened to attract . . . the great genius of Fielding, which was from nothing so averse . . . as from . . . pretension, pedantry, or conceit. SAINTSBURY, Eng. Pr. St., p. xxvi.

Conceited (VII.): Camp. to present.
 The conceited Spanish-French style. SAINTSBURY, Hist. Fr. Lit., p. 293.
Concentrated (XIX.): Lan. to present.
 Lucretius' . . . poetry is masculine, plain, concentrated, and energetic. LANDOR, IV., p. 525.
Concinnity (IV.): Lowell.
 Marlowe's Hero and Leander has . . . many lines as perfect in their concinnity as those of Pope. LOWELL, O. E. D., p. 52.
Concise (XIX.): Bacon to present.
 Poetry . . . must be more intense in meaning and more concise in style than prose. BAGEHOT, Lit. St., II., p. 351.
Concrete (VIII.) *b*: Pater to present.
 Concrete imagery of Blessed Damozel. PATER, Ap., etc., p. 215.
Condensed (XIX.): Cole. to present.

Results either from careful selection, or from intensity of feeling.

 Crabbe's . . . great selection and condensation of expression. JEFFREY, II., p. 276.
 There is no enthusiasm, no energy, no condensation, nothing which springs from strong feeling, nothing which tends to excite it. 1824. MACAULAY, IV., p. 381.
 Shakespeare's sonnets are hot and pothery; there is much condensation, little delicacy. LANDOR, IV., p. 512.
 Goldsmith was a great, perhaps an unequalled, master of the arts of selection and condensation. 1856. MACAULAY, IV., p. 51.
Confused (II.): Ascham to present
 Order helps much to perspicuity as confusion hurts. B. JONSON, Timber, p. 63.
Congenial (XIV.): Congenial case . . . of Pepys. GOSSE, Hist. Eng. Lit., III., p. 80.
CONGRUITY (IV.).

Until the present century, "congruity" was often employed in conjunction with the term "propriety," with which it was very nearly identical in meaning. The sense of the congruous, however, was perhaps more concentrated, definite, and distinct than the sense of propriety; it was more immediate in its action, and in a sense more spontaneous; it was the first flash of recognition of a propriety between specific features of a composition. As referring not to the mental process, but to the completed literary product, the two terms are exactly synonymous.

As artistic propriety.

> A solecism or incongruity. 1585. PUTTENHAM, p. 258.
> Shakespeare, to enrich his scene with that variety which his exuberant genius so largely supplied, hath deformed his best plays with prodigious incongruities. 1749. HURD, I., p. 69.

During the present century, "congruity" has represented the moral sense of symmetry and proportion in literature, the unusual or unexpected violation of which produces the ridiculous or the humorous.

As ethical harmony.

> Wit is the clash and reconcilement of incongruities. 1846. HUNT, Wit and Humour, p. 8.
> Humor in its first analysis is a perception of the incongruous, and in its highest development of the incongruity between the actual and the ideal in men and life. 1866. LOWELL, II., p. 97.
> The same want of humor which made Wordsworth insensible to incongruity may perhaps account also for the singular unconsciousness of disproportion which so often strikes us in his poetry. 1875. ID., IV., p. 410.
> Tragic incongruity arises from the disproportion between the world and the soul of man; life is too small to satisfy the soul. . . . The comic incongruity is the reverse of this. DOWDEN, Sh., his Mind & Art. p. 351.

Conscientious (XIV.): Ros., Swinburne, Es. & St. p. 86.

Conscious (VII.): S. John. to present.
> Where an unconscious energy unites itself in the artist with his conscious activity, and these interpenetrate one another, the work of art comes forth. DOWDEN, St. in Lit., pp. 408, 409.

Consentaneity (IV.): In the poems of Wordsworth, which are most distinctively Wordsworthian, there is an entire consentaneity of thought and feeling. DOWDEN, St. in Lit., p. 127.

Consistency (XIII.), cf. (XIV.): Rymer to present.

Adaptation of the parts of a composition to each other so as to produce uniformity of tone and unity of impression.

> Ben Jonson's plots are improbable by an excess of consistency. HAZLITT, Eng. Com. Writers, p. 51.
> One-ness, that is to say, consistency in the general impression, metrical and moral. HUNT, Imagination and Fancy, p. 33.
> Shakespeare alone . . . made a world-wide variety of character and incident consistent with oneness of impression. WHIPPLE, Lit. of Age of El., p. 120.

Conspicuous (XVI.), cf. (IX.): Jef., Stephen. Jeffrey, II., p. 247.

Constrained (XVIII.): K. James to Carlyle.
> The hiatus is smoother, less constrained, and so preferable to the cæsura. POPE, VI., p. 113.

Constructive (XXIII.): Saintsbury.
> Four requisites for a poet . . . creativeness, constructiveness, the sublime, the pathetic. LANDOR, VIII., p. 419.

Consummate (XXII.): Swinburne, Es. & St., p. 65.

Contemplative (XX.) *b*: Jef., Ros. Jeffrey, II., p. 451.

Continuity (XIII.): Lan. to present.

Connected; blended and fused into a close emotional unity.

> Continuous . . . united by means of connectives. ARISTOTLE, Rhet., p. 229.
> The musical in sound is the sustained and continuous; the musical

in thought is the sustained and continuous also. HAZLITT, Eng. Poets, p. 16.

The rhythmical, the continuous, what in French is called the *soutenu*. DE QUINCEY, III., p. 51.

Contorted (II.): Cole., Car.

Conventional (IV.): J. War. to present.

Wordsworth has much conventional sentiment. PATER, Ap., p. 38.

Conversational: Saintsbury, Eng. Pr. Style, p. 18.

Convincing (XXII.) *b*: H. James, Partial Portraits, pp. 251, 252.

Convolution (II.): Saintsbury, Hist. Eng. Lit., p. 42.

Copious (XI.) *b*: Put. to present.

Homer's diction, contrary to what one would imagine consistent with simplicity, is at the same time very copious. POPE, VI., p. 13.

Copy (XI.) *b*: T. Wil., B. Jon.

There is a great difference between those that, to gain the opinion of copy, utter all they can, however unfitly; and those that use election and a mean. B. JONSON, Pref. to Alchemist.

Cordial (XIV.): Swinburne, Mis., p. 67.

CORRECTNESS (I.).

"Correctness" denotes in general a conformity in literature to the known laws of language and to the established rules of composition. The term thus refers primarily to the form of expression rather than to the thought, and represents a method of restraining or controlling the immediate movement in the development of language by means of past literary attainments. The history of the term may be divided into three periods.

Until the middle of the eighteenth century, "correctness" was one of the chief active terms of criticism.

<small>As exact methodic composition.</small> In the advertising phrase, "corrected and enlarged," which was so often placed on the

title page of the early dramas, "corrected" perhaps signified merely that the drama had been revised, especially its language, so as to be more intelligible and acceptable than it had been hitherto. But in all such revision there was a constant tendency to "correct" irregularities of all kinds, whether caused by overhaste or by the moulding influence of the inspiration which had given to the drama its literary value. "Correctness," as referring to versification, denoted metrical regularity, or at least variation of meter according to method and rule. "Correct," as referring to the drama, indicated a conformity to certain traditional rules of plot construction. The term, in short, denoted exactness in language and method in composition, and even the most ardent disciples of "correctness" recognized that it was opposed to the onward movement of literary sympathy and appreciation.

> All language has three kinds of excellence, to be correct, perspicuous, and elegant. QUINTILIAN, I. p. 37.
> Jonson is the more correct poet, but Shakespeare is the greater wit. 1668. DRYDEN, XV., p. 347.
> Correct plotting . . . and decorum of the stage. 1670. DRYDEN, Vol. IV.
> It is to criticism that the sacred authors themselves owe their highest purity and correctness. SHAFTESBURY, III., p. 186.
> Correctly cold. 1711. POPE, II., p. 48.
>> Blot out, correct, insert, refine,
>> Enlarge, diminish, interline:
>> Be mindful when invention fails,
>> To scratch your head and bite your nails.
>>   SWIFT, XIV., p. 303.

From about the middle of the eighteenth century until within the first few decades of the present century, "correct," though fast passing out of favor, was still an active term in criticism. Attempts were made in two ways to modify the intensely conservative nature of the term.

As accuracy to fact. Occasionally the term was applied directly to the thought of a composition, indicating truthfulness to the historical fact represented.

> Nature in awe to Him
> Had dofft her gawdy trim.
> (Milton, On the Nativity.)
> This is incorrect . . . it was winter. 1756. J. WARTON, I., p. 39.
> Truth and correctness. HURD, I., pp. 70, 71.
> Shakespeare . . . the most correct of poets. COLERIDGE, IV.; p. 65.

More usually, in so far as the term was thought to represent any positive literary merit at all, it indicated **As economy of strength or efficiency of statement.** a certain moderation of tone in literature, which, by being adapted exactly to the taste of the audience addressed, gave evidence of great skill, and perhaps produced as great an effect as could be attained by more spontaneous and irregular methods of composition.

> Correct mediocrity, which distinguishes the lyric poetry of the French. 1756. J. WARTON, I., p. 66.
> The early productions of Pope were perhaps too finished, correct, and pure. ID., I., p. 83.
> Correctness is a vague term, frequently used without meaning and precision. The French critics declare that the English writers are generally incorrect. If correctness implies an absence of petty faults, this perhaps may be granted; if it means a just economy in fables, the notion is groundless and absurd. ID., I., p. 196.

It is . . . the criticism which the stage exercises upon public manners that is fatal to comedy, by rendering the subject matter of it tame, correct, and spiritless. 1817. HAZLITT, The Round Table, p. 14.

His imagination . . . unrestrained by a correct judgment. 1818. BRYANT, I., p. 52.

Correctness . . . is . . . skill. . . . In this sense, Scott, Wordsworth, and Coleridge are far more correct poets than Pope or Addison. 1830. MACAULAY, I., p. 470.

Coldly and stiffly, though correctly and classically. 1830. WILSON, V., p. 362.

During the greater part of the present century the term "correct" has not been applied to current literature, but has been employed as a means for explaining the literature of the seventeenth and eighteenth centuries, especially the writings of Dryden and Pope. As a retrospective term, the meaning of "correctness" has been determined, not from what the term signified to Dryden and Pope themselves, but from what, as seen in their writings, the general effect of "correctness" is, when it is made the central and organizing principle of literature. The modern interpretations of "correctness" are more general and psychological, and refer more to the thought of the composition than did "correctness" as understood in the times of Dryden and Pope.

A retrospective term.

A mind always intent on correctness is apt to be dissipated in trifles. LONGINUS, p. 63.

It is an error that Pope's distinction consisted in correctness. . . . Of all poets that have practiced reasoning in verse, Pope is the most inconsequential in the deduction of his thoughts, and the most severely distressed in any effort to effect or to explain the dependency of their parts. . . . His grammar is vicious . . .

his syntax so bad as to darken his meaning at times, and at other times to defeat it. 1848. DE QUINCEY, XI., p. 62.

Correctness in metrical composition, as I understand Pope to mean, implies obedience to the laws of imaginative thought; and therefore not only precision of poetical expression, but justice of poetical conception. COURTHOPE, Lib. Movement, etc., p. 59.

The virtue on which Pope prided himself was correctness; and I have interpreted this to mean the quality which is gained by incessant labour guided by quick feeling, and always under the strict supervision of common sense. STEPHEN, Pope, p. 195. Morley's Eng. Men of Letters.

English prose literature towards the end of the seventeenth century, in the hands of Dryden and Locke, was becoming, as that of France had become at an earlier date, a matter of design and skilled practice, highly conscious of itself as an art, and above all correct. 1886. PATER, Ap., p. 127.

Setting up correctness, that humble merit of prose, as the central literary excellence, he (Dryden) is really a less correct writer than he may seem, still with an imperfect mastery of the relative pronoun. 1888. PATER, Ap., p. 3.

Corrective: Jeffrey.
Corrupt (XIV.): Coleridge, Stephen, Eng. Thought in Eighteenth Century, II., p. 353.
Costly (V.): Spenser's style . . . is costly. None but the daintiest and nicest phrases will serve him. LOWELL, IV., p. 334.
Courtly (V.): Bolton to present.

Raleigh . . . is full of proper, clear, and courtly graces of speech. 1610. BOLTON, Hypercritica, p. 249.

Covert (III.): Put. The English have no fancy, and are never surprised into a covert or witty word. EMERSON, Rep. Men, p. 221.
Crabbed (II.): Dek. to present. Gosse, From Shak. etc., p. 118.
Creative (XXIII.): T. War. to present.

Used chiefly in theory. It represents the result of the imaginative activities of the mind, which are brought into play in the production of literature.

Imagination has something in it like creation. ADDISON, III., p. 429.
For by invention, I believe, is usually understood a creative faculty. FIELDING, T. Jones, II., p. 6.
Genius . . . the power of acting creatively under laws of its own origination. COLERIDGE, IV., p. 54.
Creeping (XVIII.): Jeff., Hal., Jeffrey, II., p. 521.
Crisp (XVIII.): Terse and crisp versification. GOSSE, From Shak., etc., p. 212.
CRITICAL (XX.) *a*: Hal., Saints.

Used chiefly in theory:
I. As an elaborative and reflective process.

Fancy was weakened by reflection and philosophy. . . . Judgment was advanced above imagination, and rules of criticism were established. T. WARTON, II. E. P., p. 627.
The critical faculty is lower than the inventive. M. ARNOLD, Cr. Es., 1st S., p. 3.

II. As a penetrative and intuitive process.

Poetry is at bottom a criticism of life. M. ARNOLD, Cr. Es., 2d S., p. 143.
A delicate and tender justice in the criticism of human life. PATER, Ap., p. 105.
Crooked (II.): Ascham, Milton.
Crude (V.): Rymer to present.
Crude work of Shelley's boyhood. DOWDEN, Tr. & St., p. 247.
Cumbrous (II.): Cole to present.
Cumbrous and clumsy. WILSON, VIII., p. 86.
Cunning (V.) *b*: Swin., Dow.
Delicate cunning. DOWDEN, Shak., etc., p. 60.
Curious (IX.): Ascham to present.

I. The odd and striking, viewed chiefly as a product.

More curiously than cleanly. PUTTENHAM, p. 28.
More careful to speak curiously than truly. SIDNEY, p. 54.

II. The desire for the strange and unusual, viewed chiefly as a mental process.

> When one's curiosity . . . overbalances the desire of beauty. PATER, Ap., p. 248.
> Not less interesting than curious. SWINBURNE, A St. of B. J., p. 137.

Currant (XVIII.): Har., Put., Webbe.
> Currant and slipper upon the tongue. PUTTENHAM, p. 24.

Cut-and-thrust (XII.): Wilson, VII., p. 404.
Cyclopean (XI.): A Titanic or Cyclopean style. SWINBURNE, Mis., p. 98.
Cynical (XIV.): Swinburne, Mis., p. 75.
Dainty (XXII.) *b*: Whipple to present. Swinburne, Mis., p. 250.
Daring (XII.): Bryant to present.
> Their style becomes free and daring. DOWDEN, Shak., etc., p. 62.

Dark (III.): Ascham to present.
> The sense is hard and dark. ASCHAM, III., p. 269.

Dazzling (V.): Jeffrey, I., p. 413; Gosse, Life of Congreve, p. 135.
Debased (XIV.): Swinburne, Es. & St., p. 251.
DECENT (IV.):

Until the latter portion of the eighteenth century, the term "decent" indicated the absence in a compo-
As moral and artistic propriety. sition of startling incongruities, which gave offence to what may be called the moral sense of order and symmetry in literature. "Decent" was a less technical term than "decorum," and more inclusive in its meaning. The presence or absence of decency in a composition was determined by "some instinct or genius," or by the known truth or fact, or by well-established literary principles and precepts derived from past usage.

> The Greeks call this good grace of everything in its kind τὸ πρεπὸν, the Latins decorum; we in our vulgar call it by a scholastic

term, decency, our own Saxon English term is seemliness, that is to say, for his good shape and utter appearance well pleasing the eye, we call it also comeliness. 1585. PUTTENHAM, p. 268.

Still methinks that in all decency the style ought to conform with the nature of the subject, otherwise if a writer will seem to observe no decorum at all. ID., p. 163.

Apt and decent framing of words. 1586. WEBBE, p. 38.

Of the indecencies of an heroic poem, the most remarkable are those that show disproportion either between the persons and their actions, or between the manners of the poet and the poem. 1650. HOBBES, IV., p. 454.

A poet ought always to have that instinct or some good genius ready to serve his hero upon occasion, to prevent these unpleasant shocking indecencies. RYMER, 1st Pt., p. 64.

Sentiments which raise laughter can very seldom be admitted with any decency into an heroic poem, whose business is to excite passions of a much nobler nature. 1711. ADDISON, III., p. 188.

It is for the most part in our skill in manners, and in the observances of time and place, and of decency in general, which is only to be learned in those schools to which Horace recommends us, that what is called taste, by way of distinction consists. 1756. BURKE, I., p. 63.

The following is indecently hyperbolical:—
    To see this fleet upon the ocean move,
    Angels drew wide the curtains of the skies, etc.
        1781. S. JOHNSON, VII., p. 317.

Occasionally throughout the whole history of the term, and especially during the present century, "decent" has indicated an absence of moral licentiousness in the literary representation. *As moral propriety.*

Like the term "purity," it has been appropriated for the expression of the growing sense of morals in literature. It has, however, been less in use than formerly when given a more technical significance.

Indecency of wounding women (on the stage). 1670. DRYDEN, IV., p. 230.

Otway's "Orphan" is the work of a man not attentive to decency, nor zealous for virtue; but of one who conceived forcibly, and drew originally, by consulting nature in his own breast. 1781. S. JOHNSON, VII., p. 176.

Since the time of Addison . . . the open violation of decency has always been considered among us as the mark of a fool. MACAULAY, III., p. 454.

Decisive: Whip. to present.
Declamation (XIX.): J. War. to present.

Highly figurative; almost bombastic. A questionable and rare form of literary excellence.

Declamation overlays and strangles poetry, and disfigures even satire. LANDOR, V., p. 116.

The change from jog-trot commonplace to almost inspired declamation. SAINTSBURY, Hist. Eng. Lit., p. 214.

Decorative (V.): Sted., Swin.

Decoration . . . is attractive, but least artistic and least proper to poetry. ARISTOTLE, Poetics, p. 25.

In works of the imagination . . . the use of decorations may be varied a thousand ways with equal propriety. S. JOHNSON, II., p. 115.

DECORUM (IV.).

The term "decorum," until within the early portion of the present century, indicated the action of a refined and conservative moral sense within the ethical circle of literary sympathy. Hence it referred primarily to the literary representation of characters, of their moral deportment, and of the incidents related of them. Only very incidentally did the term refer to the language of a literary work. In theory "decorum" was sometimes said to be determined by an instinct or intuition of the mind;

As moral refinement in literature.

but in actual criticism it was at best an instinctive conformation to the well-established usages or conventions of good society and of good literature.

> They use one order of speech for all persons, a gross indecorum. 1578. WHEATSTONE, I., p. 204.
> Spenser's due observing of decorum everywhere, in personages, in season, in matter, in speech, and generally in all seemly simplicity of handling his matter and framing his words. 1586. WEBBE, p. 53.
> So to intermingle merry jests in a serious matter is an indecorum. GASCOIGNE, p. 32.
> I will as near as I can set down which matters be high and lofty, which be but mean, and which be low and base, to the intent the styles may be fashioned to the matters, and keep their decorum and good proportion in every respect. 1585. PUTTENHAM, p. 162.
> This lovely conformity or proportion or convenience between the sense and the sensible hath nature herself first most carefully observed in all her own works, then also by kind graft it in the appetites of every creature working by intelligence to covet and desire; and in their actions to imitate and perform, and of man chiefly before any other creature as well in his speeches as in every other part of his behavior. And this in generality and by a usual term is that which the Latins call decorum. ID., p. 269.
> (Of a sister's voluntarily consenting to incest) nothing could be invented more opposite to all honesty, honour, and decorum. RYMER, 1st Pt., pp. 69, 70.
> Decorum of the stage. 1670. DRYDEN, IV.
> The venustum, the honestum, the decorum of things will force its way. SHAFTESBURY, I., p. 108.
> There is an impropriety and indecorum in joining the name of the most profligate parasite with that of an apostle. 1756. J. WARTON, II., p. 315.

During the present century, "decorum" has fallen so much out of favor that it is not even used as a retrospective term. It usually denotes a conformity in literature to conventions of all kinds, an utter lack of spontaneity and original energy in a composition. It has been very little in use.

As moral and artistic conventionalism in literature.

> The details are lost or shaped into flimsy and insipid decorum. 1825. HAZLITT, Sp. of Age, p. 102.

Defective (XXII.) *a*: Jef. to present.   Jeffrey, I., p. 213.
Definite (III.): T. War. to present.
> Concrete and definite imagery . . . of Blessed Damozel. PATER, Ap., pp. 215, 216.

Delicacy (XXII.) *b*: Put. to present.

Refined sensibility; an airy gracefulness, the result of fineness rather than strength of feeling.

> The meter of six syllables is very sweet and delicate. PUTTENHAM, p. 84.
> Delicate, classical, and polished. BRYANT, I., p. 53.
> The poetic faculty always has for its basis a peculiar temperament, an extraordinary delicacy of organization, and susceptibility to impressions. M. ARNOLD, Cr. Es., 1st S., p. 107.

Delicious (XXII.) *b*: Jef. to present.   Swinburne, Mis., p. 3.
Delightful (XXII.) *b*: Hazlitt to present.   Hazlitt, Sp. of Age, p. 315.
Delusive (VIII.): J. Wilson, VII., p. 314.
Dense (XI.): Swin., Gosse.
> Juvenal's dense and full-bodied lines. GOSSE, Life of Congreve, p. 28.

Depth (XIII.) *b*: Ascham to present.

That which gives evidence of real and essential truth, of penetration and insight into the unifying principles of separate facts and details.

> Acuteness of remark or depth of reflection. MILTON, III., p. 498.
> More truth of character, more instinctive depth of sentiment. HAZLITT, Age of El., p. 96.

Depth and clearness; a clearness that shows depth. LANDOR, II., p. 415.

Goethe combines . . . French clearness with English depth. CARLYLE, I., p. 55.

Design (XXIII.): Dry. to present.

A conscious plan or purpose, or elaborated method of composition.

Design and artifice. DRYDEN, II., p. 288.

There is no uniformity in the design of Spenser: he aims at the accomplishment of no one action. ID., XIII., p. 17.

Without design; in which the essence of humor consists. HURD, II., p. 38.

Desultory (XVIII.): Jef. to present.

Desultory and rambling. WILSON, VI., p. 238.

Detailed (VIII.): Jef. to present.

Dramatic power of detail. SWINBURNE, Es. & St., p. 74.

Detestable (XXII.)*b*: Gosse, Life of Congreve, p. 85.

Device (XXIII.): Gas. to present.

An invention; a fancy; an ingenious ornament.

Beautify the same with brave devices. WEBBE, p. 36.

Whatever devise be of rare invention they term it fantastical. PUTTENHAM, p. 34.

Furnish your imagination with great store of images and suitable devices. SWIFT, IX., p. 189.

Dexterity (V.)*b*: Nash to present.

Peele's . . . pregnant dexterity of wit and manifold dexterity of invention. 1589. NASH, in Lit. Centuria, II., p. 238.

Dictatorial: Gosse, Hist. Eng. Lit., p. 94.

DIDACTIC (XXI.): Jef. to present.

Poetry written with the evident purpose of inculcating some moral lesson. A retrospective term, referring to the poetry of the seventeenth and eighteenth centuries.

What is didactic poetry? . . . The predicate destroys the subject. . . . No poetry can have the function of teaching . . . only as nature teaches, as forests teach, . . . viz. by deep impulse, by hieroglyphic suggestion. DE QUINCEY, XI., p. 88.

The didactic . . . is a lower kind of poetry. M. ARNOLD, Cr. Es., 2d S., p. 139.

Classical, didactic, and anti-romantic. GOSSE, From Shak., etc., p. 15.

Difficult (III.): Chan. to present.

Difficult and abstract. M. ARNOLD, Cr. Es., 2d S., p. 281.

Diffuse (XIX.): Swift to present. Hazlitt, Sp. of Age, p. 204.

DIGNITY (XI.).

The word "dignity" represents great energy and strength of personal character, which is at the same *As regulated metrical movement.* time controlled and regulated by a firm self-restraint. As a critical term, "dignity," previous to the present century, was thought to consist chiefly in the restraint and regulation of energy. Occasionally the term denoted a stately regularity of metrical movement.

> The shortness of verse and the quick returns of rhyme debase . . . the dignity of style. 1693. DRYDEN, XIII., p. 112.

Often the word denoted a uniform seriousness of tone in a composition. This meaning, which occasionally *As seriousness of thought.* occurs throughout the whole history of the term, places it in alliance with the tragic, and in opposition to the comic.

> Dignity of tragedy . . . elegance of comedy. 1638. MILTON, III., p. 498.
> Dignity and state of an heroic poem. 1669. DRYDEN, IV., p. 22.
> Dignity of tragedy. 1711. POPE, VI., p. 128.
> Wit should be used with caution in works of dignity, as it is only at best an ornament. 1759. GOLDSMITH, II., p. 357.
> Dignity truly Pindarick. 1781. S. JOHNSON, VIII., p. 38.

During the present century, the term "dignity" usually denotes a certain equipoise of thought and simplicity of statement which spring from a consciousness of great power, and a regulated and restrained use of that power. *As regulated strength and energy.*

> Moral dignity. LAMB, Elia, p. 286.
> Dignity,—from finite standard of the Greeks (as against sublimity). COLERIDGE, IV., p. 29.
> Dignity,—from sobriety and greatness of mind. MACAULAY, I., p. 38.
> Severe dignity of style. Do., p. 26.
> Dignity,—from simplicity. WORDSWORTH, III., p. 245.
> Dignity of poise. LOWELL, O. E. D., p. 37.

Digression (XIII.): T. Wil. to present.
Dilatation (XIX.) *b*: Spenser's dilatation is not mere distension. LOWELL, IV., p. 331.
Dilation (XIX.) *b*: Milton's power lay in dilation. LOWELL, Prose, IV., p. 84.
Dilletantesque (VII.): Poe to present.

Having a sporadic interest in many diverse things; an extensive rather than an intensive method of appreciation. Lack of earnestness and organic development.

> Two kinds of dilettanti . . . says Goethe . . . he who neglects the indispensable mechanical part, and thinks he has done enough if he shows spirituality and feeling; and he who seeks to arrive at poetry merely by mechanism, in which he can acquire an artizan's readiness, and is without soul and spirit. M. ARNOLD, Mixed Es., p. 503.
> Petrarch . . . is a moral dilettante. LOWELL, Prose, II., p. 253.

Dilution (XIX.): De Quincey to present. Swinburne, Es. & St., p. 251.
Dim (III.): Lamb, Swin.
> Your obscurity is not the dimness of positive darkness, but of distance. LAMB, Letters, II., p. 80.

DIRECT (XVIII.).

The use of the term "direct" is confined almost exclusively to the present century, and during the last few decades it has come to be of considerable prominence in criticism. "Directness" represents both a method of thinking and a form of feeling. These are both present in every use of the term, but now one preponderates and now another. Often "directness" denotes for the most part mere logical closeness and severity of thought; an intellectual simplicity and unsuperfluousness of style.

<small>As intellectual unsuperfluousness.</small>

> Direct and explicit. GRAY, 1., p. 403.
> Simplicity and directness. 1816. JEFFREY, II., p. 448.
> Directness and clearness of speech. M. ARNOLD, Mixed Es., p. 211.
> The thought deep, lucid, direct. 1867. SWINBURNE, Es. & St., p. 126.
> The direct intelligence of simple reason. 1872. ID., p. 28.

Often the term signifies for the most part a sincere openness of emotional expression, — a sincerity so immediate and energetic that at times it becomes blunt and unrefined.

<small>As emotional unsuperfluousness.</small>

> Keen sincerity and direct force. 1870. SWINBURNE, Es. & St., p. 89.
> There is a seeming artlessness in Lodge's sonnets, a winsome directness. 1874. MINTO, Char. of Eng. Poets, p. 198.
> It was thought that the old direct manner of speaking was crude and futile. 1885. GOSSE, From Shak. to Pope, p. 10.
> A direct statement through its truth, often has exceeding beauty, — the beauty, pathetic or otherwise, of perfect naturalness. 1892. STEDMAN, Nat. of Poetry, p. 193.

Discord (X.): Saints. Swinburne, Es. & St., p. 141.
Discriminative (XX.) *b*: Jef. to present. Dowden St. in Lit., p. 208.

Discursive (XIII.): Jef. to present.
  The discursive and decorative style of Spenser. SWINBURNE, Mis., p. 10.
Discutable (VIII.): H. James, p. 376.
Disjointed (XIII.): Haz., Saints.
  Lumbering and disjointed. SAINTSBURY, Hist. Fr. Lit., p. 214.
Dislocated: Gosse, From Shak., etc., p. 101.
Dissonance (X.): Swinburne, Mis., p. 114.
Distinct (III.): Mil. to present.

The term refers primarily to mental imagery. It denotes definiteness in the different images,— a definiteness, however, which is not abstracted and isolated enough to be inconsistent with an intense unifying emotion or feeling in the literary production.

> In Ossian . . . I knew that the imagery was spurious. In nature everything is distinct, yet nothing defined into absolute independent singleness. WORDSWORTH, II., p. 122.
> In Scott . . . the intensity of the feeling is not equal to the distinctness of the imagery. HAZLITT, Eng. Com. Writers, p. 174.

Distinction (IX.): Swin., Gosse.
  Originality or distinction. Swinburne, Mis., p. 92.
Distinguished (XXII.), cf. (XIX.): Cole, Gosse. Coleridge, III., p. 462.
Distorted (II.): Distorted and exaggerated picture. JEFFREY, III., p. 100.
Diverse (XIII.): Collier to present. Swinburne, Es. & St., p. 141.
Diverting (XVII.): Hal., Mor., Gosse. Hallam, III., p. 328.
Divine (XXII.) *b*: Add. to present. Addison, III., p. 188.
Doggerel (XXII.) *b*: Put. to present.
  Dissonant doggerel. SWINBURNE, Mis., p. 114.
DRAMATIC (XXI.).

The term "dramatic" represents in a composition that which is fit to be acted; in the author, the power of losing his personality in a full realization of the motives and actions of others; but the unifying conception of the term comes from the effect which the drama produces upon the reader or hearer. The term usually charactizes those forms of literature other than the drama which produce an effect upon the mind of the reader similar to that of the drama itself. It represents character portrayal, in which the incidents are intensified, animated, vivid, and striking. Occasionally the term is employed to distinguish between those parts of dramatic composition which conform to these essential requirements, and those parts which do not.

>Dramatic poetry . . . history made visible. BACON, IV., p. 315.
>As the Iliad was written while his spirit was in its greatest vigour, the whole structure of that work is dramatic and full of action. POPE, etc.
>>Shut, shut the door, good John (fatigued I said),
>>Tie up the knocker; say I'm sick, I'm dead. (Pope.)
>This abrupt exordium is animated and dramatic. J. WARTON, II., p. 208.
>Bold, dramatic transitions of Shakespeare's blank verse. HAZLITT, Eng. Poets, pp. 56, 57.
>The dramatist must . . . keep himself out of sight and let nothing appear but his characters. MACAULAY, I., p. 24.
>In the abstract, dramatic is thought or emotion in action, or on its way to become action. In the concrete, it is that which is more vivid if represented than described, and which would lose if merely narrated. LOWELL, O. E. D., p. 25.

Drawling: Wilson, II., p. 85.
Dreamy: Jef., Mor. Dreamy and abstracted. JEFFREY, II., p. 376.
Dreary (XXII.) *b*: Swin. to present. Swinburne, Mis., p. 133.
Drivelling (XI.): Jef. to present. Swinburne, Mis., p. 82.
Droll (XVII.): Rymer to present.
>Drollery arises where the laughable is its own end, — neither inference or moral being intended. COLERIDGE, IV., p. 275.

Dry (XV.), cf. (XVI. and XVII.): Ascham to present.

>An apparent want of spirit, feeling, and penetration.

Dry, hard, and barren of effect. HAZLITT, Age of El., p. 207.
Thoreau's dry humor. BURROUGHS, Birds and Poets, p. 61.
A certain coldness or dryness in the tone. T. ARNOLD, Hist., etc., p. 604.

Dry-stick (XVII.): Hunt. Saintsbury, Es. in Eng. Lit., p. 257.
Ductile (XVIII.): Jef., Whip. Jeffrey, II., p. 194.
Dull (XX.) *b*: Mil. to present.

Locke's style . . . is bald, dull, plebeian. SAINTSBURY, Eng. Pr. St., p. xxiv.

Earnest (XIV.): Lamb to present.

In considerable use: usually opposed to formal refinement and polish.

The primary virtues of sincerity, earnestness, and a moral interest in the main object. WORDSWORTH, II., p. 54.
Decorum gives place to earnestness. T. ARNOLD, Man., etc., p. 418.

EASY (XVIII.).

Previous to the present century, there were two more or less distinct uses of the term "easy." Often it was very nearly if not quite identical in meaning with clearness and perspicuity.

As perspicuity.

Easy and plain composition. TH. WILSON, Rhet., p. 178.
History . . . aims at easiness and perspicuity. 1699. BENTLEY, I., p. 360.
Perspicuous and easy. 1778. T. WARTON, Hist. E. P., p. 965.

More often "easy" denoted a general facility in composition, the result of extensive training and practice; if applied to versification it might result from the form of verse chosen.

As facility.

Rhyme, — that vulgar and easy kind of poetry. CAMPION, p. 232.
The great easiness of blank verse renders the poet too luxuriant; he is tempted to say many things which might better be omitted, or at least shut up in fewer words. 1664. DRYDEN, II., p. 138.

> When they had so polished their piece, and rendered it . . . natural and easy. SHAFTESBURY, I., p. 183.
> True ease in writing comes from art, not chance. 1711. POPE, II., p. 56.
> Whatever is done skilfully appears to be done with ease. 1751. S. JOHNSON, III., p. 80.

During the present century "ease" has represented a certain general efficacy of statement rather than mere fluency or clearness. The author must be master of the thought that he wishes to express; he must use words and methods of expression as familiar as is consistent with an adequate representation of the subject; and to do this there is required both acquired skill and native power and ability. When applied to the versification, "ease" denotes smoothness and efficiency, the result of practice and of the native sense of rhythm and harmony.

As efficiency.

> Ease and simplicity are two expressions often confounded and misapplied. We usually find ease arising from long practice, and sometimes from a delicate ear without it; but simplicity may be rustic and awkward, of which there are innumerable examples in Wordsworth's volumes. 1826. LANDOR, IV., p. 61.
> If by classical is meant ease, precision, and unsuperfluousness of style. 1848. HUNT, A Jar of Honey, p. 158.
> A French lightness and ease of expression. 1843. WHIPPLE, Es. & Rev., p. 16.
> Too much consideration is unfavorable to the ease of letter-writing, and perhaps of all writing. 1855. BAGEHOT, I., p. 253.
> A feminine ease and grace. M. ARNOLD, Cr. Es., 1st S., p. 131.
> Familiar words make a style frank and easy. ID., p. 283.
> The seventeenth century critics . . . associated and confounded ease of composition with shallowness of endowment, and a stock of classical phraseology with creative power. 1884. T. ARNOLD, Man. of Eng. Lit., p. 280.

Ebullient (XII.): Effusive and ebullient. SWINBURNE, Es. & St., p. 271.
Eccentric (II.): Saintsbury, Hist. Eng. Lit., III., p. 278.
Eclectic (XIII.): Gosse, Pater.
  Of eclecticism, we have a justifying example in one of the first poets of our time, — Tennyson. PATER, Ap., p. 13.
Ecstasy (XV.): Ros., Gosse. Rossetti, Lives of Famous Poets, p. 60.
Edge (XX.) *b*: Swinburne, Mis., p. 303.
Effeminate (XII.): Gosson to present. S. Johnson, V., p. 133.
Effete (IV.): Swin., Gosse. Swinburne, Mis., p. 86.
Efficacy (XXII.): Camden to present.
  Skill, variety, efficacy, and sweetness, the four material points required in a poet. CAMDEN, p. 337.
Effortless (VII.): Wilson, X., p. 180.
Effusive (XIX.) *b*: Dow. Swinburne, Es. & St., p. 69.
Egotism (XIV.): Jef. to present. Swinburne, Mis., p. 110.
Elaborate (V.): Heywood to present.

Not spontaneous; that which is consciously designed and attained.

  Cultivate simplicity, banish elaborateness. LAMB, Letters, I., p. 46.
  Goldsmith wrote with elaborate simplicity. JEFFREY, I. p. 166.
  The delicate touch of the true humorist . . . is alien to De Quincey's more elaborate style. STEPHEN, Hrs. in a Lib., I., p. 376.

Elastic (XVIII.): Jef. to present. Swinburne, Es. & St., p. 250.
Elegiac (XXI.): Low. to present.
  Dante's "Inferno" . . . not sublime enough to be tragic, and not pathetic enough to be elegiac. T. ARNOLD, Hist. of Eng. Lit., p. 498.

ELEGANCE (V.).

"Elegance" in rhetorical theory is considered as one of the three or four essentials of style. In actual criticism its history may be divided into two periods. Until near the beginning of the present century, "elegance" indicated a gen- *As general elevation and refinement of style.*

eral exaltation of style out of the vulgar and commonplace, by means of refined diction, poetical figures of speech, and scholarly allusion. The term is found placed in antithesis to "dignity," to the "strong and solemn," to the "sublime," and to the "beautiful." "Elegance" thus represented the lighter graces of speech, which are the result of fanciful ingenuity, rather than the more essential qualities of style, which rest primarily upon the thought and the artistic conception of the literary work.

> Elegancies result from metaphor constructed on similar ratios, proportion, and from personification. ARISTOTLE, Rhet., p. 239.
>
> A fiction of one of the later poets is not inelegant: He feigns that at the end of the thread or web of every man's life, there hangs a little medal or collar, on which his name is stamped. BACON, IV., p. 307.
>
> Propriety must first be stated, ere any measures of elegance can be taken. 1679. DRYDEN, VI., p. 251.
>
> Elegance and grace. 1756. J. WARTON, I., p. 334.
>
> The nameless and inexplicable elegancies, which appeal wholly to the fancy, from which we feel delight but know not how they produce it. 1751. S. JOHNSON, II., p. 432.
>
> Though the following lines of Donne . . . have something in them scholastic, they are not inelegant:
>> This twilight of two years, not past nor next,
>> Some emblem is of me or I of this,
>> Who meteor-like of stuff and form perplexed,
>> Whose what and where in disputation is.
>
> 1781. ID., VII., p. 19.
>
> Those happy combinations of words which distinguish poetry from prose had been rarely attempted. We had few elegancies or flowers of speech. 1781. ID., VII., p. 308.

During the present century "elegance" has been employed to a certain extent as a retrospective term, and has not been held in very high favor. It is supposed to result from an elaborate use of the fancy, use so elaborate as to negate the higher possibilities of poetry. "Elegance" thus signifies a certain studied brilliancy, primarily of the language, secondarily of the thought, the evident result of lightness of fancy rather than depth of thought or feeling.

As elaborate brilliancy.

> An inelegant cluster of "withouts." 1810. COLERIDGE, IV., p. 386.
> Romantic grace and classic elegance. 1820. HAZLITT, Age of Eliz., p. 116.
> (Of Voltaire) That the deeper portion of our soul sits silent unmoved under all this; recognizing no universal beauty, but only a modish elegance, less the work of a poetical creation than a process of the toilette, need occasion no surprise. 1829. CARLYLE, II., p. 167.
> (Of Captain Hall) There is such a pleasure in listening to his elegant nothings. POE, I., p. 355.
> Elegant . . . is not in the nomenclature of the Lake School. Since dealing . . . with the essential principles of human nature, that school had no room . . . for those minor contrivances of thought and language, which are necessary to express the complex accumulation of little feelings, the secondary growth of human emotion. 1857. BAGEHOT, II., p. 272.
> Wit, ingenuity, and learning in verse, even elegancy itself, though that comes nearest, are one thing; true native poetry is another. 1871. (Quoted from Philipps.) LOWELL, IV., p. 2.

Elevation (XI.): Dry. to present.

Much in use. A sublimation or heightening of ordinary language.

I. Previous to the present century, by means of metrical and rhetorical expedients.

> Expedients for elevation of style, — 1. Definition instead of single name, etc. ARISTOTLE, Rhet., pp. 222, 223.

> Poetry . . . an elevation of natural dialogue. GOLDSMITH, I., p. 339.
> Cowley considered the verse of twelve syllables as elevated and majestic. S. JOHNSON, VII., p. 55.

II. During the present century, "elevation" has usually been supposed to spring from the passion, feeling, or thought expressed.

> The elevation of tone arises from the strong mood of passion rather than from poetical fancy. SCOTT, Life of Swift, p. 453.
> Milton's elevation clearly comes in the main from a moral quality in him, — his pureness. M. ARNOLD, Mixed Es., etc., p. 202.

Elliptical (XIX.) *b*: Hal. to present. Swinburne, Mis., p. 206.
Elocution (VI.): Webbe to Dryden.

Used chiefly in theory. It was a technical expression, denoting the choice of words, the selection of language for a thought already apprehended and arranged. Occasionally the term represented merely the rhetorical enhancement of the thought.

> Elocution, or the art of clothing and adorning thought, already found and varied, in apt, significant, and sounding words. DRYDEN, IX., p. 96.
> Elocution and artifices. ID., XV., pp. 304, 305.
> Lively images and elocution. ID., V., p. 120.

ELOQUENCE (VI.).

The term "eloquence" has usually been closely synonymous with the term "poetical." Like the "poeti-
<small>As strong poetical feeling.</small> cal," "eloquence" in early criticism tended to represent a heightening, and hence a falsification of the truth; later, an "imitation of nature;" and in the present century, impassioned imagination. But these different uses and changes of meaning in the term "eloquence" were not as marked as in the

term "poetical," and may be classed together as representing an impassioned and elevated method of expression, as strength rather than delicacy of poetic feeling.

> I hold eloquence venerable and even sacred in all its departments; in solemn tragedy ... in the majesty of the epic, the gayety of the lyric muse, the wanton elegy, the keen iambic, and the pointed epigram. TACITUS, II., p. 401.
> Cato ... had more truth for the matter than eloquence for the style. ASCHAM, p. 156.
> Doubtless that indeed according to art is most eloquent which turns and approaches nearest to nature. MILTON, III., p. 100.
> Plato is most celebrated for imagination, and for an eloquence highly poetical. LANDOR, III., p. 149.
> Eloquence of impassioned thought finding vent in vivid imagery. LOWELL, Lat. Lit. Es., p. 124.

In theory at least, however, the "poetical" and the "eloquent" have occasionally been distinguished from each other. Modern eloquence is not naturally so poetical as was ancient eloquence. When it becomes elevated, it usually gives the effect of rhetorical heightening rather than of sincere and native feeling.

As a heightened method of expression.

> Ancient eloquence was sublime, passionate; modern eloquence is argumentative, rational. HUME, I., p. 172.
> Poetry sprang from ease, and was consecrated to pleasure, whereas eloquence arose from necessity, and aims at conviction. GOLDSMITH, I., p. 341.
> It is the fault of the day to mistake mere eloquence for poetry; whereas in direct opposition to the conciseness and simplicity of the poet, the talent of the orator consists in making much of a simple idea. NEWMAN, Es. on Aristotle, p. 18.

Emasculate (XII.): Smooth, emasculated lyrics. GOSSE, Seventeenth Cent. St., p. 201.

Embellished (V.): Dry. to present.

Embroidered (V.): Jeffrey, I., p. 412.
Emotion (XV.): Jef. to present.

Recently in considerable use. The term usually represents a mental excitation, which is less intense and active than passion, and more so than feeling.

> True emotion is emotion ripened by a slow ferment of the mind and qualified to an agreeable temperance by that taste which is the conscience of polite society. LOWELL, II., p. 252.
> His idealism does not consist in conferring grandeur upon vulgar objects by tinging them with the reflection of deep emotion. STEPHEN, Hrs in a Lib., I., p. 280.
> Poetic passion is intensity of emotion. STEDMAN, Nat. of Poetry, p. 261.

Emphatic (XII.).

That which by any means has been made more striking than ordinary composition. This result is usually brought about by figurative language; and the "emphatic" and the "poetical" are occasionally found associated with each other.

> Emphasis, or what in an artist's sense gives relief to a passage, causing it to stand forward and in advance of what surrounds it, — that is the predominating idea in the "sublime" of Longinus. DE QUINCEY, X., p. 301.
> Poetical . . . that is figurative and emphatic. HALLAM, II., p. 207.
> Poetry should be memorable and emphatic, intense and soon over. BAGEHOT, Lit. St., II., p. 352.
> Style . . . consists mainly in the absence of undue emphasis and exaggeration. LOWELL, III., p. 353.

Enchanting (XXII.) *b*: Jef. to present. Jeffrey, II., p. 56.
Energia (XII.): Sid. to present.

> Energia of poets lies in high and hearty invention. (Quoted from Chapman.) STEDMAN, Nat. of Poetry, p. 18.

ENERGY (XII).

Previous to the present century, the term "energy," much like the Greek ἐνέργεια, signified a general vividness in composition, which manifested itself in both the thought and the language. As applying to the language of a composition, "energy" was manifested in the sound, in the meter, in rhyme, in the general diction and choice of words, and in smoothness and ease of comprehension. When the term apparently refers wholly to the language, it perhaps often applies by figure of speech to the thought also. As applying to the thought of a composition, "energy" was said to spring from concreteness, from distinctness, from dramatic power, and from brevity.

As vividness and effectiveness.

> If indeed they feel those passions, it may easily be betrayed by that same forcibleness or energeia (as the Greeks call it) of the writer. 1583. SIDNEY, p. 52.
> From burning suns when livid deaths descend,
> When earthquakes swallow, or when tempests sweep
> Towns to one grave, whole nations to the deep. (Pope.)
> I quote these lines as an example of energy of style. 1756. J. WARTON, II., p. 65.
> The foundations for a nervous or a weak style are laid in an author's manner of thinking. If he conceives an object strongly he will express it with energy. BLAIR, Rhet., p. 199.

During the present century, the term "energy" has almost uniformly referred to the active creative process in the mind of the poet. It denotes delicacy as well as vividness of conception and expression; it represents the most primal and fundamental activity of the artistic impulses and instincts.

As strength of artistic impulse.

> Motives are symptoms of weakness and supplements for the deficient energy of the living principle, the law within us. 1825. COLERIDGE, I., p. 166.

Byron possessed the soul of poetry which is energy. 1826. LAN-DOR, IV., p. 43.
For one effect of knowledge is to deaden the force of the imagination and the original energy of the whole man. 1846. RUSKIN, St. of Ven., II., p. 56.
Genius is mainly an affair of energy, and poetry is mainly an affair of genius. 1865. M. ARNOLD, Cr. Es., 1st S., p. 50.
No poet, perhaps, is so evidently filled with a new and sacred energy when the inspiration is upon him (as Wordsworth). M. ARNOLD, Cr. Es., 2d S., p. 155.
Chaucer's descriptive style is remarkable for its lowness of tone, — for that combination of energy with simplicity which is among the rarest gifts in literature. 1870. LOWELL, III., p. 353.

Engaging (XXII.) *b*: Jeffrey, II., p. 326.
English (I.): Keats' "Ode to Nightingale" . . . fresh, genuine, and English. JEFFREY, II., p. 386.
Entertaining (XXII.) *b*: Haz., Gosse. Hazlitt, Sp. of Age, p. 315.

ENTHUSIASM.

The term "enthusiasm" has varied more as to the favor with which it has been received than as to the meaning which has been given to it. *[As the passionately fanciful.]* It has always represented an excited state of the feelings, a passionate devotion to a purpose or ideal. But until the latter portion of the eighteenth century, this passion or feeling was thought to be inconsistent with the calm apprehension and presentation of truth. "Enthusiasm" represented a moral quality, having some justification for its existence, which, however, in literature produced nothing but wild and incoherent fancies.

Poetry is the language of enthusiasm . . . guard against what savours of poetry. ARISTOTLE, Rhet., pp. 222, 226.
Good humour is not only the best security against enthusiasm, but the best foundation of piety and true religion. SHAFTESBURY, I., pp. 16, 17.

> Inspiration is a real feeling of the divine presence, and enthusiasm a false one. ID., p. 40.
> True poetry . . . cannot well subsist . . . without a tincture of enthusiasm. 1756. J. WARTON, I., p. 317.

Since the latter portion of the eighteenth century, the enthusiastic has been closely synonymous with the impassioned. It represents moral sincerity and intense energy combined, to a certain extent at least, with poetical passion and feeling. *As the sympathetic and impassioned.*

> Enthusiastic and meditative imagination, poetical as contradistinguished from human and dramatic imagination. WORDSWORTH, II., p. 139.
> There is no enthusiasm, no energy, no condensation, nothing which springs from strong feeling, nothing which tends to excite it. MACAULAY, IV., p. 391.
> Enthusiasm sublimates the understanding into imagination. LOWELL, Lit. Es., I., p. 196.

Enthusiastic (XV.): Shaftes. to present.
Ephemeral (XI.): Poe. Gosse, Hist. Eng. Lit., p. 43.
Epical (XXI.): Lowell.

Used little in theory, and perhaps not at all as an active critical term.

> The Spanish tragedy inclines more towards the lyrical, the French toward the epical. LOWELL, Prose, II., p. 128.

Epigrammatic: Camden to present.

Usually regarded as a low form of literary composition.

> Little fanciful authors and writers of epigram. ADDISON, II., p. 374.
> Alexander's Feast concludes with an epigram of four lines; a species of wit as flagrantly unsuitable to the dignity, and as foreign to the nature, of the lyric, as it is of the epic muse. J. WARTON, I., p. 60.

Equable (XIX.): Haz. to present.
> Equable flow of the sentiments. HAZLITT, Age of El., p. 56.
> That monotonous equability, that often wearies us in more polished poetry. HALLAM, II., p. 232.

Equality (II.): Dry. to present. .
> I have not everywhere observed the equality of numbers in my verse . . . because I would not have my sense a slave to syllables. DRYDEN, III., p. 379.
> Hazlitt is one of the most absolutely unequal writers in English; with him the inequality is pervading, and shows itself in his finest passages. SAINTSBURY, Eng. Lit., etc., p. 137.

Equanimity (XIX.): Equanimity of conscious and constantly indwelling power . . . Wordsworth had not. LOWELL, Prose, VI., p. 109.

Erotic (XV.): Shel. to present.
> Erotic delicacy in poetry . . . correlate with softness in statuary. SHELLEY, VII., pp. 118, 119.

Erratic (II.): Swinburne, Es. & St., p. 284.

Erudite (XX.): Gosse, Life of Congreve, p. 182.

Ethereal (XXII.) *b*: Whip. to present.
> There is something a little too ethereal in all this. M. ARNOLD, Cr. Es., 1st S., p. 285.

Ethos (VI.): Dry. to present. (See "Characters" and "Manners.")

Euphuism: Whip. to present.

Has not been applied to literature enough to be given a definite meaning. The affectation of ardent and useless feelings. Chiefly a retrospective term, referring to certain foreign imitations in the time of Queen Elizabeth.

> In the romances of Greene and Lodge we have Euphuism as an affectation of an affectation. WHIPPLE, Lit. of Age of El., p. 253.
> Belated euphuism. GOSSE, Hist. Eng. Lit., p. 39.

Evanescent (XI.): Ros., Gosse.
> Spontaneous and evanescent beauties . . . of the best romantic poetry. GOSSE, Hist. Eng. Lit., III., p. 24.

Even (II.): Put. to present.
Even and harmonious excellence. SWINBURNE, Mis., p. 136.
Everydayness: Lowell, Prose, III., p. 111.
EXACT (VIII.).

Usually the term "exact" has indicated a careful and studied method of expression, the chief emphasis being placed upon the use of language and the mechanical construction of the composition. *As accuracy of language.* This use of the term was especially marked previous to the present century.

> Little exactnesses in translating. POPE, VIII., p. 107.
> To make our poetry exact there ought to be some stated mode of admitting triplets and alexandrines. S. JOHNSON, VII., p. 347.
> Where there is laxity, there is inexactness. LANDOR, V., p. 109.

Occasionally the term denotes definiteness in the use of imagery, and accuracy in the sequence of thought in a composition. *As logical accuracy.*

> An attempt to unite order and exactness of imagery with a subject formed on principles so professedly romantic and anomalous is like giving Corinthian pillars to a Gothic palace. T. WARTON, Hist. Eng. Poetry, p. 261.
> Intellectual exactness of statement. LOWELL, IV., p. 20.

Occasionally, also, exactness indicates a scrupulous accuracy to the details of the facts represented. *As accuracy to fact.*

> This exactness of detail . . . gives an appearance of truth. HAZLITT, Eng. Com. Writers, p. 159.

Exaggerated (VIII.): Bacon to present.

Much in use. An overstatement of the facts, which, however, in a mild form, as poetical emphasis, has usually been regarded, in theory at least, as possessing positive literary merit.

The chief power of an orator lies in exaggeration and extenuation. QUINTILIAN, II., p. 108.

Characters in poetry may be a little overcharged or exaggerated without offering violence to nature. GOLDSMITH, I., p. 339.

Exaggeration and as a result coldness of sentiment. MACAULAY, IV., p. 380.

The imagination is an exaggerating and exclusive faculty. HAZLITT, III., p. 50.

Exalted (XI.): J. War. to present. Swinburne, Es. & St., p. 12.
Excellent (XXI.): Jef. to present. Swinburne, Es. & St., p. 165.
Excessive (VIII.): Hume to present. Rossetti, Lives, etc., p. 106.
Excitement: Intensity and excitement in expression. GOSSE, Hist. Eng. Lit., III., p. 57.
Excrementitious (VII.): Dowden, Tr. & St., p. 287.
Excursive (XIII.): Jef., Saints. Jeffrey, I., p. 391.
Exhaustive (XXII.): Swin., Saints. Swinburne, Mis., p. 57.
Exotic (VII.): Gib., Jef., Saints.
Expansive (XIII.) *b*: Haz. to present.

Meditative expansiveness . . . of Bacon. WHIPPLE, Lit. of Age of El., p. 337.

Explicit (III.): Gray. Gosse, Hist. Eng. Lit., p. 26.
Expressive: J. War. to present.

Burns' letters . . . simple, vigorous, expressive. CARLYLE, II., p. 12.

Exquisite (XXII.) *b*: Rymer to present.

In this fable . . . there is hardly anything more exquisite and more perfect than history. RYMER, 1st Pt., pp. 57, 58.

Extraordinary (IX.): Jef. to present.
Extravagant (XIX.) *b*: Dry. to present.

Much in use. An overstrained use of figurative language, or an extremely exaggerated method of presenting facts.

Which the glad saint shakes off at his command,
As once the viper from his sacred hand. (Waller.)

This is extravagant. S. JOHNSON, VII., p. 211.

This extravagant and absurd diction. WORDSWORTH, II., p. 103.

A delicate sense of humor . . . the best preservative against all extravagance. STEPHEN, Hrs. in a Lib., p. 295.

Exuberance (XI.) *b* : Mil. to present.
  The remedy for exuberance is easy; barrenness is incurable by any labor. QUINTILIAN, II., p. 106.
  Chasten the exuberance of conceit and fancy. SHAFTESBURY, I., p. 131.
Exultation: Swinburne, Es. & St., p. 164.
FABLE (VI.) : Put. to beginning of nineteenth century.

Used in theory as a correlate expression to characters, manners, sentiment, and style. Mechanically considered, it represented the plot construction, more essentially the story or fiction embodied in a literary production. The fable was usually regarded as in itself poetical. This was the epic conception of poetry. The schematizing influence of the term, or at least of the idea which it represents, is found throughout dramatic criticism, and to a certain extent in the criticism of the novel also.

  The fable and fiction is, as it were, the form and soul of any poetical work or poem. B. JONSON, Timber, p. 73.
  Fable though the foundation . . . is not the chief thing, since pity and terror will operate nothing on our affections except the characters, manners, thoughts, and words are suitable. DRYDEN, XV., pp. 381, 382.
  The fable is properly the poet's part, since characters are taken from moral philosophy, etc. RYMER, 2d Pt., pp. 86, 87.
  In poetry, which is all fable, truth still is the perfection. SHAFTESBURY, I., pp. 110, 111.
Facetious (XXII.) *b*: Wakefield to present.
  Facetious stories. WAKEFIELD, in Lit. Cen., I., p. 20.
Facility (XVIII.), cf. (V.) *b* : Put. to present.
  The uncommon union of so much facility and force. J. WARTON, II., p. 267.
Factitious (VII.) : Jeffrey, I., p. 393.
Fade (Fr.) : Insipid; dull. Saintsbury, Es. in Eng. Lit., p. 350.
Fair: Jef. Saintsbury, Hist. Fr. Lit., p. 289.

Faithful (VIII.): T. War. to present.
    Justness and faithfulness of the representation. T. WARTON, Hist. Eng. Poetry, p. 34.
False (VIII.): Jef. to present.
    False and hollow. WILSON, VII., p. 297.
Falsetto (VII.): Jef. to present. Coleridge, VI., p. 417.
Familiar: Dry. to present.
    At once romantic and familiar. HAZLITT, Eng. Com. Writers, p. 174.
FANCY (XXIII.).

Until the present century, "fancy" and "imagination," in actual criticism, were almost synonymous expressions. "Imagination," however, was often in a vague manner the more inclusive term. "Fancy," when it was not exactly synonymous with "imagination," may be said to have varied from it in three ways: it denoted the more wild and vagrant flights of the imagination; or those lighter forms of the imagination which perhaps aid in the process of composition; or those far-fetched combinations of ideas or images which produce the feeling of the ludicrous, or what was sometimes called "comical wit."

As lightness of conceit.

    Poetical fancies and furies. 1641. B. JONSON, I., p. 201.
    His sharp wit and high fancy. 1640. WALTON, Lives, p. 53.
    Fancy . . . consisteth not so much in motion as in copious imagery discreetly ordered and perfectly registered in the memory. 1650. HOBBES, IV., p. 449.
    When fancy was yet in its first work, moving the sleeping images of things towards the light, there to be distinguished, and then either chosen or rejected by the judgment. 1664. DRYDEN, II., p. 130.
    In plotting and writing, the fancy, memory, and judgment are then extended, like so many limbs, upon the rack. 1664. ID., p. 132.

So, then, the first happiness of the poet's imagination is properly invention, or finding of the thought; the second is fancy, or the variation deriving or moulding of that thought, as the judgment represents it proper to the subject. 1666. DRYDEN, IX., p. 96.

But how it happens that an impossible adventurer should cause our mirth, I cannot so easily imagine . . . its oddness . . . to be ascribed to the strange appetite of the fancy. 1671. ID., III., p. 241.

Fancy gives the life touches and secret graces to a poem. 1671. ID., p. 252.

Fancy, I think, in poetry is like faith in religion; it makes far discoveries, and soars above reason, but never clashes or runs against it. RYMER, 1st Pt., p. 8.

Correct the redundancy of humours, and chasten the exuberance of conceit and fancy. SHAFTESBURY, I., p. 131.

The imagination or fancy, which I shall use promiscuously. 1712. ADDISON, III., p. 394.

In allegory there are always two passions opposing each other; a love of reality, which represses the flights of fancy, and a passion for the marvellous, which would leave reflection behind 1759. GOLDSMITH, IV., pp. 334, 335.

When the reader's fancy is once on the wing, let it not stoop at correction and explanation. 1765. S. JOHNSON, V., p. 152.

During the present century, "fancy" and "imagination" have been sharply distinguished from each other, "fancy" denoting that method of combining ideas or images which is intermediate between the method of imagination on the one hand and of conceit on the other. "Fancy," considered as a mental process, represents the rapid play of the mind in search of unwonted combinations, which, often by revealing essential likenesses in ideas or images that were thought to be unrelated to one another, imperceptibly shades into the imagination. Considered as a

As lightness of imaginative activity.

completed product, "fancy" denotes such combinations of mental elements as neither having any direct analogy in actual life, nor possessing sufficient æsthetic beauty to be taken up into ideals, arouse no passion or intense feeling, and find their artistic justification only in a certain delicacy of conception, which easily shades into over-refinement and conceit.

>Things that come from the heart direct, not by the medium of the fancy. 1796. LAMB, Letters, I., p. 18.
>
>Fancy, the faculty of bringing together images dissimilar in the main by some one point or more of likeness, as in such a passage as this: —
>>Full gently now she takes him by the hand,
>>A lily prisoned in a pail of snow.
>
>> 1810. COLERIDGE, IV., p. 48.
>
>Fancy has no other counters to play with but fixities and definites. The fancy is indeed no other than a mode of memory emancipated from the order of time and space, . . . while it is blended with and modified by that empirical phenomenon of the will which we express by the word choice. But equally with the ordinary memory the fancy must receive all its materials ready made from the law of association. 1817. COLERIDGE, III., p. 364.
>
>All the fancies that fleet across the imagination, like shadows on the grass of the tree-tops, are not entitled to be made small separate poems of about the length of one's little finger. (Of Tennyson's early poems.) 1832. WILSON, VI., p. 151.
>
>Imagination belongs to Tragedy or the serious muse; Fancy to the comic. 1844. HUNT, Im. & Fancy, p. 26.
>
>Wit . . . is fancy in its most wilful, and, strictly speaking, its least poetical state. 1846. HUNT, Wit & Humour, p. 8.
>
>Fancy . . . is related to color; imagination to form. 1876. EMERSON, Let. & Soc. Aims, p. 33.
>
>The fancy of young poets is apt to be superabundant. It is the imagination that ripens with the judgment, and asserts itself as the shaping power in a deeper sense than belongs to it as a mere

maker of pictures when the eyes are shut. LOWELL, Rep. Men, p. 116.

The Rape of the Lock ranks by itself as one of the purest works of human fancy; whether that fancy be strictly poetical or not is another matter. 1871. LOWELL, IV., p. 36.

The distinction between fancy and imagination is, in brief, that fancy deals with the superficial resemblances, and imagination with the deeper truths that underlie them. 1879. STEPHEN, Hrs. in a Library, p. 203.

Imagination and fancy are both intellectual faculties, and the main function of both is to detect and exhibit the resemblances which exist among objects of sense or intelligence. 1884. T. ARNOLD, Hist. of Eng. Lit., p. 558.

Fantastic (II.): Webbe to present.

Though not fantastical and full of love quirks and quiddities. 1588. MUNDAY, Har. Mis., IV., p. 220.

Little niceties and fantastical operations of art. POPE, X., p. 532.

The fantastic is dangerously near to the grotesque, while the imagination, where it is most authentic, is most serene. LOWELL, O. E. D., p. 71.

Fantasy (XXIII.): Camden to present.

Fantasy, the image-making power, common to all who have the gift of dreams. LOWELL, III., p. 31.

Farce (XXI.): Hurd to present.

Farce . . . object merely to excite laughter. HURD, II., p. 30.

The "Taming of the Shrew" for its extravagance ought rather to be called a farce than a comedy. HUNT, Wit & H., p. 117.

Far-fetched (IV.): T. Wil. to present.

Jejune, far-fetched, and frigid. HAZLITT, Age of El., p. 211.

Far-sought (VII.): Far-sought phrase of literary curiosity. LOWELL, Prose, II., p. 106.

Fascinating (XXII.) *b*: Hal. to present. Swinburne, A St. of B. J., p. 102.

Fashionable (IV.): Jef. to present. Gosse, Seventeenth Cent. St., p. 278.

Fast: Straight, fast, and temperate style. ASCHAM, III., p. 204.

Fastidious (IV.): Jef. to present. Jeffrey, I., p. 165.

Faultless (XXII.): Dowden, Tr. & St., p. 288.

Fecundity (XVI.): Whip., Low.
  Fecundity of invention. LOWELL, Prose, VI., p. 134.
Feeble (XII.): Ascham to present.
  A feeble, diffuse, showy, Asiatic redundancy. HAZLITT, Sp. of Age, p. 204.
FEELING (XV.).

The term "feeling" has grown rapidly in use during the present century. It indicates a certain delicacy of mental response or of susceptibility to the full meaning of the given facts of experience, and an equal delicacy and susceptibility in blending these given facts with the æsthetic intuitions and ideals of the mind. In so far as "feeling" merely responds to the given facts of experience, it often seems to be wholly passive and to become allied to taste and to the proprieties. But in so far as it denotes susceptibility in blending these given facts with ideals, it is active, and is allied to sympathy and the imagination. "Feeling," thus representing a general susceptibility in the mental organism, is a fundamental capacity, is always genuine, is never merely fancied or assumed. Hence it is occasionally made to stand merely for earnestness and sincerity.

> We can always feel more than we can imagine, and the most artful fiction must give way to truth. 1753. S. JOHNSON, IV., p. 79.
> Pathos and feeling. 1778. T. WARTON, p. 661.
> That same equipoise of the faculties, during which the feelings are representative of all past experience. 1810. COLERIDGE, IV., p. 75.
> Mere peculiarity of taste or feeling. 1810. JEFFREY, III., p. 292.
> Vague and unlocalized feelings, the failing too much of some poetry of the present day. 1818. LAMB, Elia, p. 293.

It may be interesting to you to pick out some lines from Hyperion, and put a ✗ to the false beauty proceeding from art, and an ‖ to the true voice of feeling. 1819. KEATS, Letters, p. 321.

In poetry . . . strong feeling is always a sure guide. It rarely offends against good taste, because it instinctively chooses the most effectual means of communicating itself to others. 1825. BRYANT, I., p. 10.

(To W. R. Hamilton.) Your verses are animated with true poetic spirit, as they are evidently the product of strong feeling. 1827. WORDSWORTH, III., p. 293.

These old songs (of Burns') were his models, because they were models of certain forms of feeling having a necessary and eternal existence. 1841. WILSON, VII., p. 100.

Felicity (IV.): Put. to present.

Much in use. That which is happy and well chosen in composition, the result of the most delicate and instinctive sense of propriety.

What instinctive felicity of versification. LOWELL, IV., p. 24.
The felicity and idiomatic naïveté . . . of Walton. MATHEWS, Lit. St., p. 7.

Feminine (XII.): Car. to present.

Feminine vehemence. CARLYLE, I., p. 122.
A feminine intensity. DOWDEN, St. in Lit., p. 408.

Ferocious (XII.): Jef. Swinburne, Es. & St., p. 281.

Fertility (XVI.): Dry. to present.

Uniformly associated with the more active artistic impulses and processes, with energy, suggestion, fancy, invention, and imagination.

Fertility of invention. T. WARTON, p. 978.
Fertility of fancy. S. JOHNSON, VII., p. 42.
Fertile imagination. SCOTT, Life of Dryden, p. 12.

Fervent (XV.): Camp. to present. Swinburne, Es. & St., p. 65.
Fervor (XV.): Swin. Dowden, Tr. & St., p. 225.
Feverish (XV.): Stephen, Swin.
FICTITIOUS (VIII.).

"Fiction," or the "fictitious," has been regarded by the critics in two different senses. Occasionally the term has indicated the poetical heightening or enhancement of the facts or historical truth represented. This use of the term occurs chiefly in theoretical discussions, and is uniformly given a positive and favorable literary significance.

<small>As poetical enhancement.</small>

> Two requisites of universal poetry, namely, that license of expression which we call the style of poetry, and that license of representation which we call fiction. The style is, as it were, the body of poetry, fiction is its soul. HURD, II., pp. 10, 11.
>
> Fiction in poetry is not the reverse of truth, but her soft and enchanted companion. CAMPBELL, I., p. 327.

As usually employed in actual criticism, however, "fiction" is by no means necessarily in alliance with the "poetical." It represents an imaginary series of events, which, previous to the present century, was looked upon with more or less disfavor as a falsification of the truth, but which in the present century has usually been regarded as a healthful form of literary art, and thus as constituting a class or species of literature.

<small>As an imaginary series of events.</small>

> There are some that are not pleased with fiction, unless it be bold; not only to exceed the work, but also the possibility of nature. 1650. HOBBES, IV., p. 451.
>
> Where there is leisure for fiction there is little grief. S. JOHNSON, VII., p. 119.
>
> The monstrosities of fiction may be found in the bookseller's shops . . . but they have no place in literature, because in literature the one aim of art is the beautiful. M. ARNOLD, Cr. Es., 1st S., p. 292.

Fidelity (VIII.): T. War. to present.
>In translating a poetical writer, there are two kinds of fidelity to be aimed at: fidelity to the matter and fidelity to the manner of the original. JEFFREY, I., p. 417.
>Fidelity to the essential truth of things. DOWDEN, Shak., etc., p. 73.

Fierce (XII.): Jef., Swin.
Fiery (XII.): Sted. Swinburne, Es. & St., p. 7.
FIGURATIVE (VIII.).

Until within the eighteenth century, figurative language was usually regarded as an ornamented falsification of the truth, the source at once of æsthetic pleasure and of the most puzzling uncertainty and obscurity. *As ornament.*

>This ornament is given by figures and figurative speeches. PUTTENHAM, p. 150.
>Shakespeare's whole style is so pestered with figurative expressions, that it is as affected as it is obscure. DRYDEN, VI., p. 255.

Occasionally, — especially during the latter half of the eighteenth century, — the "figurative" and the "poetical" have been more or less completely identified with each other. *As the poetical.*

>Poetical, that is highly figurative expression. HURD, I., p. 102.
>Poetical ... that is figurative and emphatic. HALLAM, II., p. 207.

Usually, however, — especially during the present century, — the "figurative" represents vividness of mental imagery and intensity of imaginative power, which is of itself by no means necessarily poetical. (See "Poetical.") *As vividness of imagination.*

8

Tully and Demosthenes spoke often figuratively but not poetically, and the very figures of oratory are vastly different from those of poetry. POPE, VIII., p. 218.

To say that a man is a great thinker or a fine thinker, is but another expression for saying that he has a schematizing (or, to use a plainer but less accurate expression, a figurative) understanding. DE QUINCEY, X., p. 115.

Figured (V.): Figured or poetical expressions. JEFFREY, I., p. 223.

Filthy (XIV.): Dry. to present.
Coarse and filthy. JEFFREY, I., p. 219.

Final (XXI.): Swin., Min. Swinburne, Es. & St., p. 165.

Fine (XXII.) b: T. Wil. to present.
Raleigh's Cynthia ... a fine and sweet invention. HARVEY, in Marlowe's Shak. by Boswell, II., p. 579.

Finery (V.): Byron to present.
It is in their finery that the new school is most vulgar. 1821. Life and Letters, p. 507.

Finesse: Jef. to present.
Delicacy and finesse. JEFFREY, II., p. 370.
All beauty is in the long run only finesse of truth. PATER, Ap., p. 6.

Finical (V.): Jef., Haz. Jeffrey, I., p. 222.

Finished (V.): Camp. to present.

That which gives evidence both of careful execution and of good taste.

·

The early productions of Pope were perhaps ... too finished, correct, and pure. J. WARTON, I., p. 83.
Greene ... is sometimes more laboured than finished. HUNT, Wit & Humour, p. 308.
The poetry of Gray is finished, perhaps I should rather say limited. LOWELL, Lat. Lit. Es., p. 16.

Fire (XII.): Jef. to present.
Fire and force. GOSSE, Seventeenth Cent. St., p. 183.

Firm (XI.): Haz. to present. Swinburne, A St. of B. J., p. 65.

Fitful (II.): Broken or fitful. Swinburne, Mis., p. 237.

Fitness (IV.): Ascham to present.

Used very little during the eighteenth century. Adaptation of the elements of composition to one another: a popular expression for the term "propriety," considered in a somewhat mechanical sense.

>Fitness of character . . . woman must be woman, etc. ARISTOTLE, Poetics, p. 47.
>Pleased with a work where nothing's just or fit. POPE, II., p. 50.
>There is a fitness and propriety in every part. LANDOR, VIII., p. 386.

Flaccid (XII.): Swin., Gosse.
>Flaccid and untunable verse of Byron. SWINBURNE, Mis., p. 81.

Flagging (XVIII.): Mor. Swinburne, Es. & St., p. 86.

Flagrant: Hal., Gosse.
>Flagrant absurdity. GOSSE, Hist. Eng. Lit., II., p. 262.

Flamboyant (V.): The flamboyant style in modern English prose. SAINTSBURY, Eng. Pr. St., p. xxxi.

Flashy (V.): Jef., Gosse.
>Noisy and flashy. GOSSE, From Shak., etc., p. 127.

Flat (XII.): B. Jon. to present.
>What is flat ought to be plain. LANDOR, IV., p. 64.

Flavor (XXII.) *b*: Sted. Saintsbury, Hist. Fr. Lit., p. 203.

Flawless (XXI.): Swin. Dowden, Tr. & St., p. 259.

Fleshliness: Fleshliness . . . oddly enough is found in Wordsworth. LOWELL, Prose IV., p. 371.

Fleshly: Fleshly sculpture. SWINBURNE, Es. & St., p. 65.

Fleshy: We say it is a fleshy style, carnosa, when there is much periphrasis and circuit of words. B. JONSON, Timber, p. 65.

Flexible (XVIII.): S. John. to present.
>Flexible bucolic hexameter. STEDMAN, Vic. Poets, p. 226.

Flimsy: J. War. to present.
>Flimsy and insipid decorum. HAZLITT, Sp. of Age, p. 102.

Flippant (XI.): Jef., Whip.
>Vulgar flippancy. JEFFREY, I., p. 217.

Floribund (V.): Gay and floribund. GOSSE, From Shak., etc., p. 155.

Florid (V.): Shaftes. to present.
   This painted florid style. POPE, VIII., p. 219.
      The groves appear all drest with wreaths of flowers,
      And from their leaves drop aromatic showers.
   This is in the florid style. SWIFT, XIII., p. 73.

Floundering (XVIII.): Swin., Saints.

Flowing (XVIII.): K. James to present.

Refers both to the sounds and to the thoughts of a composition.

   Sounds . . . most flowing and slipper upon the tongue. PUTTENHAM, p. 129.
   The equable flow of the sentiments. HAZLITT, Age of El., p. 56.

Flowerless (V.): Flowerless and pallid. SWINBURNE, Es. & St., p. 137.

Flowery (V.): Camp. to present. Saintsbury, Hist. Eng. Lit., II., p. 48.

Fluent (XVIII.): Dekker to present.
   The fluency which was a besetting sin of Whittier's poetry, when released from the fetters of rhyme and meter, ran into wordiness. BEERS, St. in Am. Lit., p. 160.

Fluid (XVIII.): Fluidity of meter. SWINBURNE, A St. of B. J., p. 124.

Flute-like (X.): Swin., Gosse.
   Clear flute-like notes of Cynthia. SWINBURNE, A St. of B. J., p. 56.

Fluttering: Light, airy, fluttering. WHIPPLE, Es. & Rev., II., p. 65.

Folly (XX.): Pure childishness or mere folly. JEFFREY, I., p. 271.

Foolish (XX.): Jef. Swinburne, Mis., p. 110.

FORCE (XII.).

There are no distinctly marked periods in the history of the term "force." Occasionally "force" seems to designate a general efficiency of thought and language, — an interesting thought treated in accordance with the best known rules of composition.

As effectiveness.

   Justness and force of the representation. JEFFREY, II., p. 285.
   Ease, force, and perspicuity. HAZLITT, Table Talk, p. 338.

Often the term "force" indicates a mere vividness in the impression which the literary work produces upon the mind of the reader. *As vividness.*

> Force, — from vivid imagery. T. WARTON, p. 661; also BYRON, Letters, p. 501.
> Force, — from figures of speech. T. WARTON, p. 207.

More usually, however, — especially during the present century, — "force" has been regarded as the native power of the mind, asserting itself in ways *As power.* which often run counter to regular methods of composition, which often, indeed, violate every canon of artistic refinement, and which acknowledge no law of expression except that which is immediately prompted by the intensity of the conception, and by the ethical purpose which this conception is intended to subserve.

> The uncommon union of so much facility and force. 1756. J. WARTON, II., p. 267.
> These monosyllables have much force and energy:
>> All good to me becomes
>> Bane. (Milton.) ID., I., p. 347.
> Atterbury ... writes more with elegance and correctness than with any force of thinking or reasoning. ID., II., p. 361.
> Force of poetry. 1751. S. JOHNSON, III., p. 293.
> Intensity is the great and prominent distinction of Lord Byron's writings. He seldom gets beyond force of style, nor has he produced any regular work or masterly whole. 1825. HAZLITT, Sp. of Age, p. 124.
> If by force you mean beauty manifesting itself with power, I maintain that the Abbé Delille has more force than Milton. (Quoted disapprovingly, as a *saugrenu* judgment.) M. ARNOLD, Cr. Es., 1st S., p. 279.
> What Dryden valued above all things was force, though in his haste he is willing to make a shift with its counterfeit effect. 1868. LOWELL, III., p. 183.

Forced (VII.) : Dry. to present.

The strained and unnatural; usually assumed to be the result of conscious effort.

> Forced and unnatural. GOLDSMITH, IV., p. 283.
> A forced and almost grotesque materializing of abstractions. PATER, Ap., p. 232.

FORM (II.).

The word "form" has been employed in criticism in three more or less distinct ways. Previous to the present century, and in large part during this century, the word has merely represented the mechanical expression of thought in language,—punctuation, capitalization, the grammatical relations of words, the construction of phrases, clauses, sentences, paragraphs, and perhaps the rhetorical requirements of composition as a whole. As verbal expression.

> What I can say concerning our English poetry, first in the matter thereof, then in the form. WEBBE, p. 38.
> No work of true genius dares want its appropriate form. COLERIDGE, IV., p. 54.

Often the term indicates that portion of the mechanical construction of composition which answers more or less directly to the sense of rhythm and proportion in the mind,—the metrical movement, the balance of phrases, clauses, and sentences, the harmonious adaptation of all the parts of a composition to one another, the composition, however, being considered as a completed product, and the adaptation being determined entirely, perhaps, by past attainment, by precedent, and by custom. As the sense of propriety and proportion.

> The word Form has also more limited application, as, for example, when we use it to imply that nice sense of proportion and adaptation which results in style. LOWELL, O. E. D., p. 56.
>
> I am not sure that Form, which is the artistic sense of decorum controlling the co-ordination of parts and ensuring their harmonious subservience to a common end, can be learned at all, whether of the Greeks or elsewhere. LOWELL, Lat. Lit. Es., p. 144.

Occasionally, in theory, if not in applied criticism, the term denotes the developing sense of beauty and proportion in literature, as referring to the mechanical construction of the composition, to the picturesque features of the thought presented, and perhaps in a measure to the representation of moral truths and principles. *As sensibility to the beauty of formal construction.*

> That there is an intimate relation, or at any rate a close analogy between Form, in this its highest attribute, and imagination, is evident if we remember that the imagination is the shaping faculty. LOWELL, O. E. D., p. 56.

Formality (IV): Jef. to present. Hazlitt, Sp. of Age, pp. 256, 257.
Foul (XIV.): Low. to present.
> Roderick Random ... so foul as to be fit only for a well-seasoned reader. GOSSE, Hist. Eng. Lit., III., p. 259.

Fragile: Whip., Gosse.
> Fragility of Tennyson's figures. WHIPPLE, Es. & Rev., p. 341.

Fragrance (XXII.) *b*: Swin., Beers. Swinburne, A St. of B. J., p. 4.
Frank (XIV.): Low. to present.
> Frank unconsciousness. LOWELL, Prose, I., pp. 247, 248.

Frantic (XV.): Frantic invective. JEFFREY, I., p. 217.
Free (XVIII.): Rymer to present.

Much in use. Unconstrained movement. Usually refers to the mechanical construction of composition, occasionally to the thought.

The more we attend to the composition of Milton's harmony, the more we shall be sensible how he loved to vary his pauses, his measures, and his feet, which gives that enchanting air of freedom and wildness to his versification, unconfined by any rules but those which his own feelings and the nature of his subject demanded. GRAY, I., pp. 332, 333.

A young writer can hardly afford to be quite direct and free in his movements, lest he should be violent and awkward. DOWDEN, St. in Lit., p. 129.

. Freedom being thus the dominant note of Elizabethan poetry. J. SYMONDS, Es., Sp. & Sug., p. 394.

Frenzy (XV.): Laboured frenzy of diction. WHIPPLE, Es. & Rev., p. 176.

FRESH (IX.).

The term "fresh" is largely negative in its signification. That is said to be fresh which is in no sense bookish, conventional, or pedantic. In its positive significance, the term is uniformly associated with such conceptions as sincerity, spontaneity, energy, the impassioned, and the romantic.

Fresh . . . romantic spirit. CAMPBELL, p. 81.
Fresh as from the hand of nature. HAZLITT, Sp. of Age, p. 104.
Freshness of antiquity. ID., p. 121.
Fresh and lively. HALLAM, Lit. Hist., I., pp. 130, 131.
Neither "eloquence" nor "poetry" are the exact words with which it would be appropriate to describe the fresh style of the Waverley Novels. BAGEHOT, II., p. 151.
Chaucer . . . is fresh . . . because he sets before us the world as it honestly appeared to Geoffrey Chaucer, and not a world as it seemed proper to certain people that it ought to appear. LOWELL, III., p. 361.
Bunyan was conscious that greatness had been thrust upon him; and one misses accordingly in the second part something of the delightful freshness, the naturalness, the entire unconscious devotion of heart and singleness of purpose, which are so conspicuous in the first part. T. ARNOLD, Man. of Eng Lit., p. 320.

Fresh and almost childlike. ID., p. 455.
Natural, fresh, and spontaneous. BEERS, Outline, etc., p. 90.

Frigid (XV.): Mil. to present:

A lack of sincere, genuine feeling, which may result from two causes: —

I. From a total lack of feeling of any kind.

Over-elaboration ends in frigidity. LONGINUS, p. 6.
Jejune, far-fetched, and frigid. HAZLITT, Age of El., p. 211.
Frigid and ridiculous pedantry. ID., p. 137.

II. From the affectation of too much feeling.

Those who express themselves with this poetic air, produce by their want of taste both the ridiculous and the frigid. ARISTOTLE, Rhet., p. 216.
According to the definition of Theophrastus, the frigid in style is that which exceeds the expression suitable to the subject. GOLDSMITH, I., p. 378.
The frigid . . . a failure to stir up in the reader the emotions affected in the composition. S. JOHNSON, VII., p. 36.
Frigid fervours in poetry. DOWDEN, Shak., etc., p. 63.

Frippery (V.): Macaulay to present. Whipple, Es. & Rev., p. 269.
Frivolous (XI.): Jef. to present. Jeffrey, II., p. 479.
Fruitful (XVI): Swinburne, Es. & St. p. 188.
Fugitive (XI.): Swin., Gosse. Swinburne, Mis., p. 53.
Full-bodied (XII.): Dense and full-bodied lines. GOSSE, Life of Congreve, p. 28.
Fulness (XI.) *b*: B. Jonson to present.

Refers both to the thought and to the sound of composition. As referring to the thought, it may indicate either emotional or intellectual affluence or copiousness.

The verses . . . sweet, smooth, full, and strong. RYMER, 2d Pt., p. 79.
The violin's fulness and the violin's intensity are in the sonnets from the Portuguese. DOWDEN, Tr. & St., p. 213.

Fulsome (XIV.): Mil. to present.
Fulsome doggerel. SWINBURNE, Mis., p. 211.
Fusion (XIII.): Haz. to present.

The term represents both logical and emotional coherence and continuity, the blending of all the elements of a composition so as to produce a perfect unity of effect.

> There is no principle of fusion in the work. HAZLITT, Sp. of Age, p. 179.
> Now passion, imagination, and will are fused together, and Romeo who was weak, has at length become strong. DOWDEN, Shak., etc., p. 118.

Fustian; (XIX.): Gosson to present.
Fustian of Marlowe's style. DOWDEN, Tr. & St., p. 451.
Futile (XXII.) *a*: Wil. to present.
Weak and futile. WILSON, VIII., p. 17.
Gallant: Put. to present century.

I. The excellent; noble; æsthetically good.

> Gallant verse . . . of Phaer. WEBBE, p. 34.

II. Chivalric; courteous; not really a critical term.

> The songs and smaller pieces of Dryden have smoothness, wit, and when addressed to ladies, gallantry in profusion. SCOTT, Life of Dryden, I., pp. 425, 426.

Gallic (I.): Elegancies of a Gallic style. GOSSE, From Shak., etc., p. 157.
Garrulity (XIX.) *b*. Car. to present.
Sociable garrulity. JEFFREY, I., p. 366.
Gasping: Swinburne, Mis., p. 76.
Gaudy (V.): Blair to present.
Addison's style is splendid without being gaudy. BLAIR, Rhet., p. 209.
Gay (XIV.): S. John. to present.
Gay and sportive. DOWDEN, Tr. & St., p. 278.

Generality (VIII.) b: Swift to present.

Not usually regarded as conducive to the best literary effects.

> What distinguishes Homer and Shakespeare from all other poets is that they do not give their readers general ideas; every image is the particular and unalienable property of the person who uses it. J. WARTON, I., p. 318.
>
> Cowley pursues his thoughts to the last ramifications, by which he loses the grandeur of generality. S. JOHNSON, VII., p. 38.
>
> An unaffecting generality. WILSON, VIII., p. 44.

Generous (XIV.): J. War., Swin. J. Warton, II., p. 8.

Genial (XIV.): Car. to present.

> Where there is genius there should be geniality. LANDOR, IV., p. 51.
>
> Genius — that is, geniality — dwells in unnumbered bosoms. WILSON, V., p. 352.
>
> Genius is that mode of intellectual power which moves in alliance with the genial nature. DE QUINCEY, XI., p. 382.

GENIUS (XXIII.).

The history of the term "genius" may be divided into four periods. During the first period, which continued until the middle of the eighteenth century, "genius" was closely related in meaning to the term "nature." "Genius," however, unlike "nature," denoted natural capacity or native ingenuity, not only as controlling the original impulse or inception of the literary work, but also as entering into every phase and feature of the actual process of its composition.

As native ingenuity.

> Betwixt genius (acumen) and diligence there is very little room left for art (ratio); art only shows you where to look, and where that lies which you want to find. CICERO, Orations, p. 262.
>
> A poet no industry can make if his own genius be not carried into

it. And therefore is it an old proverb: Orator fit, poeta nascitur. 1583. Sidney, p. 46.

A poet ought always to have that instinct or some good genius ready to serve his hero upon occasion, to prevent these unpleasant shocking indecencies. Rymer, 1st Pt., p. 64.

I believe it is no wrong observation, that persons of genius, and those who are most capable of art, are always most fond of nature; as such are chiefly sensible that all art consists in the imitation and study of nature. 1713. Pope, X., p. 532.

By genius I would understand that power, or rather those powers of the mind which are capable of penetrating into all things within our reach and knowledge, and of distinguishing their essential differences. These are no other than invention and judgment; and they are both called by the collective name of genius, as they are of those gifts of nature which we bring with us into the world. Fielding, T. Jones, II., pp. 5, 6.

The second period includes the last half of the eighteenth century. "Genius" represented the power of producing something new, either as to the thought or as to the method of expressing it. Hence "genius" stood opposed to the established rules of art: it was the most general and at the same time the most vague expression possible for the progressive tendencies in literature, and over the more specific terms which denoted these tendencies it exercised a strong schematizing influence.

As original impulse.

We see that the most accurate observation of dramatic rules without genius is of no effect. 1756. J. Warton, Pope, I., p. 69.

By genius is meant those excellencies that no study or art can communicate, such as elevation, expression, description, wit, humour, passion, etc. 1758. Goldsmith, IV., p. 418.

I am convinced that rules alone never made a genius. Conscious I am that all the fine reasoning and delicate remark that have been exhausted of late years upon this subject, are not equal to

> one single scene dictated by a fine imagination. (Quoted from Voltaire.) ID., p. 14.
> Genius full of resources, master of the rules, but master also of the reasons for the rules, often appears to despise them. 1759. GIBBON, IV., p. 45.
> The highest praise of genius is original invention. 1781. S. JOHNSON, VII., p. 142.

During the present century, "genius," when referring to a mental process, denotes both original impulse and native power in giving this impulse literary expression; when referring to the literary work as a completed product, it represents a constant appeal from literature to life, from established methods of composition to other possible methods, which have not yet been attempted. Moreover, in the present century, "genius" indicates not simply impulse or native force, but also a certain refinement of force which gives to it artistic value. "Genius" thus has at its command, at least in a measure, its own laws of literary expression. It not only represents progressive tendencies in art, but it represents progressive tendencies which are organic in their nature.

During the early portion of the century, "genius" was supposed to manifest itself chiefly in an increase of sensibility and in bold flights of the imagination. It evolved its own laws of art, and it was thought to be wholly unconscious, to elude all immediate detection and analysis.

As an artistic impulse.

> Of genius in the fine arts, the only infallible sign is the widening the sphere of human sensibility. 1802. WORDSWORTH, II., p. 127.

The ancients had no word that properly expresses what we mean by the word genius. They perhaps had not the thing. Their minds appear to have been too exact, too retentive, too minute and subtle, too sensible to the external differences of things, too passive under their impressions to admit of those bold and rapid combinations, those lofty flights of fancy, which, glancing from heaven to earth, unite the most opposite extremes, and draw the happiest illustrations from things the most remote. 1807. HAZLITT, Sk. & Essays, p. 424.

No work of true genius dares want its appropriate form ... for it is even this that constitutes it genius, — the power of acting creatively under laws of its own origination. 1810. COLERIDGE, IV., p. 54.

Sensibility both quick and deep ... may be deemed a component part of genius. 1817. ID., III., p. 175.

Genius is unconscious of its existence and action ... e. g. Milton's preference for Paradise Regained. 1826. HAZLITT, Pl. Sp., pp. 160–175.

All genius is metaphysical; because the ultimate end of genius is ideal, however it may be actualized by incidental and accidental circumstances. 1832. COLERIDGE, VI., p. 411.

Men of humor are always in some degree men of genius; wits are rarely so. 1833. ID., VI., p. 481.

During the latter portion of the century, "genius" has been closely related to the intellectual processes and to action. It usually refers to an intense activity of the mind, an activity which from its intensity is oblivious of itself, and thus seems to attain results of whose origin no account can be given, an activity which represents a blending, as it were, of all the powers of the mind, intellectual, æsthetic, and ethical. This concentrated intense activity of the mind, however, has not been regarded as having its origin and outcome in sensibility, so much as in a subtle intellectual analysis, and in impulses

As ethical, intellectual, and artistic power.

toward action, toward the realization in some manner of the intensely conceived thought, purpose, or ideal. Many efforts have been made to define the term "genius" in the light of modern psychological knowledge, but in criticism for the last half-century, the term has been passing rapidly out of use.

> Genius is intellectual power impregnated with the moral nature, and expresses a synthesis of the active in man with his original organic capacity of pleasure and pain. 1838. DE QUINCEY, III., p. 34.
>
> Genius is nothing less than the possession of all the powers and impulses of humanity in their greatest possible strength, and most harmonious combination. 1848. WHIPPLE, Lit. and Life, p. 159.
>
> Enough that we recognize in Keats that indefinable newness and unexpectedness which we call genius. 1854. LOWELL, Lat. Lit. Es., I., p. 242.
>
> Burns . . . possessed in as high degree, I think, as ever man possessed, the power of which Coleridge speaks in defining the term genius, the power to combine the child's sense of wonder and novelty with appearances which the experience of years had rendered familiar. 1859. BRYANT, II., p. 318.
>
> "Creative energy of genius" is said to be in opposition to "form," "method," "precision," "proportions," "arrangement," — all of them things . . . where intelligence proper comes in. 1865. M. ARNOLD, Cr. Es., 1st S., p. 54.
>
> Genius . . . is the ruling divinity of poetry. ID., p. 62.
>
> A man of genius Lessing . . . . unquestionably was, if genius may be claimed no less for force than fineness of mind, — for the intensity of conviction that inspires the understanding as much as for that apprehension of beauty which gives energy of will to imagination, — but a poetic genius he was not. 1866. LOWELL, II., p. 224.
>
> Genius lending itself to embody the new desire of man's mind as it had embodied the old. 1868. ID., III., p. 65.
>
> The term genius when used with emphasis implies imagination. 1876. EMERSON, Let. & Soc. Aims, p. 22.

Genius, therefore, manifested in any high degree, must be taken to include intellect; if the words are to be used in this sense, genius begins where intellect ends. 1879. STEPHEN, Hrs. in a Lib., p. 330.

Those dark and capricious suggestions of genius. 1880. PATER, Ap., p. 74.

Byron's poetry has two main constituents, — passion and wit. . . . The great thing in Byron is genius. 1878. ROSSETTI, Lives of the Poets, p. 307.

Humor is the overflow of genius. 1892. STEDMAN, Nat. & El. of Poetry, p. 215.

The whole belief in genius seems to me rather a mischievous superstition. . . . Does it mean anything more or less than the mastery which comes to any man according to his powers and diligence in any direction? HOWELLS, Crit. & Fiction, pp. 87, 88.

To be a genius is to find one's self capable of perceiving ulterior truths of far-reaching consequence, without passing through all the intermediate stages of approach and preparation. . . . The mental activity is of the same kind as that which comprehends a "brave attack" as "an attack by brave men." 1893. SHERMAN, Analytics of Lit., p. 121.

Gentle (XIX.): B. Jon. to present. Swinburne, Es. & St., p. 24.
Gentlemanlike (V.): Gosse, Seventeenth Cent. St., p. 66.
Gentlemanly (V.): Hal. to present.
Manly and gentlemanly. WHIPPLE, Am. Lit., etc., p. 89.
Genuine (VII.): Goldsmith to present.
Fresh and genuine. SAINTSBURY, Hist. Eng. Lit., p. 116.
Germanisms (I.): The Germanisms of Carlyle. SAINTSBURY, Eng. Pr. St., p. xxxi.
Gibberish (XXII.): Whipple, Es. & Rev., I., p. 412.
Gigantic (XI.): J. War. to present.
The Egyptians . . . mistook the gigantic for the sublime, and greatness of bulk for greatness of manner. J. WARTON, I., p. 350.
Faustus himself is a rude sketch, but it is a gigantic one. HAZLITT, Age of El., p. 43.
Glaring (V.): Pope to present. Pope, X., p. 549.

A HISTORY OF ENGLISH CRITICAL TERMS. 129

Glitter (V.) : Haz. to present.
    Glittering but still graceful conceits. HAZLITT, Age of El., p. 178.
    An unseasonable glitter of rhetoric. DE QUINCEY, V., p. 99.
Gloomy (XIV.) : Jef. to present.
    Grand and gloomy sketch. JEFFREY, II., p. 476.
Glory : Swinburne, Es. & St., p. 24.
Glossy (V.) : A meretricious gloss. HAZLITT, Sp. of Age, p. 121.
Good-sense (XX.) *a* : Jef. to present.
    The reflection of this quality of solid good sense, absolutely scorn-
    ing any aliment except that of solid facts, is the so-called realism
    of Fielding's novels. STEPHEN, Hrs. in a Lib., III., p. 72.
Gorgeous (V.) : Webbe to present.
    Gorgeous diction of Thompson. JEFFREY, II., p. 88.
GOTHIC (IX.).

"Gothic" has been employed in criticism chiefly as a schematizing term, being applied directly to literature but very seldom. Four periods may be distinguished in the history of the term.

During the first period, which extended until within the early portion of the eighteenth century, "Gothic" indicated whatever was considered as rude, *As crudity of conceit and barbarous, or crude in literature. Rhyme ornament.* was thought to be a Gothic device, an uncouth ornament. Forced conceits and wild fancies of all kinds were classed as Gothic, since they seemed designed merely to be striking, and since they caused the simplifying and unifying conception of the composition, as a whole, to be lost sight of in the over-emphasis of the separate parts and details.

    But now when men know the difference, and have the examples
    both of the best and the worst, surely to follow rather the Goths
    in rhyming than the Greeks in true versifying, were even to eat
    acorns with swine, when we may freely eat wheat bread amongst
    men. 1568. ASCHAM, III., p. 249.

Rhyme, common to all those peoples called barbarous by the Greeks; but it is the first method and most universal method, . . . which give to all human inventions no small credit. 1585. PUTTENHAM, p. 26.

Something of the stiff and Gothic did stick upon our language till long after Chaucer. RYMER, 2d Pt., p. 78.

The little Gothic ornaments of epigrammatical conceits, turns, points, and quibbles, which are so frequent in the most admired of our English poets, and practised by those who want genius and strength to represent, after the manner of the ancients, simplicity in its natural beauty and perfection. 1710. ADDISON, II., p. 146.

As the eye, in surveying a Gothic building, is distracted by the multiplicity of ornaments, and loses the whole by its minute attention to the parts, so the mind, in perusing a work overstocked with wit is fatigued and disgusted with the constant endeavor to shine and surprise. 1742. D. HUME, I., p. 241.

The second period includes the greater portion of the eighteenth century. Rhyme grew into favor with the critics. The Gothic was often placed in opposition to the classic, not as representing mere barbarity, but as being associated with such terms as strength, vividness, imagination, grandeur, and sublimity. The use of the term in this and in the succeeding period was little more than a transference into literature of the feeling and sentiment inspired by a Gothic cathedral. The cathedral was conspicuous for its gloomy massiveness, its abrupt emphasis of separate parts, and its lack of formal unity in general design. Likewise, during the eighteenth century, the term "Gothic," as employed in criticism, signified power and grandeur of thought, vivid and picturesque imagery, and a unity which lay deeper than

As strength of conceit and rugged grandeur.

mere formal design and construction, — a unity of emotional effect.

> To the Bishop of Rochester: I know you will be so gentle to the modern Goths and Vandals as to allow them to put a few rhymes upon tombs or over doors. 1718. POPE, IX.; p. 13.
>
> One may look upon Shakespeare's works in comparison of those that are more finished and regular, as upon an ancient majestic piece of Gothic architecture, compared with a neat modern building; the latter is more elegant and glaring, but the former is more strong and solemn. 1725. ID., X., p. 549.
>
> Gothic imagination . . . bordering often on the most ideal and capricious extravagance. 1778. T. WARTON, Hist. E. P., p. 257.
>
> The following portrait is highly charged, and very great in the Gothic style of painting: —
>
>> Blake was his berde, and manly was his face:
>> The circles of his eyin in his hede,
>> They glowdin betwixte yalowe and rede
>> And like a lyon lokid he about
>> With kempid heris on his browis stout. (Chaucer.)
>>   1778. T. WARTON, p. 239.

During the early portion of the present century the Gothic was regarded as in no sense crude and unrefined. Its rugged power was transformed into suggestive power. [As suggestive grandeur and sublimity.] It became more intellectual. It usually denoted a supreme intensity of conception and force in execution; a blending of the most vivid imagery with the sense of the mysterious and the infinite; a rigid subordination of definite form in literature to the thought or principle by which this form is continually redetermined.

> Wordsworth compares his works to a Gothic church: —
>> Excursion is the body of the church,
>> Prelude is the ante-chapel,
>> Smaller pieces are oratorios, etc.
>>   WORDSWORTH, II., p. 146.

Bold, rude Gothic outline (Macbeth). 1820. HAZLITT, Eliz. Lit., p. 19.

Laid the restless spirit of Gothic quaintness, witticism, and conceit in the lap of classic elegance and pastoral simplicity. ID., p. 206.

The principle of the Gothic architecture is infinity made imaginable. It is no doubt a sublimer effort of genius than the Greek style; but then it depends much more on execution for its effect. 1833. COLERIDGE, VI., p. 461.

Greek art is beautiful . . . but Gothic art is sublime. ID., IV., p. 235.

That magnificent condition of fantastic imagination which . . . is one of the chief elements of the Northern Gothic mind. 1846. RUSKIN, St. of Venice, II., p. 154.

During the last half of the present century, the terms "Gothic" and "romantic" have been employed almost interchangeably to represent one of the two general and opposing tendencies by which the development of literature has been controlled. (See Classical.) The early association of the terms "Gothic" and "romantic" was historical in origin, more or less accidental, and the terms were by no means identified with each other in meaning. In becoming a synonym for the "romantic," the "Gothic" lost the fierceness of its strength, the wildness of its suggestion. It became more general and diffused. It denotes the progressive tendencies in literature slightly intensified, perhaps, over that which is signified by the term "romantic." (See "Romantic" for quotations.)

As the romantic.

GRACEFUL (XXII.) *b.*

Throughout the history of the term, and especially previous to the latter portion of the eighteenth century, the "graceful" indicated freedom and ease in composition, resulting perhaps from choice and finish, but far more usually from spontaneous, sincere, and even negligent methods of expression. *As the spontaneous, natural, and easy.*

> Affected metaphors lose their grace. B. Jonson, Timber, p. 60.
> Horace still charms with graceful negligence. Pope, II., p. 75.
> Ovid shows himself most in a familiar story, where the chief grace is to be easy and natural. Addison, I., p. 145.
> Samson Agonistes opens with a graceful abruptness. S. Johnson, III., p. 158.

Since the latter portion of the eighteenth century, the "graceful" has usually been associated more closely than it had previously been with the conception of energy, or of movement, in composition. *As animated and free movement.* Grace consists in the absence of difficulty, the perfect union of vigor and fluency; it represents the æsthetic sense of action or the poetry of movement.

> Gracefulness is an idea not very different from beauty. . . . It belongs to posture and motion. In both these to be graceful, it is requisite that there be no appearance of difficulty. Burke, I., pp. 137, 138.
> Sweet native gracefulness . . . in Burns. Carlyle, II., p. 15.
> Impetuous, graceful power. Id., IV., p. 130.
> Grace, that charm so magical because at once so shadowy and so potent, that Will-o'-the Wisp which in its supreme development may be said to involve nearly all that is valuable in poetry. Poe, II., pp. 98, 99.
> Grace is but a more refined form of power. Lowell, III., p. 34.

Gracious (XIV.): Ros. to present.

> So bright, so tender, so gracious. Dowden, Shak., etc., p. 333.

Grammatical (I.): Dry. to present.

I. Exactness and correctness in the use of single words and phrases. Usually a primary literary requirement previous to the present century.

Shakespeare . . . was ungrammatical and coarse. DRYDEN, VI., p. 255.
Shakespeare . . . was ungrammatical, perplexed, and obscure. 1765. S. JOHNSON, V., p. 135.
Pope . . . was not grammatical. 1781. ID., VIII., p. 343.

II. An exact, clear-cut, and often puristic use of language. Usually a very secondary literary requirement during the present century.

"I've done, begin the rites."
Here it is the brokenness, the ungrammatical position, the total subversion of the period, that charms me. GRAY, II., p. 333.
The grammatical style . . . of Newman. M. ARNOLD, Cel. Lit., p. 200.

Grand (XI.): Scott to present.
The grand style, at once noble and natural. LOWELL, III., p. 173.
Shakespeare himself . . . has not of the marks of the master, this one: perfect sureness of hand in his style. Alone of English poets Milton has it; he is our great artist in style, our one first rate master in the grand style. M. ARNOLD, Mixed Es., p. 200.

Grandeur (XI.): Mil. to present.

The sublime, which is also simple; vast images or conceptions which are not complicated or over-suggestive, the limits or full import of which are somewhat definitely marked.

The grandeur of the historic style. MILTON, III., p. 498.
The simplicity of grandeur which fills the imagination. S. JOHNSON, II., p. 178.
Artless grandeur. ID., VIII., p. 336.
Sometimes . . . the intensity of his satire gives to his poetry a character of emphatic violence, which borders upon grandeur. SCOTT, Life of Swift, p. 453.
Wordsworth . . . a baldness which is full of grandeur. M. ARNOLD, Cr. Es., 2d S., p. 159.

Grandiloquent (XIX.) *b*: Put. to present.

Grandiose (XIX.) *b*: Hal. to present.
  Marlowe . . . constantly pushes grandiosity to the verge of bombast. LOWELL, O. E. D., p. 36.
Grandity (XIX.) *b*: Camden, p. 337.
Graphic (III.): Jef. to present. Wilson, VI., p. 198.
Grasp (XIII.): Swin., Mor. Swinburne, Es. & St., p. 15.
Grave (XIV.): T. Wil. to present. Much in use.
  The Georgiacs are written in a . . . grave and decent style. WEBBE, p. 29.
Great (XXII.) *a*: Haz. to present.
  The great becomes turgid in . . . Moore's . . . hands. HAZLITT, Sp. of Age, p. 325.
Grim (XIV.): J. Wil. to present.
  A certain grim irony. DOWDEN, Shak., p. 105.
Grisâtre: Saintsbury, Eng. Pr. St., p. xliv.
Gross (V.): Ascham to present.
  To bring his style from all low grossness to such firm fastness in Latin as is in Demosthenes in Greek. ASCHAM, III., p. 206.
GROTESQUE (IX.).

The term "grotesque" indicates in general an almost total lack of proportion in the parts of a composition, with special reference to the pictorial character of the mental imagery employed. Until within the early portion of the present century, the "grotesque" was considered as unnatural, inorganic, hideous in its disproportion. It was often associated with whatever was barbarous, Gothic, or Mediæval, but even after the Gothic and Mediæval had come into favor in criticism, the "grotesque" still continued for at least half a century to be thought of as something that lay wholly beyond the limits of normal, healthful literary art.

As general disproportion.

  When words or images are placed in unusual juxtaposition rather than connection, and are so placed merely because the juxtaposition is unusual, we have the odd or the grotesque. 1810. COLERIDGE, IV., p. 276.

The pure, which is called the classical; the ornate, called romantic; and the grotesque, which might be called the Mediæval. 1864. BAGEHOT, Lit. St., II., p. 352.

During the greater portion of the present century, the characteristic use of the term has been to repre- *As disproportion of imagery.* sent the healthful overflow, so to speak, of the imagination in literary production, as especially indicated in an extreme disproportion of the picturesque qualities of the mental imagery employed. The hideous now indicates the outer limits of disproportion in art, which was formerly occupied by the grotesque.

The picturesque depends chiefly on the principle of discrimination or contrast. . . . It runs imperceptibly into the fantastical and grotesque. 1819. HAZLITT, Table Talk, pp. 448, 449.

Close alongside of the normal lies the sphere of the abnormal; of the sane, lies the insane; of pleasure, lies disgust; of cohesion, lies dissolution; of the grotesque, lies the hideous; of the sublime, lies the ridiculous. . . . Victor Hugo, in his imaginative flights, is forever hovering about this dividing line, fascinated, spellbound by what lies beyond. BURROUGHS, Indoor St., p. 182.

Wherever the human mind is healthy and vigorous in all its proportions, great in imagination and emotion no less than in intellect, and not overborne by an undue or hardened pre-eminence of the mere reasoning faculties, there the grotesque will exist in full energy. . . . I think that the central man of all the world as representing in perfect balance the imaginative, moral, and intellectual faculties, all at their highest, is Dante. 1846. RUSKIN, St. of Venice, II., p. 206.

Grovelling: Dry., Ad.

Grovelling style . . . of Horace. DRYDEN, XIII., p. 88.

Guarded (XIX.): Jeffrey, II., p. 88.

Gush (XIX.) *b*: Sted., Saints. Swinburne, Mis., p. 158.
Gusto (XV.): Haz. to present.

An impulsive and passionate apprehension and literary embodiment of an image, thought, or general principle.

> Gusto in art is power or passion defining an object. HAZLITT, The Round Table, p. 109.
> Gusto of Chaucer . . . a local truth and freshness. ID., Eng. P., p. 36.
> Acuteness and gusto. HUNT, Wit & Humour, p. 5.
> Combination of gusto with sound theory. SAINTSBURY, Es. in Eng. Lit., p. 158.

Gusty: (XIX.) *b*; Swin. Gosse, Hist. Eng. Lit., III., p. 265.
Hackneyed (IX.): Cole to present.
> Hackneyed and commonplace. LOWELL, O. E. D., p. 130.

Halting (XVIII.): Hazlitt, Age of El., p. 44.
Handsome (XXII.) *b*: Jef. Gosse, Hist. Eng. Lit., p. 72.
Happy (IV.): Camden to present.
> The turn of the poem is happy. RYMER, 2d Pt., p. 79.

Hard (III.), cf. (XXII.) *b*: Ascham to present.

I. Difficult; not clear.

> The sense is hard and dark. ASCHAM, III., p. 269.
> Piers Plowman . . . hard and obscure. PUTTENHAM, p. 76.

II. Not productive of æsthetic feeling; ineffectual.

> All attempts that are new in this kind are dangerous and somewhat hard, before they be softened with use. B. JONSON, Timber, p. 61.
> Dry, hard, and barren of effect. HAZLITT, Age of El., p. 207.

HARMONY (X.).

There are two periods and three uses in the history of the term "harmony." Previous to the present century the term denoted a fixed and uniform method of combining sounds and of arrang- *As regular continuations of sound.*

ing the metrical movements of a literary production. This established harmony, it was assumed, could not fail to please the ear and arouse agreeable emotions in the mind.

> We ought to join words together in apt order that the ear may delight in hearing the harmony. T. WILSON, Rhet., pp. 175, 176.
> Poesy is a skill to speak and write harmonically. 1583. PUTTENHAM, p. 79.
> By the harmony of words we elevate the mind to a sense of devotion. 1669. DRYDEN, III., p. 377.
> To preserve an exact harmony and variety, the pause at the fourth or sixth . . . syllable of the verse . . . should not be continued above three lines together without the interposition of another. 1706. POPE, VI., p. 57.
> Our poetry was not quite harmonized in Waller's time; so that this (On the Death of the Lord Protector), which would be now looked upon as a slovenly sort of versification, was, with respect to the times in which it was written, almost a prodigy of harmony. 1767. GOLDSMITH, V., p. 160.
> After about half a century of forced thoughts and rugged meter, some advances toward nature and harmony had been made by Waller and Denham. 1781. S. JOHNSON, VII., pp. 307, 308.

During the present century, the term "harmony," when referring to the sounds and rhythms of a composition, represents such a combination of regularity and irregularity, of uniformity and variety, as shall keep expectation continually upon the wing, as shall conform to the anticipated combinations of sounds and of rhythms enough to give a certain degree of confidence to the expectation, but which shall disappoint the anticipation enough to keep the expectation continually re-forming its basis of inference.

As unity and variety of sound.

The heroic measure of Chaucer is in general not only metrically correct, but possesses considerable harmony. 1819. CAMPBELL, I., p. 47.
Spenser threw the soul of harmony into our verse. ID., p. 53.
Johnson says these are remarkably inharmonious: —
> This delicious place
> For us too large, where thy abundance wants
> Partakers, and uncropt falls to the ground. (Par. Lost.)

There are few so dull as to be incapable of perceiving the beauty of the rhythm in the last. 1826. LANDOR, IV., p. 449.
There is many a critic who talks of harmony, and whose ear seems to have been fashioned out of the callus of his foot. ID., VIII., p. 387.
In Massinger, as all our poets before Dryden, in order to make harmonious verse in the reading, it is absolutely necessary that the meaning should be understood; when the meaning is once seen then the harmony is perfect. Whereas in Pope . . . it is the mechanical meter which determines the sense. (Pub.) 1836. COLERIDGE, IV., p. 259.

Occasionally, in this century, the term "harmony" denotes a blending of all the parts of a composition into one another in such a manner as to produce a perfect unity of æsthetic effect. *As general adaptation in composition.*

Poetry . . . is the result of the general harmony and completion . . . of all the faculties. 1828. CARLYLE, II., p. 18.
We have no word but the coarse and insufficient word taste to express that noble sense of harmony and high poetic propriety shown . . . in these lyrics. 1867. SWINBURNE, Es. & St., p. 141.
Dramatic harmony. 1889. ID., A St. of B. Jonson, p. 66.

Harsh (X.): Harvey to present.

I. Rough and broken in sound or thought.

The sound which I speak of as belonging to Grammar relates only to sweetnesses and harshnesses. BACON, IV., p. 443.

II. Hard; obscure.

Harsh and obscure. WEBBE, p. 32.

III. Unfeeling; unsympathetic.

The harsh direct narrative of Defoe. GOSSE, Eighteenth Cent. St., p. 385.

Healthful (XIV.): Chan. Howells, Cr. & Fiction, p. 24.

Hearty (XII.): Walton, Saints.

Too hearty to be dissembled. WALTON, Lives, p. 119.

Heat (XV.): Lan., Swin.

Shakespeare's sonnets are hot and pothery. LANDOR, IV., p. 512.

Heavenly (XXII.) *b*: Lodge to present.

When their matter is most heavenly, their style is most lofty. LODGE, p. 11.

Heavy (XVIII.): Campion to present.

That which produces fatigue;' the tedious, the difficult, the over-condensed.

I cannot agree that this exactness of detail produces heaviness; on the contrary, it gives an appearance of truth. HAZLITT, Eng. Com. Writers, p. 159.

Milton . . . often condenses weight into heaviness. HUNT, Imagination and Fancy, p. 47.

Hectic (XV.): The water blushed into wine. (Crashaw.)

This is in his usual hectic manner. HAZLITT, Eng. Com. Writers, p. 69.

Heightened (VIII.): Heightened and elaborate air. M. ARNOLD, Cel. Lit., etc., p. 288.

Heroic (XI.): Put. to present.

Kinds of poetry,—heroic, scommatic, pastoral. HOBBES, IV., p. 444.

The personages to speak not as men but as heroes. SCOTT, Ed. of Dryden, II., p. 318.

Hideous (XXII.) *b*: Hideous and ludicrous conceits. GOSSE, Life of Congreve, p. 155.

High (XI.): Put. to present.

High and stately. PUTTENHAM, p. 164.

From style really high and pure, Milton never departs. M. ARNOLD, Cr. Es., 2d S., p. 62.

High-colored (V.): Jef. to present.

High-colored and apparently exaggerated. Jeffrey, I., p. 370.

High-toned: Swinburne, A St. of B. J., p. 79.
Historic (VIII.): Camp. to present.

I. In theory, history, representing past events and past attainments, is thought to furnish a basis for the poetic activity to which, also, in a measure, it prescribes limits.

> In an historian . . . I do not want frequent interspersions of sentiment. MILTON, III., p. 515.
> For as truth is the bound of historical, so the resemblance of truth is the utmost limit of poetical liberty. HOBBES, IV., pp. 451, 452.
> The historian, to be worthy the name, must occasionally exercise the poet's office. WALLER, II., p. 448.
> Truth to nature can be reached ideally, never historically. LOWELL, Prose, II., p. 128.

II. The "historic," in its immediate critical significance, is thought to be prosaic and tedious.

> Norman verse dwelt for a considerable time in the tedious historic style. CAMPBELL, I., p. 14.

Histrionic (VIII.): False and histrionic. SWINBURNE, Es. & St., p. 240.
Hobbling (XVIII.): Mil., Dry.
> Carmen hexametrum doth rather trot and hobble than run smoothly in our English tongue. ASCHAM, III., p. 251.

Hollow: J. Wil. to present.
> False and hollow. WILSON, VII., p. 314.

Home-bred (VII.): Swinburne, Mis., p. 49.
Homely (V.): Put. to present.
> The extreme homeliness . . . of Defoe's style. LAMB, Mrs. Leicester, p. 305.

Home-spun: Swin. to present.
> Home-spun style of Locke. GOSSE, Hist. Eng. Lit., p. 96.

Homogeneous (XIII.) *a*: Lowell, Prose, IV., p. 162.

HONEST (VII.): T. Wil. to present.

I. In early criticism, the term signified that which was not affected or over-strained; moderation and naturalness of statement.

> That is called an honest matter when either we take in hand such a cause that all men would maintain, or else gainsay such a cause that no man can well like. T. WILSON, Rhet., p. 8.
> The honesty and simplicity of the first beginners in tragedy. RYMER, 2d Pt., p. 11.
> The venustum, the honestum, the decorum of things will force its way. SHAFTESBURY, I., p. 108.

II. Later, the term has signified that which is neither affected nor conventional,— the spontaneous and natural in composition.

> Spontaneous and honest. LOWELL, Lat. Lit. Es., p. 3.
> Simple, natural, and honest. HOWELLS, Cr. & Fiction.

Horrible (XXII.) *b*: Swin., Es. & St., p. 14.
Horrid (XXII.) *b*: Gosse, Life of Congreve, p. 84.
Horse-play (V.): Hunt to present. Hunt, Wit & Humour, p. 2.
Human (XIV.): Whip. to present.

> Elizabethan literature . . . was intensely human. WHIPPLE, El. Lit., p. 5.
> I call this a good human bit of writing . . . not so high-faluting . . . as the modern style, since poets have got hold of a theory that imagination is common sense turned inside out. LOWELL, III., p. 270.
> Motives broadly human . . . such as one and all may realize. PATER, Ap., p. 241.

Humanism: The faded humanism of the taste of the day. GOSSE, Seventeenth Cent. St., p. 97.
Humble: Put. to present.

> In a style that expressed such a grave and so humble a majesty. WALTON, Lives, p. 184.
> The proper place of comparisons lies in the middle region between

the highly pathetic and the very humble style. BLAIR, Rhet., p. 184.

Humdrum: Jog-trot and humdrum, so not powerful. M. ARNOLD, Celtic Lit., etc., p. 183.

HUMOR (XVII.).

The word "humor" as employed in criticism denoted at first — in accordance with the physiological knowledge of the times — a supposed fluid or moisture of the body, which was erratic and ungovernable in its method of activity. "Humor" has come to mean an active, impulsive play of sympathy between the ideal and the actual conditions of human life. In such an extended change of meaning as this, it is evident that almost an infinite number of intermediate distinctions could be drawn. But in all such distinctions there is a common element of critical significance in the term, in that it designates a principle of variation in literature, progressive or revolutionary tendencies, which are brought about by an apparently involuntary play of the fancy upon the incongruities of actual life, accompanied, perhaps, by a spirit of sympathetic feeling. The changes of meaning in the term have resulted chiefly from the different incentives which have produced this variation and play of the fancy.

Four general stages of development of meaning may be distinguished in the history of the term.

Until the eighteenth century, the physiological origin of the term occasionally controlled its critical meaning. The humors of the body were blind and aimless. They were themselves the source of oddities and incongruities rather than the means of

As an erratic bodily humor.

reacting upon oddities and incongruities in others. Hence they furnished material for literary representation, but in the author himself they were considered as merely a disturbing influence in the organizing of this material.

> Poetry in the primogeniture had many peccant humours, and is made to have more now, through the levity and inconstancy of men's judgments. (Pub.) 1641. B. JONSON, Timber, p. 72.
> A play . . . is . . . a just and lively image of human nature, representing its passions and humours, and the changes of fortune to which it is subject, for the delight and instruction of mankind. 1668. DRYDEN, XV., p. 292.
> What force of wit and spirit in the style, what lively painting of humour, some fancy they discern there, I will not examine nor dispute. 1699. BENTLEY, II., p. 78.
> Correct the redundancy of humours, and chasten the exuberance of conceit and fancy. SHAFTESBURY, I., p. 131.
> All the varieties and turns of humour. . . . Yet the simple imitation of nature . . . through petulancy or debauch of humour . . . was set aside. ID., p. 193.

From the middle of the seventeenth century until the latter portion of the eighteenth century, "humor" usually indicated the pleasantly ridiculous, the merely laughable, the comical. But for the representation of these things, the author, it was now recognized, must himself be possessed of a sense of what was humorous, and it was this humorous sense in the author which determined the nature of the humor in the literary production. This humor was closely allied to wit. It consisted in general of a sudden feeling of contrast between the ordinary routine of life and some extravagant incident or incongruity, which was

As the agreeably ridiculous.

usually supposed to be found or to have taken place among the lower classes of society. The contrast, however, remained a contrast, and was not taken up into the unifying influence of sympathetic feeling. The purpose of the humor did not extend beyond the pleasant excitation of the moment.

> Genesis of humor from the ancients. (Summary):—
> 1. At first an odd conceit, not imitation.
> 2. Then containing only the general characters of men and manners, i. e., types; e. g. old men, lovers, courtezans, etc.
> 3. Among English, some extravagant habit, passion, or affectation . . . distinguishing its possessor from the rest of men. 1668. DRYDEN, XV., p. 350.
>
> Jonson's-comedy, "neither all wit or all humour, but the result of both." 1671. ID., III., p. 244.
> Jonson was the only man of all ages and nations who has performed it (humor) well. . . . To make men appear pleasantly ridiculous on the stage . . . was his talent. ID., p. 241.
> There is in Othello some burlesque, some humour, and ramble of comical wit. RYMER, 2d Pt., p. 146.
> Few passages in Horace are more full of humour than this ludicrous punishment of the poor creditor. 1756. J. WARTON, II., p. 215.
> As humor in writing chiefly consists in an imitation of the foibles or absurdities of mankind, so our pleasure in this species of composition arises from comparing the picture in description with the original in nature. In the works of our own countrymen we have frequent opportunities of making this comparison, as the originals are generally before us; but when we read the productions of foreigners, as their portraits are copied from manners with which we are not sufficiently acquainted, so they must often appear forced and unnatural. 1757. GOLDSMITH, IV., p. 283.

During the eighteenth century "humor" was very often regarded as a form of the comical, in which the poignancy resulted, not from the extravagant violation of social customs in general, but from any deviation whatever from good taste and cultivated feeling. "Humor" thus considered was more diffused and genial than in the preceding use of the term. It was thought of as a characteristic of the author's mind, an active influence in producing literature. It represented a conservative form of sympathy, a sympathy which included certain imperfect conditions only in order that these conditions might be corrected and improved in conformity with other conditions already well established. This form of "humor" was associated with wit and satire, not with pathos.

As the agreeably ludicrous.

> A man of urbanitas will be one from whom many good sayings and repartees shall have proceeded, and who, in common conversation, at meetings, at entertainments, in assemblies of the people, and, in short, everywhere speaks with humor and propriety. QUINTILIAN, VI., p. 455.
>
> A taste for humour is in some manner fixed to the very nature of man, and generally obvious to the vulgar, except upon subjects too refined, and superior to their understanding. SWIFT, IX., p. 88.
>
> It is not an imagination that teems with monsters, an head that is filled with extravagant conceptions, which is capable of furnishing the world with diversions of humour. 1710. ADDISON, II., p. 297.
>
> Genuine humour, the concomitant of true taste, consists in discerning improprieties in books as well as characters. 1778. T. WARTON, Hist. E. P., p. 286.
>
> Wit and humour are ever found in proportion to the progress of refinement. 1778. ID., p. 684.
>
> Addison's humour is so happily diffused as to give the grace of novelty to domestic scenes and daily occurrences. 1781. S. JOHNSON, VII., p. 472.

In fact Hawthorne was able to tread in that magic circle only by an exquisite refinement of taste, and by a delicate sense of humour, which is the best preservative against all extravagance. 1874. STEPHEN, Hrs. in a Lib., I., p. 295.

During the latter portion of the eighteenth century, humor came to be regarded as a characteristic of genius, an instinct which acted "without design," as it were, unconsciously. In the beginning of the present century, humor was distinguished from wit, — humor being the more unconscious and sympathetic, wit the more conscious and intellectual. Throughout the present century, the term "humor," with few exceptions, has represented the sense of the incongruous, which arises, when the actual is viewed in the light of ideals, which are as broad and comprehensive as human life itself. Humor thus relates to common human interests and ideals, is buoyant and filled with a sense of growth and development. Humor reaches out continually and brings into its sympathetic unity new material for literature. Though one of the most progressive of literary tendencies, the intimate relation of humor to pathos keeps it distinct from the merely incongruous, the disproportioned, the grotesque. *As the sympathetic sense of the incongruous.*

> Such, then, being demonstrably the possibility of blending or fusing, as it were, the elements of pathos and humour, and composing out of their union a third metal, I cannot but consider John Paul Richter as by far the most eminent artist in that way since the time of Shakespeare. 1821. DE QUINCEY, XI., p. 264.
>
> Whilst wit is a purely intellectual thing, into every act of the humourous mood there is an influx of the moral nature. ID., p. 270.

The essence of humour is sensibility; warm, tender fellow-feeling with all forms of existence. Nay, we may say that unless seasoned and purified by humour, sensibility is apt to run wild; will readily corrupt into disease, falsehood, or, in one word, sentimentality. 1827. CARLYLE, I., p. 14.

Humour is properly the exponent of low things; that which first renders them poetical to the mind. The man of humour sees common life, even mean life, under the new light of sportfulness and love. 1828. ID., III., p. 97.

Humor properly took its rise in the Middle Ages; and the Devil, the Vice of the mysteries, incorporates the modern humor in its elements. It is a spirit measured by disproportionate finites. (Pub.) 1836. COLERIDGE, IV., p. 279.

Humor in its first analysis is a perception of the incongruous, and, in its highest development, of the incongruity between the actual and the ideal in men and life. 1866. LOWELL, II., p. 97.

Nothing but the highest artistic sense can prevent humor from degenerating into the grotesque. 1866. ID., p. 90.

Your historian, for instance, with absolutely truthful intention, . . . must needs select, and in selecting assert something of his own humour, something that comes not of the world without, but of a vision within. 1888. PATER, Ap., p. 5.

Humor is the overflow of genius. 1892. STEDMAN, Nat. & El. of Poetry, p. 215.

Hurtling (X.): Clang of hurtling rhymes. GOSSE, Hist. Eng. Lit., p. 43.
Hybrid (VII.): Hybrid and bastard rhymes. SWINBURNE.
Hyperbolical (VIII.): Put. to present.

Hyperboles suit with the temperament of the young, for they evince a vehemence of temper. ARISTOTLE, Rhet., p. 245.

Hyperbole, the over-reacher or loud liar. PUTTENHAM, p. 200.

Figurative expressions, or hyperbolical allusions. HAZLITT, Age of El., p. 56.

Hysterical (XV.): Gosse, From Shak., etc., p. 227.
Idea: Jef. Swinburne, Es. & St., p. 165.
IDEAL (XXIII.).

The term has been employed chiefly in theory as an opposing expression to the real. It usually refers directly to the author himself rather than to his literary work. The "ideal" represents the result of the imaginative activity in heightening or transforming facts or historical truth into literary material and literary forms of expression. Two stages may perhaps be distinguished in this imaginative sublimation of the real or actual. (See Imagination and Reality.) Usually the "ideal" indicates an improvement or elevation of the common and well-known fact, a deeper conception of its meaning; the transformation of it as a fixed entity into a moving principle, accompanied, perhaps, by strong feeling and passion. As enhancement or heightening.

> Entertains in his imagination an ideal beauty, conceived and cultivated as an improvement upon nature. GOLDSMITH, I., p. 338.
> Milton has no idealism . . . Wordsworth has. WILSON, V., p. 395.
> Truth to nature can be reached ideally, never historically. LOWELL, Prose, II., p. 128.
> A figure may be ideal and yet accurate. SWINBURNE, Es. & St., p. 220.
> Every workman must be a realist in knowledge, and an idealist for interpretation. STEDMAN, Nat. of Poetry, p. 199.

Occasionally the "ideal" possesses no direct resemblance to any definite fact or historical truth. It is to be defined merely as that which is in accord with the sense of harmony and beauty in the mind. As impassioned invention.

> The ideal is that which answers to the preconceived and appetite in the mind for love and beauty. HAZLITT, Table Talk, p. 448.
> His idealism does not consist in conferring grandeur upon vulgar objects by tinging them with the reflection of deep emotion. STEPHEN, Hrs. in a Lib., I., p. 280.

150 A HISTORY OF ENGLISH CRITICAL TERMS.

Idiomatic (I.): Harvey to present.

The vernacular; a diction, common, well known, conversational. Not held in much favor by the critics until within the eighteenth century.

> Rules for avoiding the idiomatic style and attaining the sublime, — use of metaphors, etc. ADDISON, III., pp. 191, 192.
> Milton formed his style by a perverse and pedantic principle; he was desirous to use English words with a foreign idiom. S. JOHNSON, VII., p. 140.
> Spenser's language is less pure and idiomatic than Chaucer's. HAZLITT, Eng. Poets, p. 56.
> They wrote idiomatically, because they wrote naturally and without affectation. DE QUINCEY, X., p. 126.

Idiosyncrasy: Saintsbury, Eng. Pr. St., p. xxxiv.
Idyllic (XXI.): Swin. to present.
> An idyllic or picturesque mode. STEDMAN, Vic. Poets, p. 187.
> Idyllic flavor. SAINTSBURY, Es. in Eng. Lit., p. 299.

Ignoble (XIV.): Jef. to present. Jeffrey, I., p. 391.
Ill-constructed: Gosse, Hist. Eng. Lit., III., p. 9.
Ill-digested: Gosse, Seventeenth Cent. St., p. 181.
Ill-placed (IV.): Dry., J. War.
> A synchesis or ill-placing of words. DRYDEN, IV., p. 231.

IMAGINATION (XXIII.).

Five periods may be distinguished in the history of the term "imagination." During the first period, which extends to the middle of the seventeenth century, "imagination" was not an active critical term in applied criticism, though in theory it was thought to be a sufficient explanation for the origin of poetry. Imagination was a more or less independent mental activity, set over in sharp relief against the reason, and having to do with "ideas" or images, which could in no sense be derived from past

As the source of religious and poetical conceptions.

experience, which in fact had far less reference even to the present than to future experience. Imagination was regarded from the standpoint of its effect. It was the means by which poetical and religious conceptions could be attained and appreciated. These the poet and critic found existing in society as potent influences in actual conduct. The mental activity by which these conceptions were rendered possible was left almost wholly undefined.

> Art transcends nature . . . by means of the idea or fore-conceit of the work. . . . And that the poet hath that idea is manifest by delivering them forth in such excellency as he hath imagined them. Which delivering forth also is not wholly imaginative, as we are wont to say by them that build castles in the air; but so far substantially it worketh, not only to make a Cyrus which had been, but a particular excellency, as Nature might have done, but to bestow a Cyrus upon the world, to make many Cyrus's if they will learn aright why and how that Maker made him. 1583. SIDNEY, p. 8.
>
> God, without any travail to his divine imagination, made all the world of nought, nor also by any patern or mould as the Platonics with their "Ideas" do fantastically suppose. Even so the very poet makes and contrives out of his own brain both the verse and matter of his poem, and not by any foreign copy or example, as doth the translator, who therefore may well be said a versifier but not a poet. 1585. PUTTENHAM, p. 19.
>
> The poet . . . rests only in device, and issues from an excellent sharp and quick invention, holpen by a clear and bright phantasy and imagination. ID., pp. 312, 313.
>
>> Imagination bringing bravely dight
>> Her pleasing images in best array.
>>   1603. DANIEL, I., p. 238.
>
> The best division of human learning is that derived from the three faculties of the rational soul, which is the seat of learning. History has reference to the memory, poesy to the imagination, and

philosophy to the reason. And by poesy here I mean nothing else than feigned history or fables; for verse is but a character of style, and belongs to the arts of speech. BACON, IV., p. 292. Reason, when it has made its judgment and selection, sends them over to the imagination before the decree be put in execution. For voluntary motion is ever preceded and incited by imagination. . . . So . . . this Janus of Imagination has two different faces; for the face towards reason has the print of truth, and the face toward action has the print of goodness. . . . But it is not simply a messenger . . . it usurps no small authority in itself, e. g., in matters of faith it is above reason. BACON, IV., p. 406.

In a fable, if the action be too great, we can never comprehend the whole together in our imagination. 1641. B. JONSON, Timber, p. 84.

The second period extends to the middle of the eighteenth century. Imagination was considered as an imaging process, but the image received far more attention than the process. The image was thought to be the means by which the "imitation of nature" could take place. The image might be an exact reproduction of some portion of past experience, or it might be composed of such a recombination of the elements of experience, as by conforming more nearly to the sense of beauty than the actuality gave greater immediate pleasure. This immediate pleasure was the only result of the imaginative process. The imagination was unrelated to action, and hence did not arouse the feelings and passions. It opposed the integrity of the senses, and rendered impossible accuracy of knowledge; it was lawless, and tended toward over-exuberance, conceit, and mere ornament. Imagination was, indeed, in a sense, the life of

As an imaging process.

poetry, but the form in which this life revealed itself was determined almost wholly by the judgment. Imagination might furnish the poetical incentive, but judgment was the artist that gave it expression.

> For after the object is removed, or the eye shut, we still retain an image of the thing seen, though more obscure than when we saw it. And this is it the Latins call imagination, from the image made in seeing. . . . Imagination, therefore, is nothing but decaying sense. . . . This decaying sense, when we would express the thing itself, . . . we call imagination; but when we would express the decay . . . it is called memory. HOBBES, III., pp. 4–6.
>
> For imagination in a poet is a faculty so wild and lawless that, like an high ranging spaniel, it must have clogs tied to it, lest it outrun the judgment. 1664. DRYDEN, II., p. 138.
>
> Wit . . . is the faculty of imagination in the writer, which, like a nimble spaniel, beats over and ranges through the field of memory, till it springs the quarry it hunted after. 1666. ID., IX., pp. 95, 96.
>
> He affects plainness to cover his want of imagination. 1668. ID., XV., p. 288.
>
> An heroic poet is not tied to a bare representation of what is true or exceeding probable; but that he may let himself loose to visionary objects, and to the representation of such things, as depending not on sense, and therefore not to be comprehended by knowledge, may give him a freer scope for imagination. 1669. ID., IV., p. 23.
>
> Imaging is in itself the very height and life of poetry. 1674. ID., V., p. 120.
>
> The dream I am now going to relate is as wild as can well be imagined, and adapted to please these refiners upon sleep, without any moral that I can discover. SWIFT, IX., p. 56.
>
> To make brick without straw or stubble is perhaps an easier labour than to prove morals without a world, and establish a conduct of life without the supposition of anything living or extant besides our immediate fancy and world of imagination. SHAFTESBURY, III., p. 147.

Pleasures of the imagination of two kinds: —
  I. Primary, which proceed entirely from such objects as are before our eyes.
  II. Secondary, The objects are called up in our memories, or formed into agreeable visions of things that are either absent or fictitious. 1712. ADDISON, III., p. 394.

Imagination from actual view of objects arises from the sight of what is: —
  I. Great, — e. g. the desert or ocean, — a single view.
  II. Uncommon, — "Fills the soul with an agreeable surprise."
  III. Beautiful, — Most direct appeal to the soul.
1712. ID., III., p. 397.

The understanding opens an infinite space on every side of us, but the imagination, after a few faint efforts, is immediately at a stand, and finds herself swallowed up in the immensity of the void that surrounds it. ID., III., p. 427.

When the affections are moved, there is no place for the imagination. 1742. D. HUME, I., p. 242.

The force of imagination, the energy of expression, the power of numbers, the charms of imitation: all these are naturally of themselves delightful to the mind. ID., pp. 263, 264.

One obvious cause why many feel not the proper sentiment of beauty, is the want of that delicacy of imagination which is requisite to convey a sensibility of those finer emotions. ID. I., p. 272.

The last half of the eighteenth century was a period of transition. The imagination was a vivid imaging process, — a process so intense and vivid that it seemed to represent a reality, thus arousing the passions and forming, as it were, a world of beauty of its own. This was the world of poetry, which faded away before the advance of science and learning. (See "Poetical.") Imagination was thus in a sense opposed to the reason, but this opposition was viewed from the historical standpoint rather than from the

As a vivid imaging process.

psychological. It was usually far off, remote from ordinary life that the imagination painted its pictures, and produced the temporary poetical illusion. This illusion, however, was a mere illusion, it did not react upon conduct; it served only as a means of producing immediate pleasure.

> Poetry cannot dwell upon the minuter distinctions by which one species differs from another, without departing from that simplicity of grandeur which fills the imagination. 1750. S. JOHNSON, II., p. 178.
> We can always feel more than we can imagine, and the most artful fiction must give way to truth. 1753. ID., IV., p. 79.
> It is a creative and glowing imagination, and that alone, that can stamp a writer with this exalted and very uncommon character, which so few possess, and of which so few can properly judge. 1756. J. WARTON, I., p. ii.
> Such circumstances as are best adapted to strike the imagination by lively pictures . . . the selection of which chiefly constitutes true poetry. ID., p. 26.
> Pope's close and constant reasoning had impaired and crushed the faculty of imagination. ID., p. 276.
> If the imagination be lively the passions will be strong. ID., p. 102.
> Ignorance and superstition, so opposite to the real interests of human society, are the parents of imagination. 1778. T. WARTON, II. E. P., p. 626.
> The poet has a world of his own, where experience has less to do than consistent imagination. 1762. HURD, IV., p. 324.
> And as art is merely a pleasure of the imagination, it is much higher than any that is derived from a rectitude of the judgment; the judgment is for the greater part employed in throwing stumbling-blocks in the way of the imagination, in dissipating the scenes of its enchantment, and in tying us down to the disagreeable yoke of our reason. 1756. BURKE, I., p. 65.
> The imagination is the most extended province of pleasure and pain, as it is the region of our fears and our hopes, and of all our passions that are connected with them. ID., p. 58.

Waller borrows too many of his sentiments and illustrations from the old mythology, for which it is vain to plead the example of ancient poets; the deities which they introduced so frequently were considered as realities so far as to be received by the imagination, whatever sober reason might even then determine. 1781. S. JOHNSON, VII., p. 216.

During the early portion of the present century, the imagination was considered as an ideal-making process, producing ideals which were not a mere means for creating a poetical illusion, but were a constant and normal influence in all conduct, which therefore excited the passions, and which to a greater or less extent controlled even perception. As a mental process, the imagination represented a fusion or unification of the powers of the mind, a blending of all the mental capacities in the intuition or reconstruction of an ideal. As in the case of genius the intense unification of the mental powers produced results which could only be apprehended as results, and thus the imagination was said to be "unconscious," to disclose "hidden analogies," to be an instinct, a revelation, to work like nature itself. The imagination also gave the artistic sense of power and movement, — movement which carried to an undue extent resulted in the fantastic and the grotesque. The imagination, considered as a mere picturing process, was now called the passive imagination, in contradistinction to the active imagination, which transformed these pictures into living things, thus giving the basis for sympathy, which identified beauty with truth, — at least with future truth, (see "Truth"), — and which furnished a means for the mental representation not only of feel-

As an idealized artistic process.

ings and passions, which point toward the future, or of action historically considered, but also of passion growing into action and of action resolving itself into passion. Imagination thus gave a unified view of life; still it was confined to poetry, and was not usually supposed to assist in its own verbal expression.

> The primary imagination I hold to be the living power and prime agent of all human perception, and as a repetition in the finite mind of the eternal act of creation in the infinite "I Am." The secondary is an echo of the former, identical in kind, but differing in degree, and in the mode of its operation. It dissolves, diffuses, dissipates, in order to recreate. 1817. COLERIDGE, III., p. 363.
>
> The poet described in ideal perfection brings the whole soul of man into activity with the subordination of its faculties to each other according to their relative worth and dignity. He diffuses a tone and spirit of unity that blends, and, as it were, fuses each into each, by that synthetical and magical power to which I would exclusively appropriate the name of imagination. 1817. ID., p. 374.
>
> Imagination seems insufficient of itself to produce diction always vivid and poetical, without the aid of human passion and worldly observation. 1815. WILSON, V., p. 395.
>
> What the imagination seizes as beauty must be truth, whether it existed before or not. . . . The imagination may be compared to Adam's dream; he awoke and found it truth. 1817. KEATS, Letters, pp. 41, 42.
>
> This intuitive perception of the hidden analogies of things, or, as it may be called, this instinct of the imagination, is, perhaps, what stamps the character of genius on the productions of art more than any other circumstance: for it works unconsciously like nature, and receives its impressions from a kind of inspiration. 1819. HAZLITT, Eng. Com. Writers, p. 147.
>
> We want the creative faculty to imagine that which we know; we want the generous impulse to act that which we imagine. 1821. SHELLEY, VII., p. 135.

A man to be greatly good must imagine intensely and comprehensively, . . . go out of his own nature and identify himself with beauty not his own. 1821. ID., p. 111.

Among the writers of luxuriant and florid prose, however rich and fanciful, there never was one who wrote good poetry. Imagination seems to start back when they would lead her into a narrower walk; and to forsake them at the first prelude of the lyre. 1824. LANDOR, II., p. 186.

They do not create, which implies shaping and consistency. Their imaginations are not active, — for to be active is to call something into act and form, — but passive, as men in sick dreams. 1826. LAMB, Elia, p. 252.

A true work of art requires to be fused in the mind of its creator, and, as it were, poured forth (from his imagination, though not from his pen) at one simultaneous gush. 1827. CARLYLE, I., p. 18.

Poets have penetrated into the mystery of nature . . . and thus can the spirit of our age, embodied in fair imagination, look forth on us. 1827. ID., p. 56.

It is well known that we create nine-tenths at least of what appears to exist externally; and such is somewhere about the proportion between reality and imagination. 1832. WILSON, VI., p. 109.

In this way has imagination at all times blended itself with the passion of sorrow. The strong feeling in which the mind begins to work is the wound of its own loss. ID., VIII., p. 265.

Imagination . . . purely so called is all feeling: the feeling of the subtlest and most affecting analogies; the perception of sympathies in the nature of things or in their popular attributes. 1844. HUNT, Im. & Fancy, p. 26.

That magnificent condition of fantastic imagination which . . . is one of the chief elements of the Northern Gothic mind. 1846. RUSKIN, St. of Venice, p. 154.

During the latter portion of the present century, imagination has usually been considered as an artistic process, which is in close relation with the intellectual powers of the mind. It

As an artistic process.

not only gives unity to the mental conception of the literary work, but it aids also in expressing this general conception in definite images and in words. It is guarded from excesses by an inherent sense of "form," without which it ceases to be imagination. Imagination gives body, as it were, to the reason, and reason gives the general outlines to the imaginative process. The two processes are indispensable to each other. Hence the imagination finds literary expression in prose as well as in poetry. During nearly all the present century, "imagination" has been employed to explain the origin of literature, even as "imitation" had previously been employed. The distinctions between the two views, however, belong to theoretical rather than to applied criticism. As an active critical term, "imagination" has not been so much in use during the latter portion of the century as it was during the earlier portion.

> The feat of the imagination is in showing the convertibility of every thing into every other thing. Facts which had never before left their stark common sense suddenly figure as Eleusinian mysteries. 1860. EMERSON, Conduct of Life, p. 289.
> But the main element of the modern spirit's life is neither the senses and understanding, nor the heart and imagination; it is the imaginative reason. And there is a century in Greek life, the century preceding the Peloponnesian war, . . . in which poetry made, it seems to me, the noblest, the most successful effort she has ever made as the priestess of the imaginative reason. 1865. M. ARNOLD, Cr. Es. 1st S., pp. 220, 221.
> Wordsworth was wholly void of that shaping imagination which is the highest criterion of a poet. 1866. LOWELL, II., p. 78.
> In poets, this liability to be possessed by the creations of their own brains is limited and proportioned by the artistic sense, and the

imagination thus truly becomes the shaping faculty, while in less regulated or coarser organizations it dwells forever in the Nifelheim of phantasmagoria and dream. 1868. ID., p. 321.

Lamb . . . had more sympathy with imagination where it gathers into the intense focus of passionate phrase, than with that higher form of it, where it is the faculty that shapes, gives unity of design, and balanced gravitation of parts. 1868. ID., III., p. 30.

Imagination has . . . its seat in the higher reason, and it is efficient only as the servant of the will. ID., p. 31.

In that secondary office of imagination, where it serves the artist, not as the reason that shapes, but as the interpreter of his conceptions into words, there is a distinction to be noticed between the higher and lower mode in which it performs its function. It may be either creative or pictorial, may body forth the thought or merely image it forth. With Shakespeare, for example, imagination seems imminent in his very consciousness; with Milton in his memory. 1868. ID., p. 40.

There is an essential difference between imaginative production in verse, and imaginative production in prose, that will not permit both to be called by the common name of poetry. M. ARNOLD, Mixed Essays, p. 435.

A vigorous grasp of realities is rather a proof of a powerful than a defective imagination. 1874. STEPHEN, Hrs. in a Lib., p. 283.

To identify in prose what we call poetry, the imaginative power. 1888. PATER, Ap., p. 2.

There is an imagination of the intellect, and its utterance is of a very high order, — often the prophecy of inspiration itself. 1892. STEDMAN, Nature of Poetry, p. 211.

IMITATION (XXIII.).

Early in ancient criticism, poetry was defined as a result of the tendency in the mind to imitate, to reproduce or represent human life and human achievement, and this definition exerted a strong influence upon the methods of English criticism until the middle of the present century. In Latin criticism "imitation" was usually employed to designate either a copying among authors, or oratorical mimicry, — the forensic portrayal of human manners and character. The oratorical significance of "imitation" is scarcely to be found in English criticism. The term has uniformly indicated either the representation of nature, life, or experience, or the copying among authors.

As signifying the reproduction of experience in literary form four general stages may perhaps be distinguished in the history of the term. Until the middle of the seventeenth century, "imitation" was usually thought to be a sufficient explanation for all poetry. But that which was to be imitated transcended any ordinary conception of nature, life, or experience. What was imitated was really ideals, often abstract, rigid, and conventional in their nature, and this could be accomplished only by means of imagination and suggestion. *As representation of ideals.*

> Poetry is an art of imitation, for so Aristotle termeth it in his word, . . . that is to say, a representing, a counterfeiting, or figuring forth . . . three kinds:
> I. Imitate the inconceivable excellencies of God.
> II. Imitate matters philosophical.
> III. Imitate what shall be and should be to teach and delight.
> 1583. SIDNEY, p. 9.
> To imitate, borrow nothing of what is, hath been, or shall be; but range . . . into the divine consideration of what may be and should be. ID., p. 10.
> Poesy is an art not only of making but also of imitation. . . . A poet may in some sort be said a follower or imitator, because he can express the true and lively of everything is set before him. 1585. PUTTENHAM, p. 20.
> Whatsoever a man speaks or persuades, he doth it not by imitation

artificially, but by observation naturally (though one follow another), because it is both the same and the like that nature doth suggest; but if a popinjay speaks she doth it by imitation of man's voice artificially and not naturally . . . but not the same that nature doth suggest to man. ID., p. 312.

The second period extends until the middle of the eighteenth century. Characters and sentiments as manifested in action constituted the chief subject-matter of imitation. As in ancient criticism, experience was considered historically, not ideally. Imitation, however, was not usually thought to be a complete explanation for poetry, nor did the mental process, by means of which imitation takes place, receive attention.

<small>As representation of character.</small>

> The poet is a "maker" by reason of his being an imitator, and what he imitates is action. ARISTOTLE, Poetics, p. 31.
> A play is still an imitation of nature; we know we are to be deceived, and we desire to be so; but no man ever was deceived but with a probability of truth. 1668. DRYDEN, XV., p. 120.
> All that is dull, insipid, languishing, and without sinews in a poem is called an imitation of nature . . . and lively images and elocution are never to be forgiven. 1674. ID., V., p. 120.
> To imitate well is a poet's work; but to affect the soul, and excite the passions, and above all to move admiration . . . a bare imitation will not serve. 1667. ID., II., p. 384.
> I shall quote several passages (of Chevy-Chase) in which the thought is altogether the same with what we meet in several passages of the Æneid; not that I would infer from thence that the poet (whoever he was) proposed to himself any imitation of those passages, but that he was directed to them in general by the same kind of poetical genius and by the same copyings after nature. 1710. ADDISON, II., p. 384.

The last half of the eighteenth century was a period of transition. The phrase "imitation of nature" came to represent both originality and invention, and thus again "imitation" was regarded as a full explanation for poetry. The mental process of "imitation," however, was not directly defined.

As representation of "nature."

> This primary or original copying, which in the ideas of philosophy is Imitation, is, in the language of criticism, called invention. 1751. HURD, II., p. 111.
> Nothing is an imitation further than as it resembles some other thing; and words, undoubtedly, have no sort of resemblance to the ideas for which they stand. . . . Poetry is an imitation only in so far as it describes the manners and passions of men which their words can express. 1756. BURKE, I., p. 178.
> I will not presume to say . . . descriptive poetry . . . is equal either in dignity or utility to those compositions that lay open the internal constitution of man, and that imitate characters, manners, and sentiments. 1756. J. WARTON, I., p. 49.
> There are two kinds of imitations, one of nature, the other of authors. The first we call originals, and confine the term imitation to the second. 1759. GOLDSMITH, IV., p. 365.
> If the father of criticism has rightly denominated poetry . . . an imitative art, the metaphysical poets will without great wrong lose their right to the name of poets; for they cannot be said to have imitated anything; they neither copied nature nor life; neither painted the form of matter, nor represented the operations of intellect. 1781. S. JOHNSON, VII., p. 15.

During the first half of the present century the process of imitation and the imaginative activity were often identified with each other. The poet must imitate the spirit of nature, he must represent character and sentiment by means of a sympathetic appreciation of them.

As representation of life, the "spirit of nature."

When thus employed, however, the term "imitation" had evidently acquired a meaning, quite at variance with its more primary and fundamental significance. During the last half of the century, this general use of the term is scarcely to be found in actual criticism.

> The artist must imitate that which is within the thing, that which is active through form and figure, and discourses to us by symbols, the Natur-geist, or spirit of nature, as we unconsciously imitate those whom we love. 1810. COLERIDGE, IV., p. 333.
>
> The truth is, painting and sculpture are, literally, imitative arts, while poetry is metaphorically so. . . . I would rather call poetry a suggestive art. 1825. ID., Prose, I., p. 5.
>
> The objects of the imitation of poetry are the whole external and the whole internal universe, the face of nature, the vicissitudes of fortune, man as he is in himself, man as he appears in society, all things which really exist, all things of which we can form an image in our minds by combining together parts of things which really exist. The domain of this imperial art is commensurate with the imaginative faculty. 1830. MACAULAY, I., p. 476.
>
> Sympathy is one of the strengths of the poet's soul; and sympathy, at its height and depth, works into imitation. Imitation, therefore, is proof, power, test, trial, growth, and result, cause and effect, of original genius. 1832. WILSON, VIII., p. 266.

The second general meaning of "imitation"— its use to represent the influence of authors upon one another — occurs in actual criticism far more frequently than the use of the term just given. *As free translation.* The imitation of authors is found mentioned in two different connections, giving to the term, perhaps, slightly different shades of meaning. In early English criticism, "imitation" often denoted a free method of translation in opposition to a more literal method,— a translation, as it were, of the spirit of an author rather than of his exact words.

> There be six ways appointed by the best learned men for the learning of tongues, and increase of eloquence: as, 1. Translatio

linguarum; 2. Paraphrasis; 3. Metaphrasis; 4. Epitome; 5. Imitatio; 6. Declamatio. 1568. ASCHAM, III., p. 174.

The unaptness of our tongues and the difficulty of imitation disheartens us. CAMPION, p. 233.

Three ways of translating: 1. Metaphrase, exact, literal; 2. Paraphrase; 3. Imitation, where the translator assumes the liberty, not only to vary from the words and sense, but to forsake them both as he sees occasion, and taking only some general hints from the original, to run divisions on the groundwork as he pleases. 1680. DRYDEN, XII., p. 16.

Imitation gives us a much better idea of the ancients than ever translation could do. 1767. GOLDSMITH, V., p. 155.

Imitation of authors, however, is usually made an opposing term, not to literal translation, but to originality. Discredit is thrown upon the imitation in so far as it is restricted to mere form *As copying of one author by another.* of expression; but in so far as the imitation is a reproduction of the general method, thought, and spirit of an author, the disapproval tends to pass away from the term. But the highest gifts of authorship, it has been universally recognized, are not to be attained even by this form of imitation. This use of imitation occurs more frequently at some periods of English criticism than at others, but there has perhaps been no variation in its meaning.

A great portion of art consists in imitation, since though to invent was first in order of time, and holds the first place in merit, yet it is of advantage to copy what has been invented with success. QUINTILIAN, II,, p. 278.

Three kinds of imitation:

1. A fair, lively painted picture of the life of every degree of man. Cf. Plato III., "De Republica."
2. To follow for learning of tongues and sciences the best authors.

3. Whether to follow one or more, . . . which way, . . . in what place, by what mean, and order, e. g., as Virgil followed Homer. ASCHAM, III., p. 213.

Describe not the morning and rising of the sun in the preface of your verse; for these things are so oft and so diversely written upon by poets already, that if ye do the like, it will appear ye but imitate, and that it comes not of your own invention, which is one of the chief properties of a poet. 1585. K. JAMES, pp. 112, 113.

It is not reading, it is not imitation of an author, which can produce this fineness; it must be inborn. 1693. DRYDEN, XIII., p. 97.

What Tacitus has said in five words, I imagine I have said in fifty lines. Such is the misfortune of imitating the inimitable. 1742. GRAY, II., pp. 109, 110.

To admire on principle is the only way to imitate without loss of originality. 1817. COLERIDGE, III., p. 203.

Shakespeare's style never curdles into mannerism, and thus absolutely eludes imitation. LOWELL, III., p. 36.

It is the nature of man to select the worst parts of his models for imitation. · SAINTSBURY, Eng. Pr. St., p. xxxiv.

The exquisite grace and charm of Lamb, springing in part no doubt from an imitation of the unreformed writers . . . had . yet in it so much of idiosyncrasy that it has never been and is never likely to be successfully imitated. ID., p. xxxiv.

Impalpable (XXII.) *b*: Impalpable and indefinable. SWINBURNE, Es. & St., p. 11.

IMPASSIONED (XV.).

The term "impassioned," as employed during the present century, denotes poetical passion which is intense and sustained. (See "Passion.") The emotion which it represents is not usually impetuous, but is so diffused as to give coherency and unity to the whole literary production. The impassioned designates the emotion which accompanies an intense interest in the beauty of mental imagery, and of ideals. It does not incite to the realization of an ideal so much as to the most perfect conception and statement of that ideal.

    Bold and impassioned elevations of tragedy. T. WARTON, p. 886.
    Poetry is the impassioned expression which is in the countenance of all science. 1798. WORDSWORTH, II., p. 91.
    Impassioned lines:
        Then let me hug and press thee into life,
        And lend thee motion from my beating heart. — L. WINCHELSEA. 1830. ID., III., p. 300.
    Impassioned, lofty, and sustained diction. COLERIDGE, III., p. 365.
    Impassioned poetry is an emanation of the moral and intellectual part of our nature, as well as of the sensitive, — of the desire to know, the will to act, and the power to feel. 1818. HAZLITT, Eng. Poets, p. 8.
    Poetical and impassioned. ID., El. Lit., p. 56.
    Spirited and impassioned. ID., Table Talk, p. 245.
    The soul of poetry is impassioned imagination. WHIPPLE, Lit. of Age of El., p. 217.
    Impassioned contemplation. PATER, Ap., p. 59.
    Impassioned meditation. MINTO, Char. of Eng. Poets, p. 169.

Impeccable (XXII.) *a*: Impeccable ideal line. ROSSETTI, Lives, p. 78.
Imperial (XI.): Swinburne, Es. & St., p. 65.
Impetuous (XII.): Blair to present.
    Impetuous, graceful power. CARLYLE, IV., p. 130.
Imposing (XI.): Jef., Chan. Jeffrey, II., p. 55.
Impressive (XI.): Poe to present. Stephen, Hrs. in a Lib., p. 57.
Impulsive (XII.): Hunt to present.
    Richardson's nature is always the nature of sentiment and reflection, not of impulse or situation. HAZLITT, Eng. Com. Writers, p. 160.
Inanity (XII.): Inanity and careless workmanship. GOSSE, Seventeenth Cent. St., p. 233.
Inavertible (XXII.) *a*: Gosse, From Shak., etc., p. 103.
Inchoate (II.): Ros., Saints.
    Inchoate method of execution. ROSSETTI, Pref. to Blake, p. cxvii.

Incisive (XX.) *b*: Swin. to present. Swinburne, Es. & St., p. 138.
Inconstant (XIX.): The first defect of Wordsworth's poems is the inconstancy of the style. Coleridge, III., p. 462.
Indefinable (III.): Impalpable and indefinable. Swinburne, Es. & St., p. 11.
Individual: Jef. to present. Gosse, From Shak., etc., p. 144.
Indolence (XII.): Jef., Gosse.
  A golden indolence, akin to the hazy beauty of a summer afternoon. Gosse, Seventeenth Cent. St., p. 67.
Ineptitude: Gosse, From Shak., etc., p. 216.
Inevitable (VIII.): Swinburne, A St. of B. J., p. 5.
Infantile (XII.): Gosse, From Shak., etc., p. 187.
Inflated (XIX.) *b*: J. War. to present.
  Unnatural, false, inflated, and florid style. J. Warton, II., p. 200.
Ingenious (XXIII.): Mil. to present.
  With an ingenious flattery of nature. Dryden, II., p. 296.
Ingenuous (VII.): T. Arn. to present. Much in use.
  Simplicity being true is ingenuous. Ingenuousness is the countenance of truth. Rossetti, Lives, p. 62.
Inimitable (XXII.) *a*: Jef. to present.
  The inimitable note of instinct. Swinburne, Es. & St., p. 62.
Ink-horne (I.): T. Wil., Ascham, Put.
  Never affect strange inkhorn terms. T. Wilson, Rhet., p. 171.
  Many inkhorne terms so ill-affected, brought in by men of learning, as preachers and schoolmasters. Puttenham, p. 158.
Innocence (XIV.): Jef. Gosse, Hist. Eng. Lit., III., p. 70.
Insight (XXIII.): The harsh direct narrative of Defoe, without sympathy or insight. Gosse, Eighteenth Cent. St., p. 385.
  As spontaneous as insight. Stedman, Nature of Poetry, p. 47.
Insipid (XII.): Hobbes to present.

That which fatigues from being too commonplace; without originality or feeling.

  The phrases of poetry, as the airs of music, with often hearing, become insipid. Hobbes, IV., p. 455.
  Flimsy and insipid decorum. Hazlitt, Sp. of Age, p. 102.
  Cold and insipid works. Howells, Crit. & Fiction, pp. 62, 63.

Inspired (XV.): Shaftes. to present.
   There is more of Rhetoric than of inspiration about him. JEFFREY, II., p. 405.
Instructive.(XX.): Dry. Saintsbury, Es. in Eng. Lit., p. 268.
Integrity: J. War. Gosse, Seventeenth Cent. St., p. 89.
INTELLECTUAL (XX.) *b.*

For about a century the word "intellectual" has been very generally employed in defining wit and sentiment, and as a complementary expression to the imagination, the emotions, and occasionally to the will. Its unity with the other mental powers has usually received emphasis rather than its opposition to them. It represents not so much conscious elaboration and abstraction as a careful meditative attitude of mind, and native logical acuteness and penetration. The use of the word "intellectual" as an active critical term marks the transference of psychological terminology and methods into criticism.

>Impassioned poetry is an emanation of the moral and intellectual part of our nature as well as of the sensitive. HAZLITT, Eng. Poets, p. 8.
>
>Tennyson's poetry is characterized by intellectual intensity as distinguished from the intensity of feeling. WHIPPLE, Es. & Rev., I., p. 339.
>
>Sentiment is intellectualized emotion. LOWELL, II., p. 252.
>
>Perhaps the main constituent of Longfellow, as a poetical writer, is intelligence . . . a certain openness to information of all sorts, and a readiness at turning it to practical accounts. ROSSETTI, Lives, p. 388.
>
>Intellect, which in the highest poets co-operates with the affections and the imagination, in Victor Hugo is deficient. DOWDEN, St. in Lit., pp. 429, 430.
>
>The absence of large intellectual power, is also the absence of a seat of moral sensibility. ID., p. 433.

170　*A HISTORY OF ENGLISH CRITICAL TERMS.*

Intelligible (III.): Gold. to present.
Intense (XII.): Haz. to present.

Much in use. Strength both of thought and of emotion. Sometimes one is emphasized, sometimes the other; but the term seems to represent their complete union or synthesis, and to be measured by the force of the impression which the literary work, as a whole, produces on the mind of the reader.

> Intensity is the great and prominent distinction of Lord Byron's writings. He seldom gets beyond force of style. HAZLITT, Sp. of Age, p. 124.
> Strength and intensity of thought. LANDOR, IV., p. 56.
> Poetry must be intense in meaning. BAGEHOT, Lit. St., II., p. 351.
> Wordsworth . . . a meditative and intensive poet. ROSSETTI, Lives, p. 216.
> Wordsworth is never intense for the very reason that he is spiritually massive. DOWDEN, St. in Lit., p. 66.

Interesting (XXII.) *b*: Hume to present.

> Most pathetic and most interesting, and by consequence the most agreeable. HUME, I., p. 264.

Interminable: Jef. Gosse, Life of Congreve, p. 18.
Intimate: Swin. Gosse, From Shak., etc., p. 60.
Intonation (X.): Swinburne, Es. & St., p. 7.
Intrepidity (XII.): Force and intrepidity. JEFFREY, I., p. 209.
Intricate (II.): J. War. to present. Swinburne, Es. & St., p. 65.
Intrigue: Swin., Gosse. Swinburne, A St. of B. J., p. 36.
Invective (XXI.): Jef. to present.

> Bitter cry of invective and satire. SWINBURNE, Es. & St., p. 20.

INVENTION (XXIII.).

Previous to the present century the term "invention" is to be defined far more as a product than as a process. Invention was the result of imaginative activity, when the object of representa-

As imitation of "nature."

tion was either historical truth, or something at variance with it. Invention, considered as the portrayal of the likeness of truth, occurs chiefly in connection with the theory of oratory and the drama. Used in this manner, "invention," when regarded as a product, is a means to the "imitation of nature;" when regarded as a process, it is synonymous with imitation. This is the chief use of the term until near the beginning of the present century.

> Invention is a searching out of things true, or things likely, the which may reasonably set forth a matter, and make it appear probable. T. WILSON, Rhet., p. 6.
> Invention, — finds matter;
> Disposition, — places arguments;
> Elocution, — getteth words to set forth invention. ID., p. 170.
> The invention of speech or argument is not properly an invention; for to invent is to discover that we know not, and not to recover or resummon that which we already know; and the use of this invention is no other but, out of the knowledge, whereof our mind is already possessed, to draw forth or call before us that which may be pertinent to the purpose which we take into our consideration. So as to speak truly it is no invention, but a remembrance, or suggestion, with an application. 1605. BACON, Ad. of L., p. 155.
> So then the first happiness of the poet's imagination is properly invention, or finding of the thought. 1666. DRYDEN, IX., p. 96.
> In inventing characters, it is better to attach some probable fact to a person who really existed. RYMER, 1st Pt., p. 17.
> By invention is really meant no more (and so the word signifies) than discovery, or finding out; or, to explain it at large, a quick and sagacious penetration into the true essence of all the objects of our contemplation. This, I think, can rarely exist without the concomitancy of judgment; for how we can be said to have discovered the true essence of two things, without discerning their difference, seems to me hard to conceive. 1749. FIELDING, T. Jones, II., p. 6.

What we call invention in poetry, is in respect of the matter of it simply, observation. 1751. HURD, II., p. 158.

Powers requisite for the production of poetry: 1. Observation and description; 2. Sensibility; 3. Reflection; 4. Imagination and fancy; 5. Invention, by which characters are composed out of materials supplied by observation; 6. Judgment. 1802. WORDSWORTH, II., p. 130.

Occasionally, however, "invention" signified some combination of circumstances which was not in con-
<small>As fabrication of possibilities.</small> formity with truth. This use of the term became somewhat prominent in the eighteenth century. Invention, when thus employed, is to be identified with the fancy or imagination as exercised in conceits and romances.

> An excellent, sharp, and quick invention, holpen by a clear and bright phantasy and imagination . . . is not . . . to counterfeit the natural by the like effects . . . but even as nature herself working by her own peculiar virtue and proper instinct, and not by example or meditation or exercise as all other artificers do. 1585. PUTTENHAM, pp. 312, 313.
>
> His own invention and manufacture. 1699. BENTLEY, II., p. 81.
>
> There is a kind of writing wherein the poet quite loses sight of nature, and entertains his reader's imagination with the characters and actions of such persons as have many of them no existence but what he bestows on them. Such are fairies, witches, magicians, demons, and departed spirits. This way of writing is more difficult than any other, since the poet has no pattern to follow in it, and must work altogether out of his own invention. 1712. ADDISON, III., p. 422.
>
> In dreams invention works with that ease and activity that we are not sensible when the faculty is employed. ID., p. 2.
>
> For by invention, I believe, is generally understood a creative faculty, which would indeed prove most romance writers to have the highest pretensions to it. 1749. FIELDING, T. Jones, II., p. 6.

The essence of poetry is invention; such invention as by producing something unexpected surprises and delights. 1781. S. JOHNSON, VII., p. 213.

During the present century "invention" has been regarded as a process rather than as a product. It has at times been more or less completely identified with the imaginative activity. Usu- ally, however, it indicates that part of the imaginative activity which has to do primarily with the coherency in mental images, and with the combination of circumstances, and only secondarily with the relation of these images and circumstances to the personal feelings of the author. "Invention" is thus, in a sense, an intellectual intuition, and is perhaps not directly influenced by passion or impulse.

As a form of the imagination.

> Invention regularly comes before judgment, warmth of feeling before correct reasoning. 1825. JEFFREY, I., p. 258.
>
> Inventiveness of genius. 1826. HAZLITT, Pl. Sp., pp. 484, 485.
>
> Briefly the power of the human mind to invent circumstances, forms, or scenes, at its pleasure, may be generally and properly called, imagination. 1843. RUSKIN, Modern Painters, II., p. 3.
>
> I should say of a work of art that it was well "fancied" or well "invented" or well "imagined" with only some shades of different meaning in the application of the terms. ID., p. 2.
>
> B. Jonson works by effort rather than by inspiration, and leaves the impression of ingenuity rather than inventiveness. 1859. WHIPPLE, El. Lit., p. 115.
>
> The highest reach of science is, one may say, an inventive power a faculty of divination, akin to the highest power exercised in poetry. 1865. M. ARNOLD, Cr. Es., 1st S., p. 51.
>
> Endowed with an imagination of remarkable power and beauty, Wordsworth is deficient in the highest of all poetical qualities, Invention. COURTHOPE, Lib. M. in E. Lit., pp. 170, 171.

Heine, a pagan of the lyrical rather than of the inventive cast. STEDMAN, Nature of Poetry, p. 18.
A lofty if not inventive imagination. ID., p. 202.
Invertebrate (II.): Amorphous and invertebrate. GOSSE, From Shak., etc., p. 22.
Involution (II.): Car. to present.
Bulwer is atrociously involute. POE, I., p. 347.
Irony (XVII.): J. War. to present.
Irony is akin to cavil. LANDOR, III., p. 149.
Wit and humor stand on one side, irony and sarcasm on the other. ID., IV., p. 282.
Hence a grand irony in the tragedy of Lear; hence all in it that is great is also small. DOWDEN, Shak., etc., p. 258.
Irresistible (XXII.) *b*: Gosse, Hist. Eng. Lit., p. 17.
Jactation: Tedious jactation. SAINTSBURY, Es. in Eng. Lit., p. 272.
Jagged (II.): Jagged and diffuse . . . blank verse. STEDMAN, Vic. Poets, p. 107.
Jarring (X.): Swinburne, Es. & St., p. 73.
Jaunty (V.): Whip. to present.
Languid jauntiness of style. WHIPPLE, Es. & Rev., II., p. 250.
Jejune (XII.): Goldsmith to present.
Jejune, far-fetched, and frigid. HAZLITT, Age of El., p. 211.
Jingle (X.): Byron's verse halts and jingles. SWINBURNE, Es. & St., p. 246.
Joyous (XIV.): Bryant. Swinburne, Es. & St., p. 68.
JUDGMENT (XX.).

The term has been employed almost wholly in theory. Three periods may perhaps be distinguished in its history. Until the middle of the eighteenth century, "judgment" represented all the discrimination and ingenuity exercised in giving to a composition a literary or artistic form of expression.

As artful choice.

> When the fancy was yet in its first work, moving the sleeping images of things towards the light, there to be distinguished and then either chosen or rejected by the judgment. DRYDEN, II., p. 130.

Judgment is indeed the master workman in a play. ID., XV., p. 376.

During the latter half of the eighteenth century, wit, representing the more acute discriminating powers of the mind, was distinguished from the judgment. Judgment was not so essential a factor in the production of literature. It was an elaborate and intellectual expression of taste, of the cultured instinct of order and propriety. As methodic taste.

> I mean by the word taste no more than that faculty or those faculties of the mind which are affected with, or which form a judgment of the works of imagination and the elegant arts. BURKE, I., p. 54.
> Judgment implies a preserving that probability in conducting or disposing a composition that reconciles it to credibility and the appearance of truth. GOLDSMITH, IV., p. 418.
> Judgment in the operations of intellect can hinder faults but not produce excellence. S. JOHNSON, VIII., p. 20.
> Wit and judgment are seldom united. KAMES, El. of Crit., p. 33.

In the present century the term has been little used. It seems to indicate a careful, deliberative attitude of mind, which gives to the more purely literary activities a certain steadiness, and perhaps to the composition a certain breadth and finish. As elaborate method.

> Taste is the very maker of judgment. HUNT, Im. & Fancy, p. 56.
> There must be wisdom as well as wit, sense no less than imagination, judgment in equal measure with fancy, and the fiery rocket must be bound fast to the poor wooden stick that gives it guidance if it would mount and draw all eyes. LOWELL, II., p. 81.

Judicious (XX.): Dry. to present.

Little in use since the early portion of the present century, and also not very much in favor. (See "Judgment.")

The judicious obscurity . . . of Milton's description of Death in the second book. BURKE, I., p. 90.

A judicial attitude of mind is highly unreceptive, for it necessarily implies a restraint of sympathy. MOULTON, Shak., etc., p. 7.

Jumping (X.); cf. (XVIII.): Jumping verses. BROOKE, Tennyson, p. 54.

Just (XX.): Gascoigne to present.

A careful, restrained, and more or less refined method of expression.

The just proportion of our spirits. DANIEL, I., p. 231.

Nothing is truly sublime that is not just and proper. DRYDEN, VI., p. 401.

True wit may be defined as a justness of thought and a facility of expression. POPE, VI., p. 16.

The close and reciprocal connection of just taste and pure morality. COLERIDGE, IV., p. 52.

Keen (XX.) *b*: Goldsmith to present.

Keen truthfulness. SWINBURNE, Es. & St., p. 71.

Keeping (IV.): Camp. to present.

Perfect keeping . . . of Rape of Lock. LOWELL, Prose, III., p. 34.

Labored (VII.): Ascham to present.

In Sallust's writing is more art than nature, and more labour than art. ASCHAM, III., p. 264.

No matter how slow the style, so it be laboured and accurate. B. JONSON, Timber, p. 54.

Laborious: Camp. to present. Swinburne, A St. of B. J., p. 131.

Lachrymose (XV.): Lachrymose and sentimental tragedy. GOSSE, Life of Congreve, p. 93.

Laconic (XIX.) *b*: Car., Poe.

Laconic pith . . . of Burns. CARLYLE, II., p. 17.

Lame (XVIII.): Gib. to present.

Lame, stiff, and prosaic. SAINTSBURY, Hist. Fr. Lit., p. 202.

Languid (XII.): S. John. to present.

"Ah, mark!" is rather languid. I would read, "heard ye?" GRAY, III., p. 73.

Largeness (XI.): Swin., Dow.
   So large and clear and calm an utterance. SWINBURNE, Es. & St., p. 127.
   The first word of criticism which the poetical works of Edgar Quinet suggest, — a really important word, although it does not imply profound critical insight, — is that they are very large. DOWDEN, St. in Lit., p. 285.
   The largeness and veracity of George Eliot's art proceed from the same qualities which make truth-seeking a passion of her nature. ID., p. 295.
Lascivious (XV.): Whet., Put., Webbe.
Latinism (I.): Lan., Saints.
   This pedantic quibbling Latinism. LANDOR, IV., p. 454.
Laxity (XII.); cf. (XIX.): T. War. to present.
   Where there is laxity there is inexactness. LANDOR, V., p. 109.
Leaping (XVIII.): Wil., Gosse.
   Luminous and leaping Greek words. WILSON, VIII., p. 420.
Learned (XX.) *b*: Haz., Gosse.
   Learned and precise. GOSSE, From Shak., etc., p. 180.
Lengthy: Low. to present.
   Prosing lengthiness. ROSSETTI, Lives, p. 217.
Level: Haz. to present.
   Pedestrian, unimaginative, level, neutral. GOSSE, Hist. Eng. Lit., p. 73.
Levity (XIV.): Daniel to present.
   Volubility and levity. S. JOHNSON, II., p. 447.
Liberality (XIV.): T. War., Jeffrey, I., p. 169.
Liberty: Swinburne, Es. & St., p. 98.
License (IV.): Swinburne, Mis., p. 52.
Licentious (I.): Harvey to present.

I. Previous to the present century, any innovation or wide departure from the good usage of separate words and in the mechanical construction of composition.

   A mixed and licentious iambic. HARVEY, I., p. 21.
   None are more licentious than Pope and Dryden, who perpetually borrow foreign idioms, derivatives, etc. GRAY, II., p. 108.

II. Extreme moral impurity, later; not really a critical term.

Life (XII.): Gold. to present. Swinburne, Mis., p. 93.
Life-like (VIII.): Pater. Swinburne, A St. of B. J., p. 13.
Light (XVIII.): Ascham to present.

Much in use. Usually regarded as a characteristic of French literature; airiness of conception and movement; acuteness and suppleness rather than depth.

> A French lightness and case of expression. WHIPPLE, Es. & Rev., I., p. 16.
> Light and thin. ID., p. 57.
> Singular grace, lightness, and elegance. SAINTSBURY, Hist. Fr. Lit., p. 102.

Lilting (X.): Lilting measure. LAMB, II., p. 107.
Limited: Jef., Low. Jeffrey, I., p. 223.
Limpid (X.): Low. to present.
> The limpidity ... of the style of Malebranche. SAINTSBURY, Hist. Fr. Lit., p. 378.

Limping (XVIII.): Limping paraphrase. GOSSE, From Shak., etc., p. 85.
Linked (XIII.): Jef., Sted.
> Linked sweetness. JEFFREY, II., p. 434.

Literal: Jef. to present.
> Exactness primarily of translation; occasionally to the fact. Literal ... power of detail. SWINBURNE, Es. & St., p. 74.

Literary (VII.): Low. to present.
> Artificial and literary. M. ARNOLD, Cel. Lit., etc., p. 228.

Lithe (XVIII.): Swinburne, Es. & St., p. 98.
Little (XI.): Puerile and little. J. WARTON, II., p. 202.
Lively (XII.): Ascham to present. Much in use.
> The iambic and trochaic are lively meters. ARISTOTLE, Poetics, p. 79.
> Minot is an easy and lively versifier. CAMPBELL, II., p. 27.
> Fresh and lively. HALLAM, Lit. Hist., I., pp. 130, 131.

Living (VII.): Jef. to present.
> Living and organic style. DOWDEN, St. in Lit., p. 151.

Lofty (XI.): Lodge to present.

Represents a conception intermediate between elevation and sublimity: requires both depth of feeling and intellectual acumen.

> When their matter is most heavenly, their style is most lofty. LODGE, p. 11.
> Peerless sublimity and loftiness of style. NEWTON, Pref. to Tr. of Seneca. Spenser Society, XLIII., p. 2.
> Arnold's . . . intellectual processes . . . are spontaneous, and sometimes rise to a loftiness which no mere lyrist, without unusual mental faculty, can ever attain. STEDMAN, Vic. Poets, p. 91.

Logical (XX.) *b*: Hazlitt.

Used almost wholly in theory. Represents the syllogistic and intellectual relations of the different statements of a composition to each other.

> It may be questioned whether his wit was anything more than an excess of his logical faculty: it did not consist in the play of fancy, but in close and cutting combinations of the understanding. HAZLITT, Sp. of Age, p. 80.
> The logical faculty has infinitely more to do with poetry than the young . . . ever dreams of. WORDSWORTH, III., p. 292.
> Men profess to reach their philosophical conclusions by some process of logic; but the imagination is the faculty which furnishes the raw material upon which the logic is employed, and unconsciously to its owners, determines, for the most part, the shape into which their theories will be moulded. STEPHEN, Hrs. in a Lib., pp. 18, 19.

Long-drawn: Minto to present.
Long-winded (XIX.) *b*: Long-winded verbosities. CARLYLE, II., p. 82.
Loose: Ascham to present.
Loose-jointed (XIII.): Loose-jointed octosyllabic lines. WHIPPLE, Es. & Rev., p. 258.
Loquacity (XIX.) *b*: Car., Saints.

Lovely (XXII.) *b*: Hunt to present. Swinburne, Es. & St., p. 98.
Low (XIV.): Ascham to present.

I. Mean, grovelling.

> Low grossness. ASCHAM, III., p. 206.
> The low style of Horace is according to his subject, that is, generally grovelling. DRYDEN, XIII., p. 88.

II. Simple and naïve.

> Chaucer's descriptive style is remarkable for its lowness of tone,— for that combination of energy with simplicity which is among the rarest gifts in literature. LOWELL, III., p. 353.

Lucid (III.): J. War. to present. Swinburne, Es. & St., p. 64.
Ludicrous (XVII.): Shaftes. to present.

The native "flash" of wit viewed as a product; the more intellectual phase of the sense of humor, somewhat elaborated toward the droll.

> The ridiculous . . . contrary to custom, sense, and reason. HAZLITT, Eng. Com. Writers, p. 5.
> Delight in blending the pathetic with the ludicrous is the characteristic of the true humorist. STEPHEN, Hrs. in a Lib., II., p. 349.

Lumbering (XVIII.): Scott to present.

> Lumbering and disjointed. SAINTSBURY, Hist. Fr. Lit., p. 214.

Luminous (III.): Jef. to present. Swinburne, Es. & St., p. 24.
Lurid: Low. to present.

> A series of lurid pictures. LOWELL, Prose, II., p. 89.

Luscious (XXII.) *b*: Hal., Saints.

> Sweet even to lusciousness. HALLAM, IV., p. 282.

Lusty (XII.): Ascham, Whip.

> Marlowe . . . in his lustiness. WHIPPLE, Es. & Rev., II., p. 18.

Luxuriant (XIX.) *b*: Dry. to present.

> Ariosto's style is luxurious, without majesty or decency. DRYDEN, XIII., p. 15.
> In the department of luxurious ornament, the example of Mr. Ruskin may be said to have rendered all other examples comparatively superfluous. SAINTSBURY, Eng. Pr. St., p. xxxii.

LYRICAL (XXI.).

Four periods may be distinguished in the history of the term "lyrical." Until about the middle of the seventeenth century, the word "lyrical" was employed merely to designate a class of poetry which was thought to be no better and no worse than poetry in general. The accusations made against poetry were levelled at the drama rather than at the lyric, though in the amative songs of the dramas themselves, the lyric came in for its share of blame. *As passion adapted to song.*

> Which we may call lyrical, because they are apt to be sung to an instrument. CAMPION, p. 252.
>
> Lyrical kind of songs and sonnets . . . singing the praises of the immortal beauty, the immortal goodness of God. SIDNEY, p. 52.
>
> If thou mislike the lyrical, because the chiefest subject thereof is love, I reply that love being virtuously intended and worthily placed, is the whetstone of wit and spur to all generous actions. 1602. DAVISON, in Lit. Centuria, I., p. 107.

During the second period, which extended until about the middle of the eighteenth century, lyrical poetry was not in good repute with the critics. Their attention was centred chiefly upon heroic, dramatic, and didactic poetry. The lyric received very little notice. It was considered as too crude, primitive, impulsive, and passionate. *As passion.*

> Tasso confesses himself too lyrical . . . beneath the dignity of heroic verse. DRYDEN, XIII., p. 15.

During the latter half of the eighteenth century, the lyric was thought to be of equal importance with the other species or divisions of poetry. Its early crude passion may be said to have *As musical emotion.*

become refined into emotion. The term "lyrical" began to exercise a schematizing influence over other critical terms which were in active use, but its own critical significance was as yet quite incidental to its use as a classifying term.

> Alexander's Feast concludes with an epigram of four lines; a species of wit as flagrantly unsuitable to the dignity, and as foreign to the nature of the lyric, as it is of the epic muse. J. WARTON, I., p. 60.
> Lyric poetry especially should not be minutely historical. ID., I., p. 374.
> Extreme conciseness of expression, yet pure, perspicuous, and musical, is one of the grand beauties of lyric poetry. GRAY, II., p. 352.
> The true lyric style with all its flights of fancy, ornaments, and heightening of expression, and harmony of sound, is in its nature superior to any other style; which is just the cause why it could not be borne in a work of great length. GRAY, II., p. 304.
> Lyric sweetness. T. WARTON, p. 646.

During the fourth period, which includes the present century, the lyric has been in greater favor than the other species of poetry. A great develop-

As intense emotion.

ment of poetry has taken place in this century, which is neither epic nor dramatic in its nature. Hence there has been a tendency to broaden the definition of the lyric both in theory and in actual criticism. In theory, the lyric has often been made to include all poetry which deals with the thoughts and emotions of the mind. But in actual criticism it includes only such a part of this subjective poetry as is written with the intensity and unity of feeling that characterizes the older lyric, — the lyric that had chiefly for its themes the passions of love and of heroism. There is thus an extension of themes in the modern lyric, but little or no change in the method of dealing with these themes. The lyric is an intensification of poetical feeling. The feeling must be simple and more or less impulsive. It must embody itself in vivid images which are directly related to the feeling, but not to each other. Even dramatic poetry, when in its effect it produces an intense æsthetic unity, is sometimes classed as lyrical.

> Some of these pieces are essentially lyrical; and therefore cannot have their due force without a supposed musical accompaniment; but in much the greatest part, as a substitute for the classic lyre or romantic harp, I require nothing more than an animated or impassioned recitation, adapted to the subject. WORDSWORTH, p. 880, Morley's edition of 1893.
> The whole of the Midsummer Night's Dream is one continued specimen of the dramatized lyrical. COLERIDGE, IV., p. 63.
> The highest lyric work is either passionate or imaginative. SWINBURNE, Es. & St., p. 275.
> The true lyric, — short, at unity with one thought, with one cry of joyful or sorrowful passion. BROOKE, Early Eng. Lit., p. 7.
> Bright, spontaneous, almost lyrical feeling. DOWDEN, Shak., etc., p. 333.
> A lyrical purity and passion. DOWDEN, Tr. & St., p. 167.

Magazinish (IX.): The mediocrity . . . is most miserably magazinish. COLERIDGE, Letters, I., p. 117.

Magical (XXII.) *b*: Jef. to present.
> Magical potency. ROSSETTI, Lives, p. 388.

Magnetic (XXII.) *b*: Low., Ros.
> Wordsworth was not a magnetic poet. ROSSETTI, Lives, p. 216.

Magnificent (XI.): Put. to present. Macaulay, I., p. 126.

Magniloquence (XIX.) *b*: Magniloquence and amplitude of phrase. GOSSE, Hist. Eng. Lit., p. 99.

MAJESTIC (XI.).

Previous to the eighteenth century, the term "majestic" signified a commanding sweep of thought and expression, a thought simple, elevated, authoritative, a form of expression — usually a metrical movement — imposing, stately, regulated.

As authority and magnitude.

> The majesty of God's holy word. ASCHAM, III., p. 227.
> Majesty of the holy style. HOBBES, IV., p. 445.
> Words borrowed of antiquity do lend a kind of majesty to style, for they have the authority of years. 1641. B. JONSON, Timber, p. 61.
> Ariosto's style is luxurious, without majesty or decency. 1693. DRYDEN, XIII., p. 15.
> The language . . . of Waller's poem on the Navy . . . is clean and majestic. RYMER, 2d Pt., p. 79.
> The Alexandrine adds a certain majesty to the verse, when it is used with judgment, and stops the sense from overflowing into another line. 1696. DRYDEN, XIV., p. 208.
> Majesty — offended by rhyme. ID., XV., p. 360.
> Denham's Cooper's Hill, — an exact standard for majesty of style. ID., II., p. 137.
> Cowley considered the verse of twelve syllables as elevated and majestic, and has therefore deviated into that measure when he supposes the voice heard of the Supreme Being. 1781. S. JOHNSON, VII., p. 55.

During the eighteenth and nineteenth centuries, the "majestic" has often been used to characterize a lower form of sublimity. It has referred more than formerly to the imagery and thought of the composition. It has occasionally denoted the literary representation of great personal strength. It has always represented strength of some kind or magnitude which could never attain to the sublime because

As supreme strength and magnitude.

it was more simple and direct, less mysterious and suggestive.

> The sentiments of Chevy-Chase are extremely natural and poetical, and full of the majestic simplicity which we admire in the greatest of the ancient poets. 1710. ADDISON, II., p. 384.
> There.is in his negligence a rude inartificial majesty. 1751. S. JOHNSON, III., p. 83.
> Majesty which approaches sublimity. 1760. GRAY, I., p. 401.
> Majesty, characteristic of Greek finiteness. COLERIDGE, IV., p. 29.
> Majesty, not complete loftiness of thought. DE QUINCEY, X., p. 423.

Malleability: He strikes after the iron is cold, and there is want of malleability in the style. HAZLITT, Sp. of Age, p. 179.

Manly (XIV.): B. Jon. to present.

> The tone of Shakespeare's writings is manly and bracing. HAZLITT, Age of El., p. 109.
> It is not fastidiousness, but manliness and good feeling, which are outraged by such vulgarities. DE QUINCEY, XI., p. 340.

Mannered (II.): Mannered sentimentality . . . of the Arcadia. DOWDEN, Tr. & St., p. 282.

Mannerism (IV.): Scott to present.

Much in use. Elaborate and formal methods of writing, not derived from a genuine interest and feeling for the subject treated of, but from the imitation and manipulation of the more mechanical elements of style.

> Mannerism and affectation. HAZLITT, Eng. Com. Writers, p. 163.
> In poetry I have sought to avoid system and mannerism. SHELLEY, VIII., p. 186.
> Until imitation has run into a spiritless mannerism. WHIPPLE, Es. & Rev., I., p. 224. .
> Perhaps I ought to have used the word "mannerism" instead of "style," for Chapman had not that perfect control of his matter which "style" implies. On the contrary, his matter seems

sometimes to do what it will with him, which is the characteristic of mannerism. LOWELL, O. E. D., p. 96.

MANNERS (VI.).

The Greek ἦθος was expressed in early English criticism by the two words "manners" and "character."
<small>As cultivated instinct and inclination.</small> (See "Character.") Until the latter part of the eighteenth century, the word "manners" frequently denoted the instincts and inclinations of the mind which tend toward fixed habits of conduct; a certain refinement of the native bent of character toward custom and uniformity; the sense of propriety turned toward action and thus exciting perhaps even the passions. As the word "manners" gradually came to refer more to the fixed habit and less to the native inclination, it tended to represent an activity which was more physical than mental in its nature; and by the latter portion of the eighteenth century, though it was still occasionally applied to the "internal constitution of man," it had already become separated from all the essential and spontaneous powers of the mind. It had been opposed to "action," to the "tragic," and "passion," to "character," to "sentiment," and to the "poetical."

> The manners in a poem are understood to be those inclinations, whether natural or acquired, which move and carry us to actions, good, bad, or indifferent, in a play; or which incline the persons to such actions. 1679. DRYDEN, VI., pp. 266, 267.
> Under this general head of manners, the passions are naturally included, as belonging to the characters. ID., p. 274.
> Manners, under which name I comprehend the passions, and in a larger sense the descriptions of persons and their very habits. 1699. ID., XI., p. 220.

And my idea of comedy requires only that the pathos be kept in subordination to the manners. 1751. HURD, II., p. 95.

Compositions that lay open the internal constitution of man, and ... imitate characters, manners, and sentiments. 1756. J. WARTON, Pope, I., p. 49.

Pope ... stuck to describing modern manners; but those manners, because they are familiar, artificial, uniform, and polished, are in their very nature unfit for any lofty effort of the muse. ID., II., p. 402.

The manners of men ... shew themselves most usually in action. 1751. HURD, II., p. 38.

Manners, those sentiments which mark and distinguish characters. ID., II., p. 133.

Actions are the province of tragedy, manners that of comedy. 1762. GIBBON, IV., p. 137.

The sentiments, as expressive of manners, or appropriated to characters, are for the greater part unexceptionably just. 1781. S. JOHNSON, VII., p. 130.

By the beginning of the present century the word "manners" was thought to represent something wholly external to the mind. The fixed habit of conduct was regarded as a formal method of behavior, which in a sense stood over in opposition to man himself,—at least to man as furnishing either the subject or the inspiration for literary production.

<small>As formal method of behavior.</small>

> The excellence of Pope ... consisted in just and acute observations on men and manners in an artificial state of society. 1817. COLERIDGE, III., p. 155.
>
> We find ... in novels ... a close imitation of men and manners; we see the very web and texture of society as it really exists, and as we meet with it when we come into the world. 1819. HAZLITT, Eng. Com. Writers, p. 142.

Many-colored (V.): Saints. Dowden, St. in Lit., p. 382.
Marvelous (XXII.) *a*: Stephen. Swinburne, Es. & St., p. 66.

Masculine (XII.): Dry. to present.
    Masculine though irregular versification. Scott, Life of Dryden, p. 400.
    Masculine, plain, concentrated, and energetic. Landor, IV., p. 525.
Massive (XI.): Macaulay to present.
    Gothic massiveness of thought. Poe, I., p. 550.
Masterly (XXII.) *a*: Dry. to present. Jeffrey, II., p. 25.
Mawkish (XV.): Jef., Saints.
    Solemn mawkishness of Cato. Jeffrey, II., p. 88.
Meager (XII.): Haz. to present.
    Meager and dry. Hazlitt, Sp. of Age, p. 320.
Mean (V.): Ascham to present.

> A humble, familiar, and extremely simple method of writing.

> The metre and verse of Plautus and Terence be very mean, and not to be followed. Ascham, III., p. 248.
> Cowley's expressions have sometimes a degree of meanness that surprises expectation; e. g.: —
>> Nay, gentle guests, he cries, since now you're in,
>> The story of your gallant friend begin.
>>   S. Johnson, VII., p. 45.

Measured (X.): Jef. to present.
Mechanical (VII.): Dry. to present.
Mediocrity: Cole to present.
    Easy and sensible mediocrity. Gosse, Seventeenth Cent. St., p. 88.
Meditation (XX.) *b*: Swinburne, Es. & St., p. 165.
Meetely (IV.): Meetely currant style . . . of Lydgate. Webbe, p. 32.
Melancholy (XIV.): Wil. to present.
    Such melancholy strain. Wilson, VI., p. 138.
Mellifluous (X.): Jef. to present. Jeffrey, II., p. 112.
Mellow: J. War. to present.
    All are mellowed, refined, made exquisite. Dowden, Shak., etc., p. 333.

Melo-drama: Haz to present.
> This is not dramatic but melo-dramatic. There is a palpable disappointment and falling off where the interest had been worked up to the highest pitch of expectation. HAZLITT, El. Lit., p. 45.
>
> He indulges more frequently than could be wished in downright melodrama, or what is generally called sensational writing. STEPHEN, Hrs. in a Lib., I., p. 322.
>
> Beauty has not come to lift the tale out of the melodrama. DOWDEN, Tr. & St., p. 380.

Melody (X.): Put. to present.

Much in use in the present century.

I. Previous to the present century, the melodious was usually a smooth and regular combination of elementary sounds and syllables.

> That verse may be melodious and pleasing, it is necessary not only that the words be so ranged as that the accent may fall on its proper place, but that the syllables themselves be so chosen as to flow smoothly into one another. This is to be effected by a proportionate mixture of vowels and consonants, and by tempering the mute consonants with liquids and semivowels. S. JOHNSON, II., p. 413.

II. During the present century, melody has represented harmony in elementary sounds, especially vowels, resulting both from regularity of arrangement and from variation.

> Halleck's poetry is not the melody of monotonous and strictly regular measurement. BRYANT, Prose, I., p. 383.

Melting (X.): Campion, Swin.
> Silent and melting consonants. CAMPION, p. 259.

Memorable (XVI.): Haz. to present.
> As a work of genius, Gorboduc may be set down as nothing, for it contains hardly a memorable line or passage. HAZLITT, El. Lit., p. 31.
>
> Poetry should be memorable and emphatic, intense and soon over. BAGEHOT, Lit. St., II., p. 352.

Mendacious (VIII.): Swinburne, A St. of B. J., p. 143.
Meretricious (V.): Haz., Poe.
    A meretricious gloss. HAZLITT, Sp. of Age, p. 121.
Meritorious (XXII.) *a*: Jef., Wil.
    We feel it to be amusing, and therefore are inclined to believe that it is meritorious. WILSON, V., p. 366.
Metallic: Gosse, Life of Congreve, p. 137.
Metaphorical (VIII.): Hal.
    Metaphor must be the language when we travel in a country beyond our senses. RYMER, 2d Pt., p. 44.
    Bacon is sometimes too metaphorical and witty. HALLAM, III., p. 65.
Metaphysical: J. War. to present.
    Petrarch's sentiments are metaphysical and far-fetched. J. WARTON, I., p. 65.
Metrical (X.): Ros., Saints.

The rhythmical considered as a product, as a sequence of accented and unaccented sounds capable of being reduced to exact rule and method.

    The metrical pomp is made . . . effectually to aid the pomp of the sentiment . . . in Milton. DE QUINCEY, XI., p. 456.
    The language alike of poetry and prose attains a rhythmical power independent of metrical combinations, and dependent rather on some subtle adjustment of the elementary sounds, of words themselves to the image or feeling they convey. PATER, Ap., p. 57.
Might (XI.): Swinburne, Mis., p. 203.
Mild (XIX.): Ascham to present.
    The mild or rough polemic of Halifax and Bentley. SAINTSBURY, Eng. Pr. St., p. xxiv.
Mimicry: Macaulay, I., p. 21.
Mincing (XII.): Mincing sweetness of versification. GOSSE, Seventeenth Cent. St., p. 15.
Minute (VIII.) *b*: J. War. to present.
    A minute and particular enumeration of circumstances, judiciously selected, is what chiefly discriminates poetry from history. J. WARTON, I., p. 47.

Prolixity, produced by this finical minuteness of language, ends by distressing one's nerves. STEPHEN, Hrs. in a Lib., I., pp. 365, 366.
Miraculous (XXII.) *a*: Jeffrey, II., p. 73.
Misty (III.): Ossianic tumidity and mistiness. ROSSETTI, Pref. to Blake, p. cxiii.
Mock-heroic: Jef. to present.
Model (XXII.) *a*: Swinburne, Mis., p. 10.
Moderation (XIX.) *b*: M. Arnold to present.
Sureness of hand and moderation of work. ROSSETTI, Life of Keats, p. 180.
Modern (IV.): J. War. to present.

The term has always designated a departure from the spirit of the ancient classics in this century; occasionally it has denoted a departure from the spirit of Mediævalism.

See, Nature hastes her earliest wreaths to bring,
With all the incense of the breathing spring.
These lines have too much prettiness and too modern an air. J. WARTON, Es. on Pope, I., p. 11.
A pretty modernism. GRAY, II., p. 353.
Werther . . . is in the modern style. HAZLITT, El. Lit., p. 266.
Heine's intense modernism, his absolute freedom, his utter rejection of stock classicism and stock romanticism. M. ARNOLD, Cr. Es., 1st S., p. 178.
Modest (XIX.) *b*: Blair to present.
Modulation (X.): Jef. to present.
Carefully modulated expression. GOSSE, Hist. Eng. Lit., p. 89.
Monochordic (X.): "In Memoriam" is monochordic but not monotonous. T. ARNOLD, Man. of Eng. Lit., p. 454.
Monotonous (II.): Rymer to present. Recently much in use.
The monotony of Johnson's style produces an apparent monotony of ideas. HAZLITT, Eng. Com. Writers, p. 135.
Monotonous and disgusting. SAINTSBURY, Eng. Pr. St., p. xxvii.
Monumental: (V.); The Dunciad is the most absolutely chiselled and monumental work "exacted" in our country. RUSKIN, Lectures on Art, pp. 86, 87.

MORAL (XIV.).

The history of the term "moral" may be divided into three periods. Until within the eighteenth century the term "moral" denoted certain fixed rules and ideals of conduct, derived in part from Scriptural authority, in part from custom and precedent, and in part perhaps from instincts of the mind which were thought to be permanent and unchangeable. But from whatever source derived, morality, composed of fixed, eternal principles, stood over against and entirely independent of literature considered merely as literature. During the first century of English criticism, in all the charges made against poetry and in the defences of it alike, the common assumption was made that literature could justify its existence only by inculcating some moral lesson which was more or less completely foreign to the nature of literature as such. During the latter portion of the seventeenth and early portion of the eighteenth century, the opposition between morality and poetry, though still continuing, was perhaps viewed from a slightly different standpoint. The imagination in poetry was thought to do violence to the world of reality, of order, of moral action; and yet by means of satire and direct teaching, poetry could be thoroughly permeated by the didactic spirit and purpose, — could be made to do duty for the cause which of itself it would violate.

[sidenote: As conventional principles of conduct.]

> Gorboduc is full of notable morality, which it doth most delightfully teach. SIDNEY, p. 47.

> To make brick without straw or stubble is perhaps an easier labour than to prove morals without a world, and establish a conduct of life without the supposition of anything living or extant besides our immediate fancy and world of imagination. SHAFTESBURY, III., p. 147.
>
> Nor will a man, after the perusal of thousands of these performances, find his knowledge enlarged with a single view of nature, not produced before, or his imagination amused with any new application of those views to moral purposes. 1750. S. JOHNSON, II., p. 177.

During the eighteenth century — especially the latter portion of it — morality was often identified with the more conservative tendencies in literature. The moral was that which was most useful from the external and mechanical point of view; and to this general spirit of utilitarianism, literature could in a measure be made to conform in so far as the imagination was kept under constant restraint by the judgment. *As effective principles of conduct.*

> A due sentiment of morals is wanting which alone can make us knowing in order and proportion, and give us the just tone and measure of human passion. SHAFTESBURY, I., p. 218.
>
> Virtue is the foundation of taste, etc. GOLDSMITH, I., p. 331.

During the present century the moral sense and literary intuitions have been very generally identified with each other as forming parts of one and the same mental process. The difference between the ethical impulse to do and the artistic impulse to create is recognized as one of degree and not of kind. It has thus become the business of literature, not to preach morals, but to be moral, and to be moral simply because it is literature. *As developing principles of conduct.*

A pathetic reflection, properly introduced into a descriptive poem, will have greater force and beauty, and more deeply interest a reader, than a moral one. 1756. J. WARTON, I., p. 32.

Impassioned poetry is an emanation of the moral and intellectual part of our nature, as well as of the sensitive. 1818. HAZLITT, Eng. Poets, p. 8.

A man to be greatly good must imagine intensely and comprehensively, — go out of his own nature and identify himself with beauty not his own. The great secret of morals is love. 1821. SHELLEY, VII., p. 111.

If you insist on my telling you what is the moral of the Iliad, I insist upon your telling me what is the moral of a rattlesnake, or the moral of a Niagara. 1847. DE QUINCEY, XI., p. 455.

All the virtues of style are in their roots moral. They are a reverberation of the soul itself, and can no more be artificially acquired than the ring of silver can be acquired by lead. MATHEWS, Lit. St., p. 29.

Poetry is interpretative both by having natural magic in it and by having moral profundity. 1865. M. ARNOLD, Cr. Es., 1st S., p. 111.

Though it is not the business of art to preach morality, still I think that, resting on a divine and spiritual principle, like the idea of the beautiful, it is perforce moral. HOWELLS, Crit. & Fiction, pp. 60, 61.

Morbid (VII.): Ros. to present.
Morbid tone. ROSSETTI, Lives, p. 208.

Motion (XVIII.): The Ancient Mariner has . . . more of material force and motion than anything else of the poet's. SWINBURNE, Es. & St., p. 264.

Motive (XIII.): Pater.
Motives are symptoms of weakness and supplements for the deficient energy of the living principle, the law within us. COLERIDGE, I., p. 166.

Motley (II.): J. War., Gosse.
Motley discourse. GOSSE, Hist. Eng. Lit., III., p. 100.

Mot-propre: Saintsbury.

Movement (XVIII.); Poe to present.
The peculiar effect of a poet resides in his manner and movement. M. ARNOLD, Cel. Lit., etc., p. 153.

Moving (XVII.): J. War. to present.
> That moving is of a higher degree than teaching, it may by this appear, that it is wellnigh both the cause and the effect of teaching. SIDNEY, p. 22.
> Tragical and moving. GOSSE, Seventeenth Cent. St., p. 279.

Mundane: Mundane and vulgar in style. GOSSE, From Shak., etc., p. 225.

Muscular (XII.): Whip., Gosse.
> Sentences full of muscular life . . . in Coleridge. WHIPPLE, Es. & Rev., I., p. 417.

MUSICAL (X.).

During the latter portion of the eighteenth century the term "musical" denoted combinations of sounds and of metrical movements, which were smooth and agreeable to a cultivated and critical ear. When the term referred to the metrical movement, it represented that which was agreeable in sound because it was regular and methodic. When the term referred to the mere combinations of sounds, it perhaps indicated a slight appeal to the native sense of hearing and harmony. *As smooth and agreeable combinations of sound.*

> Waller's numbers are not always musical, as —
>> Fair Venus in thy soft arms
>> The god of rage confine,
>> For thy whispers are the charms
>> Which only can divert his fierce design.
>> 1781. S. JOHNSON, VII., p. 207.
> A musical close in our language requires either the last or the last but one to be a long syllable. BLAIR, Rhet., p. 140.

During the early portion of the present century, the "musical" often denoted that blending and continuity of sound — and perhaps of thought — which is in harmony with the spirit of song. The æsthetic effect upon the reader was the only *As simple elevated harmony of thought and language.*

test as to whether or not this blending and continuity had been attained.

> The musical in sound is the sustained and continuous; the musical in thought is the sustained and continuous also. 1818. HAZLITT, Eng. Poets, p. 16.
> Rousseau is . . . the only musical composer that ever had a tolerable ear for prose. Music is both sunshine and irrigation to the mind; but when it occupies and covers it too long, it debilitates and corrupts it. 1826. LANDOR, IV., p. 273.
> Milton is not a picturesque but a musical poet. 1810. COLERIDGE, IV., p. 304.
> Spenser's best thoughts were born in music. 1859. WHIPPLE, El. Lit., p. 215.

During the latter portion of the present century, the term "musical" has directly referred only to the sounds and rhythms of a composition,— more directly perhaps to the sounds than to the rhythms. It denotes primarily a harmonious blending of sounds, incidentally of rhythms, and occasionally, perhaps, it still indirectly represents a lyrical strain of thought.

As harmony of sound.

> Happy coalescence of music and meaning (in Spenser). LOWELL, IV., p. 308.
> In all poetry, the very highest as well as the very lowest that is still poetry, there is something which transports, and that something in my view is always the music of the verse, of the words, of the cadence, of the rhythm, of the sounds superadded to the meaning. 1889. SAINTSBURY, Eng. Lit., pp. 26, 27.
> Such gift of appreciation depends on the habitual apprehension of men's life as a whole . . . the musical accordance between humanity and its environment. 1878. PATER, Ap. pp. 118, 119.
> Prose literature and music are the characteristic arts of the century. They are in one sense the opposite terms of art; the art of literature presenting to the imagination, through the intelligence, a range of interests as free and various as those which music presents to it through the sense. ID., p. 35.

Mystical (III.): T. Wil., Jef. to present.

I. Viewed as to its purpose the "mystical," or mysticism, often represents the attempt to give more or less concrete expression to things purely spiritual and in themselves incomprehensible.

> Some do use after the literal sense to gather a mystical understanding, and to expound the sayings spiritually. T. WILSON, Rhet., p. 118.
>
> Novalis . . . had an affinity with mysticism, in the primary and true meaning of that word, exemplified in some shape among our own Puritan divines. CARLYLE, II., p. 201.
>
> Mysticism proper is the abuse of this tendency which prompts to the impossible feat of soaring altogether beyond the necessary base of concrete realities. STEPHEN, Hrs. in a Lib., II., p. 38.

II. Viewed as to its effect, the "mystical" often, perhaps usually, represents indefiniteness of mental imagery, and extreme remoteness of suggestion in composition; obscurity, which is neither verbal nor logical in its origin.

> Parabola . . . resemblance mystical. PUTTENHAM, p. 251.
>
> The presence of a mystical element is the mark of all lofty imaginations. STEPHEN, Hrs. in a Lib., II., p. 37.

Naïve (VII.): Put., Blair to present.

> The naïve . . . opposed to self-consciousness. SYMONDS, Es., etc., p. 175.

Naïveté (VII.): Hume to present.

Ingenuous simplicity and naturalness, so extreme as to be more or less amusing, and supposed to represent a revelation of character in its native beauty and truth.

> The absurd naïveté of Sancho Pancho. HUME, I., p. 240.
>
> Naïveté . . . is no other than beautiful nature, without affectation or extraneous ornament. GOLDSMITH, I., p. 328.
>
> Naïveté and truth of local coloring. HAZLITT, El. Lit., p. 119.

Naïveté, which becomes wit to the bystander, though simply the natural expression of the thought to him who utters it. DE QUINCEY, V., p. 156.

The French naïveté always expresses a discovery of character. BLAIR, Rhet., p. 207.

The felicity and idiomatic naïveté . . . of Walton. MATHEWS, Lit. St., p. 7.

Naked (XVI.): Swin., Saints. Swinburne, Es. & St., p. 65.

Namby-Pamby (XV.): Pope to present.

> The cock is crowing,
> The stream is flowing, etc. (Wordsworth.)

This is Namby-Pamby. BYRON, Life and Letters, p. 669.

Burns was not a sickly sentimentalist, a Namby-Pamby poet. HAZLITT, Eng. Poets, p. 170.

A seven-syllabled measure, which earned Philipps . . . the name of Namby-Pamby. GOSSE, Hist. Eng. Lit., III., p. 138.

Narrow (XIII.) *b*: Stephen. Swinburne, Es. & St., p. 170.

Native (VII.): Pope to present. Swinburne, Es. & St., p. 75.

Naturalism: Swinburne, Es. & St., p. 10.

NATURAL (VII.).

The history of the adjective "natural" does not coincide by any means with that of the noun "nature." The term "natural" has perhaps undergone no change of meaning whatever in English criticism. It signifies that which in the light of present inclination and of past habit seems least abrupt and unexpected, that which produces least jar and surprise in its apprehension. Since, however, one always expects a certain amount of change, since without this change, in fact, expectation cannot be awakened in the mind, the "natural" sometimes denotes the spontaneous, the unartificial, the sincere.

As the spontaneous.

> The Georgiac, which is not to appear in the natural simplicity and nakedness of its subject, but in the pleasantest dress that poetry can bestow on it. ADDISON, I., p. 158.

Dryden . . . had so little sensibility of the power of effusions purely natural that he did not esteem them in others. 1781. S. JOHNSON, VII., p. 340.

What has since been called Artificial Poetry was then flourishing, in contradistinction to natural; or Poetry seen chiefly through art and books, and not in its first sources. 1844. HUNT, Im. & Fancy, p. 39.

Simple, natural, and honest. HOWELLS, Crit. & Fiction.

More often, however, in applied criticism "natural" represents that which is most habitual and therefore most to be expected. It is often closely synonymous with probability. **As the usual or probable.**

    Natural propriety . . . of verse. WEBBE, p. 63.
    An apter and more natural word. PUTTENHAM, p. 189.
    Unnatural . . . and constrained. DRYDEN, XV., p. 362.
    Whether the practice of soliloquizing on the stage be natural or no to us . . . we ought to make it so by study and application. SHAFTESBURY, I., pp. 124, 125.
    Natural and easy. ID., p. 183.
    Easy and natural. ADDISON, I., p. 145.
    Natural and probable. BLAIR, Rhet., p. 508.
    Distorted and unnatural. J. WARTON, II., p. 22.
    Naturally and gracefully. HAZLITT, Sp. of Age, p. 179.
    Naturally and necessarily to accomplish the order of events. LANDOR, IV., p. 444.
    Bizarre or unnatural. WHIPPLE, Lit. of Age of El., p. 232.
    Non-natural, twisted, allusive. SAINTSBURY, Eng. Pr. St., p. xliv.

NATURE (VII.).

The history of the term "nature" exhibits a development along two almost independent lines of meaning. The variation in these two general lines of meaning does not occur at the same time, and hence it is impossible to divide the history of the term into well defined periods. In general, however, five such periods may be distinguished, which are more or less exclusive of one another.

The first period, which extends until the latter part of the seventeenth century, includes two uses of the term. Its first use was similar to that which it possessed in ancient criticism. Nature represented those primary activities of the mind which precede, underlie, and for the most part determine all conscious elaboration, study, and effort. Even these primary activities, however, were conceived of in two ways. On the one hand, they were thought to be instincts, which acted according to fixed and given methods, and which thus set up unchangeable laws and principles for literature. On the other hand, these primary activities were regarded as impulses, which followed no law or method so far as known, but tended to disregard existing methods in view of possibly better ones. There were thus, in a sense, two meanings in this primary use of the term "nature."

As human life, its primal impulses and instincts.

> Nature herself teaches us to choose the fit meter, the heroic. ARISTOTLE, Poetics, p. 15.
>
> In art we admire exactness, in the works of nature magnificence; and it is from nature that man derives the faculty of speech. LONGINUS, p. 70.
>
> All arts depend upon nature. Only the poet, disdaining to be tied to any such subjection, lifted up with the vigor of his own invention, doth grow in effect into another nature . . . freely ranging within the zodiac of his own wit. 1583. SIDNEY, p. 7.
>
> The poet is not as the painter to counterfeit the natural by the like effects . . . but even as nature herself working by her own peculiar virtue and proper instinct, and not by example or meditation or exercise as all other artificers do. 1585. PUTTENHAM, pp. 312, 313.

Nature is always the same, like herself; and when she collects her strength is abler still. Men are decayed, and studies: she is not. 1641. B. JONSON, Timber, p. 7.

In his amorous verses where nature only should reign. 1692. DRYDEN, XIII., p. 6.

It is not reading, it is not imitation of authors, which can produce this fineness; it must be inborn; it must proceed from a genius, and particular way of thinking which is not to be taught, and therefore not to be imitated by him who has it not from nature. 1693. ID., p. 97.

The second early meaning of the term is closely connected with its use during the eighteenth century. Nature indicated whatever comes to the mind through the special senses, the outer existence, whether consisting of present facts or of past events. *As external fact.*

Art and Nature (summary).
1. Art an exact imitator of nature.
2. Art heightens the beauties of nature.
3. Art covers defects of nature.
4. Art develops forms wholly beyond nature. 1585. PUTTENHAM, pp. 308–312.

Poetry . . . commonly exceeds the measure of nature, joining at pleasure things which in nature would never have come together. BACON, IV., p. 292.

Nature, a thing so almost infinite and boundless as can never be fully comprehended, but where the images of all things are always present. 1664. DRYDEN, II., p. 132.

With an ingenious flattery of nature, to heighten the beauties of some parts and hide the deformities of the rest. 1667. ID., p. 296.

The obstacles which hindered the design or action of the play once removed, it ends with that resemblance of truth and nature that the audience are satisfied with the conduct of it. 1668. ID., XV., pp. 303, 304.

All that is dull, insipid, languishing, and without sinews in a poem is called an imitation of nature. 1674. ID., V., p. 120.

From the latter portion of the seventeenth century to the middle of the eighteenth century, "nature" usually represented that part of external fact which relates to human action and achievement. The term was often employed in the discussion of the plots or characters of a drama. Hence it became associated with such expressions as "possibility, probability, and historical truth." When thus employed, the term derived its meaning wholly from the past, and indicated the ordinary course of human affairs, the established methods of action and performance. During the first half of the eighteenth century this was almost the only meaning given to the term "nature."

As human life, externally and historically considered.

> There are some that are not pleased with fiction, unless it be bold; not only to exceed the work, but also the possibility of nature. 1650. HOBBES, IV., p. 451.
> Ariosto's . . . adventures are without the compass of nature and possibility. 1693. DRYDEN, XIII., p. 15.
> There is nothing of nature and probability in all this. . . . It may be Romance, but it is not Nature. RYMER, 1st Pt., p. 125.
>> Those rules of old discovered, not devised,
>> Are nature still, but nature methodised,
>>   1711. POPE, II., p. 38.
> Imitation of nature and uniformity of design. SWIFT, XIII., p. 33.

During the third period, which includes the latter half of the eighteenth century, the term "nature" was employed in three ways. Often it was employed, like the term "genius," to explain any bold and successful departure from the ordinary and established methods of composition. Nature represented the primary native capacities of the mind,

As native impulse or capacity.

which, by asserting themselves in literature, widened its range of sympathy and interest. Nature was thought of as lawless, rather than as the source of new law and method.

> Shakespeare was naturally learned: he needed not the spectacle of books to read nature; he looked inwards and found her there. ... He is always great when some great occasion is presented to him; no man can say he ever had a fit subject for his wit, and did not then raise himself high above the rest of poets. 1765. S. JOHNSON, V., p. 153.

As regards external nature, the last half of the eighteenth century was decidedly a period of transition. Nature was not considered in so exclusively historical a light as formerly. It usually indicated an outer uniformity and order, which could have been determined only from past experience, but still it had some vague reference to present fact, and the ascertained uniformity and order was not always taken as authoritative in literature.   *As external order.*

> Characters in poetry may be a little overcharged or exaggerated without offering violence to nature. 1761. GOLDSMITH, I., p. 339.
> By nature we are to suppose can only be meant the known and experienced course of affairs in this world. Whereas the poet has a world of his own, where experience has less to do than consistent imagination. 1762. HURD, IV., p. 324.
> In Lycidas there is no nature, for there is no truth. ... Its inherent improbability always forces dissatisfaction on the mind. 1781. S. JOHNSON, VII., p. 120.
> After about half a century of forced thoughts and rugged meter, some advances toward nature and harmony had been made by Waller and Denham. 1781. ID., pp. 307, 308.

Throughout all of the eighteenth century, and especially during the latter half of it, there may be traced _{As external form and color.} in criticism a growing sense of form and color, of beauty in external nature. This conception of nature, however, was not regarded with much favor in criticism, and had very little influence upon the use of "nature" as an actual critical term.

> It may be observed in general that description of the external beauties of nature is usually the first effort of a young genius, before he hath studied manners and passions. 1756. J. WARTON, I., p. 35.
> Three sources of beauty, —
> 1. Man, e. g., Euripides, etc.
> 2. Nature, as vast as it is, has furnished few images to poets.
> 3. Art. 1759. GIBBON, IV., p. 23.
> Congreve . . . draws a great deal more from life than from nature. 1758. GOLDSMITH, IV., p. 427.

The fourth period includes the first few decades of the present century. Historical nature disappeared _{As life, the essence of being.} from criticism. The sense of external beauty in nature was considered as an inner sense rather than as beauty which was external to the mind. Nature denoted life, inner and outer, the growing principle of all existence, inner impulse and outer development, which were perhaps in some manner to be identified with each other, and whose representative in literature was the imagination.

> The wonderful twilight of the mind, and mark Cervantes's courage in daring to present it, and trust to a distant posterity for an appreciation of its truth to nature. 1810. COLERIDGE, IV., p. 274.
> From copying the artificial models, we lose sight of the living principle of nature. 1820. HAZLITT, El. Lit., p. 20.

Poetry is an imitation of nature, but the imagination and the passions are a part of man's nature. ID., Pl. Sp., p. 4.

Poets have penetrated into the mystery of Nature . . . and thus can the spirit of our age, embodied in fair imagination, look forth on us. 1827. CARLYLE, I., p. 56.

Examine nature accurately, but write from recollection; and trust more to your imagination than to your memory. 1833. COLERIDGE, VI., p. 346.

During the latter portion of the present century, "nature" seems to have become very largely a retrospective term, being applied especially to the writings of the Lake School of poets. In so far as actively employed in criticism, "nature" represents the external world, a world which unites in a manner the scientific conception of orderly development with the artistic conception of beauty. In this meaning of the word "nature," however, it can scarcely be said to have been employed as a critical term. *As external law and beauty.*

> If in the realistic tide that now bears us on there are some spirits who feel nature in another way, in the romantic way or the classic way, they would not falsify her in expressing her so. HOWELLS, Crit. & Fiction, p. 63.
>
> The old formula of Greek philosophy, ζῆν κατὰ φύσιν, "to live according to nature," might be accepted as our rule, if "nature" be understood to include the action of the higher part of our humanity in controlling or modifying the lower and grosser part. DOWDEN, St. in Lit., p. 117.
>
> Nature is indeed the teacher of all true poets, but like a wise teacher she does not put all scholars through the same course of study. ID., p. 181.
>
> Of the things of nature the mediæval mind had a deep sense; but its sense of them was not objective, no real escape to the world without us. 1883. PATER, Ap., p. 218.

Nauseous (XXII.) *b*: Dowden, Tr. & St., p. 134.

Neat (V.): Lodge to present.
  Pope had a sense of the neat rather than of the beautiful. Lowell, Prose, IV., p. 34.
Negligent (XIX.): Pope to present.
  Horace still charms with graceful negligence. Pope, II., p. 75.
Nemesis: Retribution as it appears in the world of art. Moulton, Shak., etc., p. 107.
Neo-Classicism:/Saintsbury, Eng. Pr. St , p. xxxi.
Nerveless (XII.): Whip. to present.
  Nerveless and hysterical verses. Swinburne, Es. & St., p. 269.
Nervous (XII.): J. War. to present.

Sustained strength and energy of style.

  Nervous and energetic. J. Warton, II., p. 113.
  Keats entirely fails of Milton's nervous severity of phrase. Lowell, IV., p. 86.
  Daudet's style has taken on bone and muscle and become conscious of treasures of nervous agility. H. James, Par. Portraits, p. 231.
Neutral (XV.): Jef., Gosse. Jeffrey, III., p. 48.
New (IX.): Rymer to present.

Refers both to the thought and to the emotion or feeling of a literary work; more usually, however, to the thought.

  The thoughts new and noble. Rymer, 2d Pt., p. 79.
  Keats . . . has that indefinable newness and unexpectedness which we call genius. Lowell, Lat. Lit. Es., I., p. 242.
  The problem is to express new and profound ideas in a perfectly sound and classical style. M. Arnold, Cr. Es., 1st S., p. 65.
Niaiserie (XI.): Poe, M. Arn. M. Arnold, Cel. Lit., etc., p. 235.
Nicety (V.): Dry. to present.
  In this nicety of manners does the excellence of French poetry consist. Dryden, V., p. 329.
  The little niceties and fantastical operations of art. Pope, X., p. 532.
  Trifling distinctions and verbal niceties. Gray, II., p. 147.
Noble (XI.): Hobbes to present.
  The grand style, at once noble and natural. Lowell, III., p. 173.

Noisy (XIX.) *b*: Noisy alexandrines. GOSSE, Life of Congreve, p. 85.
Nonsense (XX.) *a*: Jef. Saintsbury, Hist. Eng. Lit., p. 168.
NOVELTY (IX.).

The term "novelty" was in greatest use in criticism during the latter part of the eighteenth century and the first few decades of the present century. *As extravagant strangeness.* There is found mentioned novelty of language, of images, and more often of thought; but far more usually the term "novelty" has designated merely a general impression, which the literary composition as a whole makes upon the mind of the reader. Previous to the present century, the term was not very much in favor. It was employed to characterize extravagant conceits, and all abrupt violations of regularity and unity in composition. Novelty was thought to be opposed to nature, to propriety, and even to variety; it was an affectation and a conceit, it stirred the passions, led to excess, and "violated essential principles of literature." Novelty was recognized, however, as a legitimate element of the comical or humorous.

> Those writers (Cowley, etc.) who lay on the watch for novelty could have little hope of greatness. . . . Their attempts were always analytic; they broke every image into fragments. 1781. S. JOHNSON, VII., pp. 16, 17.
>
> Addison's humour is so happily diffused as to give the grace of novelty to domestic scenes and daily occurrences. ID., p. 472.

During the present century "novelty" has usually represented the intellectual surprise which is more or less consequent upon all change in literature. *As stimulating intellectual strangeness.* In the early part of the present century "novelty" frequently indicated the general sense of newness which resulted from the revolution in literature that was then taking place. But in so far as the sense of change is not general, in so far as it arises from the modification of some specific feature of the composition, and can be localized, so to speak, the term "novelty" tends to denote mere intellectual restlessness on the part of the writer, a desire for change for the sake of change, a conscious search for the unexpected, the striking, the surprising.

> In philosophy as in poetry, it is the highest and most useful prerogative of genius to produce the strongest impression of novelty, while it rescues admitted truths from the neglect caused by the very circumstance of their universal admission. 1825. COLERIDGE, I., p. 117.
>
> The native spirit of novelty and movement. 1865. M. ARNOLD, Cr. Es., 1st S., p. 175.

Numbers (X.): Gib., Gosse.
> Ripened into ease, correctness, and numbers. GIBBON, Life and Writings, I., p. 254.

Numerous (X.): Campion to Emerson.
> His prose is numerous and sweet. J. WARTON, II., p. 8.

Objective: R. Browning, Sted.
> Shelley . . . is a subjective, Shakespeare an objective poet. R. BROWNING, Essay on Shelley in The Browning Society Papers, 1881-84, Pt. I., p. 5.
>
> Elizabethan style objective rather than subjective. STEDMAN, Vic. Poets, p. 47.

Obscene (XIV.): Dry., Jef. to present.
Obscure (III.): Ascham to present.

I. Until the middle of the eighteenth century the term "obscure" uniformly indicated the indistinctness and confusion which results from an inexact use of words, or from an imperfect logical sequence of statement.

> The worst kind of obscurity is that . . . when words that are plain in one sense have another sense concealed in them. QUINTILIAN, II., p. 84.
> An ambitious obscurity of expression. HOBBES, IV., p. 454.
> Shakespeare's whole style is so pestered with figurative expressions that it is as affected as it is obscure. DRYDEN, VI., p. 255.
> Obscurity bestows a cast of the wonderful, and throws an oracular dignity upon a piece which hath no meaning. SWIFT, XIII., p. 70.

II. Since the middle of the eighteenth century, the term "obscure" has often represented the indistinctness and suggestive mystery of the more profound problems of human life; images which produce sublime æsthetic effects because of their indistinctness.

> Your obscurity . . . is that of too much meaning . . . not the dimness of positive darkness, but of distance. LAMB, II., p. 80.
> You ought to distinguish between obscurity residing in the uncommonness of the thought, and that which proceeds from thoughts unconnected, and language not adapted to the expression of them. COLERIDGE, Letters, I., pp. 194, 195.
> The obscurity itself is a vital part of the work of art which deals not with a problem, but with a life. DOWDEN, Shak., etc., p. 127.

Obsolete (I.): Dry. to present. Rossetti, Lives, p. 88.
Obvious (III.): Jef. to present. Jeffrey, II., p. 52.
Occasional: Jef., Saints. Jeffrey, I., p. 208.
Oceanic (XI.): Lan., Dow.
> Such an oceanic writer as Shakespeare. DOWDEN, Tr. & St., p. 252.

Odd (IX.): Har., Jef. to present.
> When words or images are placed in unusual juxtaposition rather than connection, and are so placed merely because the juxtaposition is unusual, we have the odd or grotesque. COLERIDGE, IV., p. 276.

Offensive (XXII.) *b*: Swin. to present. Saintsbury, Hist. Eng. Lit., p. 369.

Old-fashioned (IX.): Old-fashioned and thin. GOSSE, Life of Congreve, p. 40.
Operose (XII.): Bent., Ros.
Stiffness and stateliness and operoseness of style. BENTLEY, II., p. 84.
Oppressive (XXII.) *b*: Jef. to present.
Prosaically oppressive. SWINBURNE, Mis., p. 40.
Opulent (XI.) *b*: De Quin. to present.
Wilson's humour is broad, overwhelming, riotously opulent. DE QUINCEY, III., p. 88.
Oratio-obliqua: Saintsbury, Eng. Pr. St., p. xxiii.
ORDER (II.).

The term "order" derives its original significance and continually draws illustration from moral conduct and from external nature. It represents the conception of things as subject to law and method,—part of these laws and methods being thought to be known, part of them being merely assumed to have an existence. As employed in criticism, the unknown laws assumed by the term when referring to the sounds of a composition, are to be traced to the native sense of harmony in the ear. But when referring to the more highly developed and subtle characteristics of literature, the validity of the known laws themselves has been constantly held in question, being continually opposed by "nature," by passion, by imagination, by the general romantic and Gothic spirit. The term seems to be better adapted to scientific than to literary discussions, and it has been employed but very little by the critics of the present century.

All composition has three necessary particulars: Ordo, Junctura, Numerus. QUINTILIAN, II., p. 216.

Passion requires a certain disorder of language, imitating the agitation and commotion of the soul. LONGINUS, p. 44.

The ordering of things invented . . . called in Latin "dispositio." TH. WILSON, Rhet., p. 6.

We ought to join words together in apt order that the ear may delight in hearing the harmony. ID., pp. 175, 176.

If you will be good scholars, and profit well in the art of music, shut your fiddles in their cases, and look up to heaven. The order of the spheres . . . variety of seasons, etc. 1579. GOSSON, p. 26.

Ovid . . . pictures nature in disorder, with which the study and choice of words is inconsistent. 1666. DRYDEN, IX., pp. 96, 97.

A due sentiment of morals is wanting, which alone can make us knowing in order and proportion. SHAFTESBURY, I., p. 218.

An attempt to unite order and exactness of imagery with a subject formed on principles so professedly romantic and anomalous, is like giving Corinthian pillars to a Gothic palace. 1778. T. WARTON, Hist. Eng. Pr., p. 261.

An orderly and sweet sentence, by gaining our ear, conciliates our affections. 1824. LANDOR, III., p. 146.

Organic (VII.): Cole. to present.
Living and organic style. DOWDEN, St. in Lit., p. 151.

Organ-like (X.): Organ-like roll and majesty of numbers. LOWELL, Prose, IV., p. 338.

Oriental (XIX.): Haz., Mac.
Affected Orientalism of . . . Moore's style. HAZLITT, Sp. of Age, p. 324.

ORIGINAL (XXIII.).

The term "original" signified at first the "imitation of nature" as opposed to the imitation of authors. (See Imitation.) As referring to the author, the term is wholly negative in its meaning, denoting merely that the author criticised does not borrow his sentiments or form of expression from another author. As referring to the completed literary product, or to its effect upon the mind of the reader, originality denotes that which is new and more or less unexpected, but which is at the same time an organic development of that which is already well known and familiar.

> The most original poetry is in fact imitation, — imitation of nature. 1762. GIBBON, IV., p. 144.
> Every author, as far as he is great and at the same time original, has had the task of creating the taste by which he is to be enjoyed. WORDSWORTH, II., p. 125.
> To admire on principle is the only way to imitate without loss of originality. COLERIDGE, III., p. 203.
> Original, masculine, and striking. HAZLITT, Sp. of Age, p. 205.
> All originality is relative. Every thinker is retrospective. EMERSON, Rep. Men, pp. 189, 190.
> An original author . . . modifies the influence of tradition, culture, and contemporary thought upon himself by some admixture of his own. LOWELL, II., p. 84.
> Originality . . . that quality in a man which touches human nature at most points of its circumference. LOWELL, IV., pp. 356, 357.
> Every great original writer brings into the world an absolutely new thing, — his own personality. DOWDEN, Tr. & St., p. 239.

ORNAMENT (V.).

Three periods may be distinguished in the history of the term "ornament." In early English criticism, *As figurative falsification of the truth.* almost everything which varied from ordinary conversational prose was characterized as an ornament, — amplification, comparisons, epithets, and proverbs in verse, verse itself, and poetical figures of speech. Poetical figures, in fact, and ornament were almost identical with each other, and the charge of untruthfulness, which was often brought against poetry and figurative language, applied with even greater force to ornament.

> Verse is but an ornament and no cause to poetry. SIDNEY, p. 11.
> This ornament is given by figures and figurative speeches, which

> be the flowers, as it were, and colours, that a poet setteth upon his language of art. 1585. PUTTENHAM, p. 150.
>
> Figurative speech is a novelty of language. ID., p. 171.
>
> Figures be the instruments of ornament in every language . . . and be occupied of purpose to deceive the ear and also the mind, drawing it from plainness and simplicity to a certain doubleness, whereby our talk is the more guileful and abusing. ID., p. 166.
>
> Many good sentences are spoken by Danus to shadow his knavery; and written by poets as ornaments to beautify their work, and set their trumpery to sale without suspect.¹ 1579. GOSSON, p. 20.
>
> And for all that concerns ornaments of speech, similitudes, treasury of eloquence, and such like emptinesses, let it be utterly dismissed. BACON, IV., p. 254.

During the seventeenth and the greater part of the eighteenth century no critical term reflected more clearly the false glitter of current literature than did the term "ornament." By means of conventional epithets and brilliant figures of speech, the language of poetry had become utterly estranged from the language of conversational prose. The facts of life, it was thought, suitable for literary treatment, had already been treated of. It remained only to vary these facts by ingenious recombinations and by ingenious methods of expression. This ingenuity, when held subservient to the sense of past literary attainment, produced in composition the quality of style known as ornament.

As refined methods of statement.

> Some words are to be culled out for ornament and colour, as we gather flowers to strew houses or make garlands. 1641. B. JONSON, Timber, p. 61.
>
> The episodes give it more ornament and more variety. 1693. DRYDEN, XIII., p. 36.
>
> It is to be considered that the essence of verse is regularity, and its ornament is variety. 1781. S. JOHNSON, VII., p. 346.

Since the latter portion of the eighteenth century, "ornament" has been to a great extent a retrospective term, referring to the literature of the seventeenth and eighteenth centuries. As an active term it lies upon the extreme limits of positive and favorable use in criticism. The facts or subject-matter of literary representation, now thought to consist chiefly of feelings and conflicting motives and passions in the mind, require not ingenuity for their combination, but insight for their detection. The facts for literary representation are thus inexhaustible. These feelings and passions can often be expressed only by means of figurative language. Figurative language is thus in a sense the most direct method of statement possible for the facts to be represented. "Ornament" has fallen into partial discredit during the present century, not because it indicates figurative language, but because it indicates figurative language which is labored and studied, and because it tends to denote the literary polishing of facts externally given.

As elaborated or conventional fancies.

> Poetical ornaments are foreign to the purpose; for they only shew a man is not sorry. 1751. GRAY, II., p. 225.
> An ornament . . . an incongruity which would shock the intelligent reader, should the poet interweave any foreign splendor of his own with that which the passion naturally suggests. 1798. WORDSWORTH, II., p. 87.

Ornate (V.): Scott to present.
> Tennyson's Enoch Arden . . . is ornate. BAGEHOT, Lit. St., II., p. 330.

Ostentation (XIX.): B. Jon. to present.
Over-castigated (IV.): Over-castigated artificial literary tone of the period. ROSSETTI, Lives, p. 157.

Over-charged: J. War. to present. J. Warton II., p. 205.
Overflow: The term "overflow" to be used for these verses in which the sense is not concluded at the end of one line or of one couplet, but straggles on at its own free will, until it naturally closes. Gosse, From Shak., etc., p. 6.
Over-jewelled (V.): Gosse, Seventeenth Cent. St., pp. 200, 201.
Over-languaged: Keats was over-languaged at first. Lowell, Prose, I., p. 241.
Over-mannered (IV.): Over-mannered style of the eighteenth century. Gosse, Hist. Eng. Lit., p. 34.
Overshining (V.): Swinburne, Es. & St., p. 16.
Overworked: Jeffrey, II., p. 428.
Overwrought: Blair to present.
  Ambitious and overwrought. Jeffrey, II., p. 476.
Padding: Padding in Cooper's novels. Whipple, Am. Lit., p. 50.
Painted (V.): Pope to present.
  This painted florid style. Pope, VIII., p. 219.
Pale (V.): H. James to present.
  Pale, pretty washed out work. Brooke, Tennyson, p. 54.
Pallid (V.): Flowerless and pallid. Swinburne, Es. & St., p. 137.
Palpable (XXII.) *b*: Tangible and palpable outline. Swinburne, Mis., p. 9.
Panegyrical (XXI.): Swin., Gosse. Swinburne, Mis., p. 74.
Parade (V.): Without strain or parade. Rossetti, Lives, p. 391.
Paradoxical (VIII.): Jef. to present. Jeffrey, I., p. 166.
Particular (VIII.): J. War. to present.

Used chiefly in connection with the theory of poetry. (See Poetical.)

I. As characteristic of history rather than poetry.

> Clarendon's narration . . . is stopped too frequently by particularities. S. Johnson, III., p. 83.

II. As characteristic of the poetical as against the historical.

> In Homer and Shakespeare . . . every image is the particular and unalienable property of the person who uses it. J. Warton, I., p. 318.

III. As representing merely the "picturesque" elements of the poetical.

> By poetic expression I do not mean merely a vividness in particulars, but the right feeling which heightens or subdues a passage or a whole poem to the proper tone, and gives entireness to the effect. LOWELL, Lit. Es., I., p. 245.

PASSION (XIV.).

Until the latter portion of the eighteenth century the term "passion" was used chiefly in two ways. <small>As mental excitation.</small> Often the term was placed in antithesis to "manners" and "characters," — passions, manners, and characters being the three chief features of dramatic representation. According to this use of the term, which was derived from ancient criticism, passion included anger, lust, mirth, pity, grief, fear, any emotion, in fact, or mental excitation of which human conduct gives evidence.

> Poets, after they have lost their power of depicting the passions, turn naturally to the delineation of character, e. g., the picture of the palace of Odysseus may be called a sort of comedy of manners. LONGINUS, pp. 20, 21.
>
> Passion contributes as largely to sublimity as the delineation of character to amusement. ID., p. 56.
>
> .Under this general head of manners the passions are naturally included as belonging to the characters. 1679. DRYDEN, VI., p. 274.
>
> Sentiments which raise laughter can very seldom be admitted with any decency into an heroic poem, whose business is to excite passions of a much nobler nature. 1711. ADDISON, III., p. 188.
>
> Description of the external beauties of nature is usually the first effort of a young genius, before he hath studied manners and passions. 1756. J. WARTON, I., p. 35.

> William Brown's poetry is not without beauty; but it is the beauty of mere landscape and allegory, without the manners and passions that constitute human interest. 1819. CAMPBELL, I., p. 218.

Often, also, the term "passion" was employed to designate the primary desires and appetites, especially love between the sexes. This use of the term is occasionally found even to the present time, chiefly in connection with the criticism of the novel. When thus employed "passion" was thought to be wholly active and impulsive, but also crude and unrefined. It might furnish a fit theme for literary treatment, but as to the active production of literature, it was thought to be unregulated and uncreative. When the native sense of beauty had come to be distinguished from artifice, this use of the term "passion" was looked upon with less disfavor by the critics.

As appetite.

> Passions are spiritual rebels and raise sedition against the understanding. 1641. B. JONSON, Timber, p. 4.
> Any sudden gust of passion (as an ecstasy of love in an unexpected meeting). 1668. DRYDEN, XV., p. 314.
> Thus by a little affectation in love matters, and with the help of a romance or novel, a boy of fifteen or a grave man of fifty may be sure to grow a very natural coxcomb, and feel the belle passion in earnest. SHAFTESBURY, I., pp. 2, 3.
> Wit and passion are entirely incompatible. When the affections are moved, there is no place for the imagination. 1742. D. HUME, I., p. 242.
> By beauty I mean that quality or those qualities in bodies by which they cause love or some passion similar to it. 1756. BURKE, I., p. 113.
> If the imagination be lively; the passions will be strong. J. WARTON, I., p. 102.
> By genius is meant those excellencies that no study or art can

communicate, — such as ... humour, passion, etc. 1758. GOLDSMITH, IV., p. 418.

To take the passion out of a novel is something like taking the sunlight out of a landscape. 1874. STEPHEN, Hrs. in a Lib., p. 239.

If a novel flatters the passions and exalts them above the principles, it is poisonous. HOWELLS, Crit. & Fiction, p. 95.

Previous to the present century, it was occasionally recognized that passion in an author would lead to earnestness, sincerity, and directness in his methods of composition. Passion guarded against false ornaments and conceits; still it was not considered as an integral part of the actual process of composition. It might be an ethical prerequisite for art, but it was not art, nor artistic; it was too primitive and unrefined.

As sincerity and directness.

But if my faith, my hope, my love, my true intent,
My liberty, my service vowed, my time and all be spent. (Dyer.)
This is ... vehement, swift, and passionate. PUTTENHAM, p. 244.
Raleigh is ... lofty, insolent, passionate. ID., p. 77.
To which poetry would be made subsequent, or indeed rather precedent, as being less subtle and fine, but more simple, sensuous, and passionate. 1644. MILTON, Mis., III., p. 473.
No poet ... can do anything great in his own way, without the imagination or supposition of a divine presence, which may raise him to some degree of this passion we are speaking of. SHAFTESBURY, I., p. 39.
Earl Percy's lamentation over his enemy is generous, beautiful, and passionate. 1710. ADDISON, II., p. 378.
Passion runs not after remote allusions. S. JOHNSON, VII., p. 119.

During the present century, especially during the early portion of it, passion has been very generally considered as one of the two or three essential characteristics of poetry, imagination

As intense poetical feeling.

and rhythm being the other requirements. Passion represents an ardent devotion to a principle, an ethical purpose, an æsthetic ideal. It is impulse and desire almost wholly disconnected from the primal appetites, and permeated, as it were, with the highest æsthetic feelings and intuitions.

> The only qualities I can find in Dryden that are essentially poetical are a certain ardour and impetuosity of mind, with an excellent ear. . . . A great command of language he certainly has . . . but it is not poetical, being neither of the imagination nor of the passions; I mean the amiable, the ennobling, or the intense passions. 1805. WORDSWORTH, III., p. 253.
> But passion — the all in all in poetry — is everywhere present, raising the low, dignifying the mean, and putting sense into the absurd. 1808. LAMB, Poems, P. & Es., p. 257.
> The elevation of tone arises from the strong mood of passion. 1814. SCOTT, Life of Swift, p. 453.
> Imagination is as the immortal God which should assume flesh for the redemption of mortal passion. 1819. SHELLEY, II., p. 14.
> Poetry is . . . the natural impression of any object or event, by its vividness exciting an involuntary movement of imagination and passion. 1818. HAZLITT, Eng. Poets, p. 1.
> M. Coppée's poetry . . . possesses sentiment, but hardly passion. DOWDEN, St. in Lit., p. 421.
> The writings of the romantic school, of which the æsthetic poetry is an afterthought, mark a transition, not so much from the pagan to the mediæval ideal, as from a lower to a higher degree of passion in literature. 1883. PATER, Ap., p. 214.
> But for positive passion, for that absolute fusion of the whole nature in one fire of sense and spirit. 1869. SWINBURNE, Es. & St., p. 307.

During the latter portion of the present century the use of the term "passion" in criticism has been very largely influenced by psychological thought and discussion. Passion, considered as an *As intense feeling.*

integral portion of the æsthetic activity of the mind, is stimulated almost wholly by the mental imagery; passion, as defining its relations to the other mental capacities, may be indeed identified in part with poetical feeling, but it represents also the more primal impulses, the sense of power, the appetites. Passion is often placed in antithesis to the imagination and the reason, and from this antithesis it obtains a more general meaning than it possessed in the early portion of the century. This meaning of the term is perhaps little more than its preceding use viewed from a different standpoint; but the critics have not as yet identified the two uses with each other in actual criticism.

> The excellence of writing, whether in prose or verse, consists in a conjunction of Reason and Passion. 1811. WORDSWORTH, II., p. 65.
>
> Men act from passion, and we can only judge of passion by sympathy. 1826. HAZLITT, Plain Speaker, p. 59.
>
> Passion of any kind may become in some degree ludicrous when disproportioned to its exciting occasions. 1848. DE QUINCEY, XI., p. 69.
>
> Our passions in general are to be traced more immediately to the active part of our nature, to the love of power, or to strength of will. 1850. HAZLITT, Sk. & Essays, p. 344.
>
> Our very passion has become metaphysical, and speculates upon itself. LOWELL, Prose Works, II., p. 136.
>
> A passion, of which the outlets are sealed, begets a tension of nerve, in which the sensible world comes to one with a reinforced brilliancy and relief, — all redness is turned into blood, all water into tears. Hence a wild, convulsed sensuousness in the poetry of the Middle Ages, in which the things of nature begin to play a strange, delirious part. 1883. PATER, Ap., p. 218.

Pastoral (XXI.): Jef. to present.
> Kinds of poetry . . . heroic, scommatic, pastoral. HOBBES, IV., p. 444.
>
> Pastoral . . . which, not professing to imitate real life, requires no experience. S. JOHNSON, VIII., p. 325.

PATHOS (XVII.).

The term "pathos" has, in general, always denoted the sympathy which is produced in the mind of the reader by the representation of feeling or passion in a literary production. Until the *As the exciting or stirring.* latter portion of the eighteenth century, the representation of any passion whatever was said to be pathetic if only the representation were made sufficiently striking and impressive. It was, however, at the same time recognized that this impressiveness was more likely to be attained by the representation of the more violent and conflicting passions,—those which would lead to tragical situations and tragical resolutions of plot development. The critical value of the term "pathos" during this early period of its history may be designated by some such series of expressions as "exciting," "stirring," "affecting," and "moving,"— words which may express compassion and pity, but need not necessarily do so.

>The moving pathetical figure, Pottyposis. 1580. HARVEY, p. 24.
>Virgil always fitteth his matter in hand with words agreeable unto the same affection, which he expresseth, as in his Tragical exclamations, what pathetical speeches he frameth! 1586. WEBBE, p. 46.
>The most delightful beauty, the most engaging and pathetic, is that which is drawn from real life, and from the passions. SHAFTESBURY, I., p. 105.
>Most pathetic and most interesting, and by consequence the most agreeable. 1742. D. HUME, I., p. 264.
>The sublime and the pathetic are the two chief nerves of all genuine poesy. What is there transcendentally sublime or pathetic in Pope? 1756. J. WARTON, I., p. vi.

> Rowe's genius was rather delicate and soft than strong and pathetic. ID., p. 268.
>
> Cato wants action and pathos; the two hinges on which a just tragedy ought to turn. 1756. ID., p. 257.
>
> Whence it comes to pass that the action, having an essential dignity, is always interesting, and by the simplest management of the poet becomes in a supreme degree pathetic. 1751. HURD, II., p. 34.
>
> Three kinds of pathos: —
> 1. Sympathy for humble pity and contrition.
> 2. Sympathy for distresses of love.
> 3. Another kind of pathos arises from magnanimity in distress, which, managed by a skilful hand, will touch us even where we detest the character which suffers. GRAY, I., p. 400.
>
> As human passions did not enter the world before the fall, there is, in Paradise Lost, little opportunity for the pathetic.

During the present century the term "pathos" has occasionally indicated a pensive meditation, a sympathetic contemplation of human life in general, a brooding over the broader traits of actual life in view of ideals which react little or none into actual conditions, and which might or might not be applicable to any special condition or event.

As meditative compassion.

> A pathetic reflection, properly introduced into a descriptive poem, will have greater force and beauty, and more deeply interest a reader, than a moral one. 1756. J. WARTON, I., p. 32.
>
> There is a meditative as well as a human pathos ... a sadness that has its seat in the depths of reason. 1802. WORDSWORTH, II., p. 128.
>
> To give to universally received truths a pathos and spirit, which shall readmit them into the soul like revelations of the moment. 1811. ID., p. 63.
>
> Wordsworth has a meditative pathos, a union of deep and subtle thought with sensibility. 1817. COLERIDGE, III., p. 493.
>
> Pathetic meditation. M. ARNOLD, Mixed Essays, p. 441.

Usually, however, the pathetic refers to concrete and specific events. From the standpoint of an ideal or of ideals, the mind dwells upon the essential incongruities in these specific facts and events, and sympathy and compassion go out to those characters or persons whose fortunes and destinies are thus affected. Pathos is sympathy for the passions and feelings represented in a literary production, when those passions and feelings are displayed in a manner which the reader from his experience must regard as destructive of natural growth and development, and when his sympathy and interest are made to centre upon these imperfect conditions rather than upon their possible amelioration and improvement. *As compassion and pity.*

> Yet so it is, that, though the feelings of pathos and ridicule seem so widely different, a certain tincture of the pitiable makes comic distress more irresistible. 1819. CAMPBELL, I., p. 71.
> Man is the only animal that laughs and weeps; for he is the only animal that is struck with the difference between what things are and what they ought to be. 1819. HAZLITT, Eng. Com. Writers, p. 1.
> But humour in men of genius is always allied to pathos. 1841. WILSON, VII., p. 78.
> Straightforward pathos . . . too sternly touched to be effusive and tearful. LOWELL, IV., p. 260.

Pedantic (VII.): Dekker to present.

I. An inappropriate elaboration and display of learning.

> Pedantry is the unseasonable ostentation of learning. S. JOHNSON, III., p. 314.
> If by pedantry is meant that minute knowledge which is derived from particular sciences and studies, in opposition to the general

notions supplied by a wide survey of life and nature, Cowley certainly errs by introducing pedantry far more frequently than Tasso. ID., VII., p. 47.

II. More usually an inappropriate conscious elaboration of any kind.

Stiffest pedantry and conceit. SHAFTESBURY, I., p. 202.
Pedantry consists in the use of words unsuitable to the time, place, and company. COLERIDGE, III., p. 272.
Pedantry, which consisted in unnecessary, and perhaps unintelligible references to ancient learning, was afterwards combined with other artifices to obtain the same end. HALLAM, III., p. 240.

Pedestrian (XVIII.): Saints., Gosse.
Pedestrian, unimaginative, level, neutral. GOSSE, Hist. Eng. Lit., III., p. 73.

Peerless (XXII.) *a*: Swinburne, Es. & St., p. 45.

Pellucid (III.): Hal., Low.
Calm and pellucid as mountain tarns. LOWELL, Lat. Lit. Es., p. 36.

Penetrative (XX.) *b*: M. Arn. to present.
Penetrative and sympathetic imagination. LOWELL, Lat. Lit. Es., I., p. 243.
The tender, penetrating fiction of Richardson. GOSSE, Eighteenth Century, p. 385.
A penetrativeness half pleasurable, half melancholy. LOWELL, O. E. D., p. 20.

Pensive (XIV.): T. War. to present.

Perfect (XXII.) *a*: Rymer to present.
There is hardly anything more exquisite and more perfect than history. RYMER, 1st Pt., pp. 57, 58.

Perfume: The perfume of the delicately chosen phrase. GOSSE, Life of Congreve, p. 135.

Periodic (II.): De Quin., Min.

Perplexed (II.): Dry. to present.

Personal: Swin. Gosse, From Shak., etc., p. 56.

Personality: In our approach to the poetry, we necessarily approach the personality of the poet. R. BROWNING, Browning Society Papers, 1881–84. Pt. I., p. 5.

Perspicacity (III.): Camp. to present.
  This botanizing perspicacity. CAMPBELL, p. 116.
  Perspicacity and perspicuity. SWINBURNE, A St. of B. J., p. 116.

PERSPICUITY (III.).

"Perspicuity" is the technical expression for clearness in composition, being, according to rhetorical theory, one of the three or four cardinal requirements for style. In early English criticism it resulted chiefly from the mere choice of words, and from the simplest elements of grammatical construction. Literary works, especially translations, were characterized as perspicuous, which, to us at least, are hopelessly vague and obscure. *From grammatical construction.*

> I have delivered mine author's meaning with as much perspicuity as so mean a scholar . . . was well able to perform. THOS. NEWTON (Pref. to Tr. of Seneca), Spenser Society, XLIII., p. 2.
> Frame your style to perspicuity and to be sensible; for the haughty, obscure verse doth not much delight, and the verse that is too easy is like a tale of a roasted horse. GASCOIGNE, p. 36.

During the greater part of the seventeenth and eighteenth centuries, perspicuity was thought to depend chiefly upon an orderly and methodic arrangement of the sentences and of the thought expressed in a composition. This is perhaps the more common use of the term even up to the present time. *From logical construction.*

> Order helps much to perspicuity, as confusion hurts. 1641. B. JONSON, Timber, p. 63.
> In the better notion of wit considered as propriety, surely method is necessary for perspicuity and harmony of parts. 1707. POPE, VI., p. 34.
> Sheffield . . . had the perspicuity and elegance of an historian, but not the fire and fancy of a poet. 1781. S. JOHNSON, VII., p. 485.

Occasionally, however,—especially in the present century,—perspicuity evidently arises chiefly from the vividness of the mental imagery employed, rather than from the merely grammatical and logical features of a composition.

<small>From mental imagery.</small>

> Have images of nature in the memory distinct and clear . . . a sign of this is perspicuity, propriety, and decency. 1650. HOBBES, IV., p. 453.
>
> The natural and perspicuous expression, which spontaneously rises to the mind. 1824. MACAULAY, IV., p. 454.
>
> Perspicuity,—the only question is, Will it tell? BAGEHOT, I., p. 31.

Persuasive (XXII.) *b*: Gosse.
> The poets were from the beginning the best persuaders. PUTTENHAM, p. 25.

Pert (XVIII.): Gray to present.
> Pert familiarity. JEFFREY, I., p. 266.

Petty (XI.): Hunt, Stephen. Hunt, Wit & Humour, p. 115.

PHILISTINISM (XXII.) *b*: Car. to present.

Primarily, and in theory, the term indicates insensibility to beauty. In actual criticism the term indicates a lack of that which the critic considers as most fundamental or essential in literary composition. Thus "philistinism" has represented:—

> Insensibility to propriety. 1781. S. JOHNSON, VIII., p. 29.
> Utilitarianism. CARLYLE, I., p. 58.
> Lack of imagination. LOWELL, II., p. 359.
> Insensibility to beauty. M. ARNOLD, Cr. Es., 1st S., pp. 162–67.
> Want of "openness to ideas." ID., p. 176.
> The apparent rhetorical truth of things. ID., p. 304.
> Indifference to the higher intellectual interests. STEPHEN, III., p. 306.
> Lack of the realistic spirit. HOWELLS, Crit & Fiction, p. 107.
> Lack of "exaltation of sentiment and thought." SAINTSBURY, Es. in Eng. Lit., p. 88.

Philosophical (XX.) *b*: Newton, Wil.
   Gravity of philosophical sentences . . . in Seneca. T. NEWTON, Spenser Society, Vol. XLIII., p. 2.
Photographic (III.): Saints., Gosse.
   Photographically minute. GOSSE, Seventeenth Cent. St., p. 128.
Picaresque (XXI.): Hal., Mac.
   The picaresque or rogue style, in which the adventures of the low and rather dishonest part of the community are made to furnish amusement for the great. HALLAM, I., pp. 248, 249.
Pictorial (III.): Hunt to present. Recently much in use.
   Artists err in the confounding of poetic with pictorial subjects. LAMB, Mrs. Leicester's School, p. 312.
   Gray is pictorial in the highest sense of the term, much more than imaginative. LOWELL, Lat. Lit. Es., p. 17.
   That double command at once of the pictorial and the musical elements of poetry in which no English poet is Spenser's superior. SAINTSBURY, Hist. Eng. Lit., p. 86.

PICTURESQUE (XVI.).

Three periods may be distinguished in the history of the term "picturesque." Previous to the present century, occasionally to the present time, it represented mental imagery which was vivid, full of color, and more or less suggestive of strength and power,—images which were "fit for a picture," a picture, however, always "in the Gothic style of painting." *As striking pictorial effects.*

   Mr. Philipps has two lines which seem to me what the French call very picturesque:—
      All hid in snow, in bright confusion lie,
      And with one dazzling waste confuse the eye.
                  1712. POPE, VI., p. 178.
   Such circumstances as are best adapted to strike the imagination by lively pictures . . . the selection of which chiefly constitutes true poetry. 1756. J. WARTON, I., p. 26.
      His sea-green mantle waving with the wind.
   This is . . . highly picturesque. ID., p. 24.

> In these *lone* walks (their days eternal bound),
> These *moss-grown* domes, with *spirey* turrets crowned,
> Where *awful* arches make the noonday night,
> And the *dim* windows shed a *solemn* light. (Pope.)
> The epithets are picturesque. ID., p. 313.
> There is great picturesque humour in the following lines: —
> He buffeted the Breton about the cheeks,
> That he looked like a lantern all his life after.
> 1778. T. WARTON, Hist. Eng. Poetry, p. 187.

During the early portion of the present century the picturesque represented a high degree of contrast in the poetical imagery, which, however, by suggestion could still be taken up into an æsthetic unity, — a unity higher than that of pictorial effects.

As contrasting pictorial effects.

> The picturesque contrasts of Character in Othello are almost as remarkable as the depth of the passion. 1817. HAZLITT, III., p. 31.
> The picturesque depends chiefly on the principle of discrimination or contrast. . . . It runs imperceptibly into the fantastical and grotesque. 1819. ID., Table Talk, pp. 448, 449.
> How significant, how picturesque. 1828. MACAULAY, I., p. 142.
> Spenser's descriptions are exceedingly vivid . . . not picturesque in the true sense of the word, but composed of a wonderful series of images, as in our dreams. COLERIDGE, IV., p. 249.
> In the Greek drama one must conceive the presiding power to be Death; in the English, Life. What Death? What Life? That sort of death or life locked up or frozen into everlasting slumber, which we see in sculpture; that sort of life, of tumult, of agitation, of tendency to something beyond, which we see in painting. The picturesque, in short, domineers over English tragedy; the sculpturesque or the statuesque over the Grecian. 1838. DE QUINCEY, X., p. 315.
> Picturesque: the ancients had neither the word or the thing which it represents. ID., pp. 308, 309.

More recently the term has occasionally been given a somewhat unfavorable meaning. When vivid contrasts are made for the sake of the contrasts, and not for the purpose of bringing into relief their ulterior unity, when highly colored images are unnecessarily scattered throughout a literary production, then the picturesque comes to be regarded as a sensuous play upon mere color and form, as something which negates the higher ethical and æsthetic purposes of art. *As mere pictorial effects.*

> Carlyle's . . . innate love of the picturesque . . . is only another form of the sentimentalism he so scoffs at, perhaps as feeling it a weakness in himself. 1866. LOWELL, II., p. 92.
> Where he is imaginative, it is in that lower sense which the poverty of our language, for want of a better word, compels us to call picturesque. 1868. ID., III., p. 170.
> A mere luxurious dreaming, where the beautiful very speedily degenerates into the pretty or picturesque. 1874. STEPHEN, Hrs. in a Lib., I., p. 121.
> They have come to please us at last as things picturesque, being set in relief against the modes of our different age. 1878. PATER, Ap., p. 117.

Piquant: Car. to present.
Pithey (XVI.): T. Wil. to present.

Much in use in early criticism. Full of meaning; pointed and sententious.

> Sensibly, pithily, bitingly. T. NEWTON, Spenser Society, XLIII., p. 3.
> Pithey and wise sentences. WEBBE, p. 44.
> Pith and point. LOWELL, Prose, II., p. 221.
> Compactly and pithily. ID., Lat. Lit. Es., p. 1.

Placid (XIX.): Hunt to present.
> Placid and decorous. GOSSE, From Shak., etc., p. 57.

Plagiarism: Jef., Poe.
   Plagiarist or imitator. JEFFREY, II., p. 245.
PLAIN (III.).

The term "plain" refers chiefly to the use of words and of mental imagery in composition. Until about the middle of the eighteenth century, "plain" denoted such a choice and arrangement of words as to make evident at once to the reader the thought intended. No distinction was perhaps drawn by the critics between the grammatical and logical means for the attainment of this purpose. The imagination was considered as a hindrance to plainness, producing in the composition a false glitter and ornamentation which rendered the thought difficult and obscure.

<small>From grammatical and logical construction.</small>

> Easy and plain composition. T. WILSON, Rhet., p. 178.
> The matter is good, the words proper and plain; yet the sense is hard and dark. 1568. ASCHAM, III., p. 269.
> Plain sense. 1586. WEBBE, p. 46.
> He affects plainness to cover his want of imagination. 1668. DRYDEN, XV., p. 288.

Since about the middle of the eighteenth century imagination and plainness have not been considered as necessarily opposed to each other. Plainness has indicated an unornamented method of statement, obtained chiefly by distinctness of imagery and unsuperfluousness of language. During the early portion of the present century the term was very frequently employed in opposition to the conventional adornments of the eighteenth-century lit-

<small>From mental imagery and logical construction.</small>

crature: more recently the term has been used chiefly in connection with the criticism of prose literature.

> Plain, blunt, and unartificial style of so rude an age. 1808. SCOTT, Ed. of Dryden, VIII., p. 1.
> Works of imagination should be written in a plain language. 1830. COLERIDGE, VI., p. 326.
> In short, the merit of De Foe's narrative bears a direct proportion to the intrinsic merit of a plain statement of the facts. STEPHEN, Hrs. in a Lib., p. 47.

Plaintive (XIV.): Bry., Swin.
Platitude (XII.): Poe to present.
> Too great proportion of sentence is . . . an encouragement to sonorous platitude. SAINTSBURY, Eng. Pr. St., p. xxviii.

Plausible (VIII.): Plausible description of physical wonders . . . in Gulliver. JEFFREY, I., p. 213.
Playful (XVIII.): Jef. to present. In considerable use.
> Light and playful. LANDOR, III., p. 471.
> Richter's satire is . . . playful . . . never bitter, scornful, or malignant. DE QUINCEY, XI., p. 271.

Pleading (XXII.)*b*: Pleading tones. WHIPPLE, Es. & Rev., p. 83.
Pleasantry (XVII.): J. War. to present.

The "flash" of wit turned especially toward social life, and giving to incidents and customs a more or less ludicrous appearance.

> A gross pleasantry or profane witticism. SCOTT, Life of Dryden, p. 61.
> The humour, and in general the pleasantry of our nation has very frequently a sarcastic and even misanthropic character, which distinguishes it from the mere playfulness and constitutional gaiety of our French neighbors. JEFFREY, I., p. 131.
> Voltaire's wit . . . is at all times mere logical pleasantry, a gaiety of the head, not of the heart. CARLYLE, II., p. 167.

Plebeian (V.): Locke's style is bald, dull, and plebeian. SAINTSBURY, Eng. Pr. St., p. xxiv.
Plentiful (XVI.): Plautus is more plentiful, Terence more pure and proper. ASCHAM, III., p. 247.

Pleonastic: Jef., Poe.
POETICAL (XXII.) b.

Until within the first half of the eighteenth century, "poetical," as a critical term, usually possessed a significance which was quite at variance with the general theoretical conception of poetry. In theory, poetry was of divine inspiration.

> Poesy in his perfection cannot grow but by some divine inspiration; the Platonics call it furor. PUTTENHAM, p. 20.
> There was never a great poet without a larger portion of the divine inspiration. B. JONSON, Timber, p. 76.

In actual criticism the poetical usually denoted an *As emotional falsification of truth.* enthusiastic and fantastical falsification of truth.

> To elevate the style, illustrate the subject by metaphor and epithets, guarding, however, against what savours of poetry. ARISTOTLE, Rhet., p. 222.
> Poetry is the language of enthusiasm. ID., p. 226.
> Those who express themselves with this poetic air, produce by their want of taste both the ridiculous and the frigid. ID., p. 216.
> Some will be . . . so fine, so poetical . . . that everybody else shall think them meeter for a lady's chamber than for an earnest matter. T. WILSON, Rhet., p. 176.
> Poetical . . . and fantastical. PUTTENHAM, p. 34.
> Poetical fancies and furies. B. JONSON, I., p. 210.
> What a base humour is this in you poetical needy brains. 1641. In J. B. Harleian Miscellany, IX., p. 201.

Since the early portion of the eighteenth century, the theory of the "poetical," and the actual use of the term in criticism, have usually been in close agreement with each other. Until the middle of the eighteenth century, the poetical in theory was the variation and ornamentation of truth in order to make it more pleasing and acceptable to the reader. The fancy produced the variation; reason and understanding held to the truth, and furnished for the poetical activity its motive or incentive, — the desire to teach.

> Poetry commonly exceeds the measure of nature, joining at pleasure things which in nature would never have come together. BACON, IV., p. 292.
>
> Poesy serveth . . . to magnanimity, morality, and to delectation. ID., Adv. of L., p. 30. (Oxford, 1891.)
>
> Poetry speaks to the understanding; painting to the sense. B. JONSON, Timber, p. 49.
>
> The great art of poets is either the adorning and beautifying of truth, or the inventing, pleasing, and probable fictions. DRYDEN, XV., p. 408.
>
> No man can be a true poet who writes for diversion only. These authors should be considered as versifiers and witty men rather than as poets. 1710. POPE, VI., p. 116.

With such a theory of poetry, the "poetical" was little used as a critical term. When it was thus employed, it denoted language which was figurative, ornamented, and elevated. *As an ornamented falsification of truth.*

> The diction is poetical. 1699. DRYDEN, XI., p. 239.
>
> Tully and Demosthenes spoke often figuratively but not poetically, and the very figures of oratory are vastly different from those of poetry. 1726. POPE, VIII., p. 218.

During the latter portion of the eighteenth century, the poetical, both in theory and in actual criticism, was closely related to the picturesque. The poetical was whatever in literary representation stirred and excited the emotions. This was thought more likely to be attained by particularity *As intensity of conception and vividness of imagination.*

and vividness. Poetry, however, was considered as the product of an imagination which faded away with the growth of science and knowledge. It was not clearly defined whether the ethical significance of poetry inheres in the poetical process itself, or whether it consists in a didactic purpose foreign to the nature of poetry as such.

> Poetical, that is, highly figurative expression. 1749. HURD, I., p. 102.
> Four classes of poets: —
> 1. Sublime and Pathetic, e. g., Spenser, Shakespeare, Milton.
> 2. True poetic genius in moderate degree, — moral, ethical, panegyrical poets, e. g., Dryden, Addison, Cowley.
> 3. Men of wit, of elegant taste, and lively fancy, e. g., Butler, Swift, Donne.
> 4. Mere versifiers, e. g., Pitt, Sandys, etc. 1756. J. WARTON, I., p. vii.
>
> A minute and particular enumeration of circumstances, judiciously selected, is what chiefly discriminates poetry from history. ID., p. 47.
> True poetry, after all, cannot well subsist, at least is never so striking, without a tincture of enthusiasm. ID., p. 317.
> Words are divided into three classes: —
> 1. Those which represent many simple ideas united by nature, e. g., man, sky, etc.
> 2. Those representing one of such simple ideas, e. g., blue. . . .
> 3. Those representing a union of the two former by the mind, e. g., virtue, magistrate, etc.
> The latter class call up no definite image in the mind, and are the especial expression of the emotions, and hence of poetry. 1756. BURKE, I., p. 170.
> As knowledge and learning increase, poetry begins to deal less in imagination. 1778. T. WARTON, Hist. Eng. Poetry, p. 310.
> One of the great sources of poetical delight is . . . the power of presenting pictures to the mind. 1781. S. JOHNSON, VII., p. 44.
> That cannot be unpoetical with which all are pleased. ID., p. 129.

During the present century poetry has usually been regarded not so much as an intuition of obscure relations which afterward develop into knowl- As intensity of impassioned imagination. edge, and thus cease to be poetry, as the culmination and unification of knowledge in feeling which always tends more or less directly toward action. Ethics and the poetical process thus become fundamentally associated with each other. Poetry, facing toward conduct instead of toward knowledge, becomes intimately related with passion, and not with the reason or understanding. Imagination gives a new sense of beauty; the first impulsive wish to realize this is poetic passion. Together imagination and passion constitute what in the present century has generally been regarded as the poetical. Since the rhythmical qualities of poetry have come to be referred to the mind for explanation rather than to the mechanism of verse, rhythm in theory has often been included as an integral portion of the conception of the poetical. In actual criticism, however, this perhaps does not hold true to an equal extent.

> As the sensible world is inferior in dignity to the rational soul, Poesy seems to bestow on human nature those things which history denies to it. BACON, IV., p. 315.
>
> Poetry is the impassioned expression which is in the countenance of all science. 1798. WORDSWORTH, II., p. 91.
>
> Poetry is the spontaneous overflow of powerful feelings. ID., p. 82.
>
> It is not language that is in the highest sense of the word poetical, being neither of the imagination nor of the passions. 1805. ID., III., p. 253.
>
> Passion the all in all in poetry. 1808. LAMB, P. P. & Es., p. 257.
>
> Impassioned poetry is an emanation of the moral and intellectual

part of our nature as well as of the sensitive. 1818. HAZLITT, Eng. Poets, p. 8.

Poetry . . . is the result of the general harmony of all our faculties. 1828. CARLYLE, II., p. 18.

Humour is properly the exponent of low things; that which first renders them poetical to the mind. ID., III., p. 97.

Everything is poetry which is not mere sensation. We are poets at all times when our minds are makers. 1832. WILSON, VI., p. 109.

No poetry can have the function of teaching. . . . Poetry, or any one of the fine arts (all of which alike speak through the genial nature of man and his excited sensibilities) can teach only as nature teaches, as the sea teaches, as forests teach, as infancy teaches, viz., by deep impulse, by hieroglyphic suggestion. 1848. DE QUINCEY, XI., p. 88.

And by poetic expression I do not mean merely a vividness in particulars, but the right feeling which heightens or subdues a passage or a whole poem to the proper tone, and gives entireness to the effect. 1854. LOWELL, Lit. Es., I., p. 245.

The essential mark of poetry is that it betrays in every word instant activity of mind, shown in new uses of every fact and image, in preternatural quickness or perception of relations. 1876. EMERSON, Let. & Soc. Aims, p. 22.

Genius is mainly an affair of energy, and poetry is mainly an affair of genius. M. ARNOLD, Cr. Es., 1st S., p. 50.

Poetry at all times exercises two distinct functions: it may reveal, it may unveil to every eye, the ideal aspects of common things . . . or it may actually add to the number of motives poetic and uncommon in themselves, by the imaginative creation of things that are ideal from their very birth. 1886. PATER, Ap., p. 242.

Poetic Justice: Rymer, S. John.

Poetical justice requires that the satisfaction be complete and full, ere the malefactor goes off the stage, and nothing left to God Almighty and another world. RYMER, 1st Pt., p. 26.

In striking contrast to Shakespeare . . . Middleton has no kind of poetic morality in the sense in which the term poetical justice is better known. SAINTSBURY, Hist. Eng. Lit., p. 268.

Poetic License: This poetical license is a shrewd fellow, and covereth many faults in a verse . . . it turneth all things at pleasure. GASCOIGNE, p. 37.

Poignant (XVII.): Dry. to present.

Stimulating; breezy; more or less amusing, — the result of a keen sense of congruity in the more external and transitory relations of things, combined with sprightliness and a certain amount of energy.

> Poignancy and propriety. J. WARTON, I., p. 330.
> Speak, dead Maria! breathe a strain divine. (Pope.)
> This is . . . too poignant and transitory. WORDSWORTH, II., p. 63.
> His wit is poignant though artificial. HAZLITT, Eng. Com. Writers, p. 163.
> An obsoleteness of language which gives a kind of poignancy. HALLAM, Lit. Hist., I., p. 35.

Point (V.): Dry. to present.
> Point and antithesis. J. WARTON, II., p. 396.
> Love of conceit and point. SCOTT, Ed. of Dryden, IX., p. 83.

Poised (II.): Ros. Brooke, Tennyson, p. 114.

Polished (V.): Whetstone to present.

Refinement considered wholly as a product, and as attained by means of conscious effort, by careful and repeated revision.

> Polished from barbarousness. WEBBE, p. 18.
> Chaucer is a rough diamond and must be polished ere he shines. DRYDEN, XI., p. 233.
> The high polish of French poetry is all that keeps out decay. LOWELL, III., p. 158.

Polite (V.): Jef. to present.
> The use of banter never disjoins banter itself from politeness, from felicity. M. ARNOLD, Cr. Es., 1st S., pp. 60–67.

Pomp (XIX.) *b*: Daniel to present.
> Wise men would be glad to find a little sense couched under all these pompous words. DRYDEN, VI., p. 280.

Dryden . . . had a pomp which . . . became pompousness in his imitators. LOWELL, III., p. 185.

Ponderous (XI.): Low. to present.

Ponderosity is not the note of Greek eloquence. Yet two great poets — Pindar and Æschylus — revealed the possibilities of a massive Greek style. SYMONDS, Es., Sp. & Sug., p. 194.

Poor (XII.): Jef. to present.

Tameness and poorness. JEFFREY, I., p. 167.

Possibility (VIII.): Whetstone to J. Warton.

Always associated either with probability or with nature considered historically. (See "Probability" and "Nature.")

Ariosto's adventures are without the compass of nature and possibility. DRYDEN, XIII., p. 15.

Potent (XII.): Ros. to present.

Magical potency. ROSSETTI, Lives, p. 388.

Pothery (XV.): Shakespeare's sonnets are hot and pothery. LANDOR, IV., p. 512.

Poverty (XII.): Rymer, Jef. to present.

Baldness and poverty of language. WHIPPLE, Es. & Rev., II., p. 194.

POWER (XII.): Jef. to present.

Much in use in the present century. Sustained force or energy, thought of as inhering for the most part in the composition itself, rendering it effective and moving.

The Bible is not the poetry of form, but of power. 1818. HAZLITT, Eng. Poets, p. 22.

Space, again, what is it in most men's minds? The lifeless form of the world without us; a postulate of the geometrician, with no more vitality or real existence to their feelings than the square root of two. But if Milton has been able to inform this empty theatre, peopling it with Titanic shadows . . . so that from being a thing to inscribe with diagrams, it has become under his hands a vital agent on the human mind, — I presume that I may justly express the tendency of Paradise Lost by saying that it communicates power . . . as opposed to that which communicates knowledge. DE QUINCEY, X., p. 49.

Our knowledge of power comes from our own personality. . . . Our conception of power cannot be explained by the philosophy which derives all knowledge from sensation and reflection. FLEMING, Vocabulary of Philosophy, pp. 316, 317.

Preciosity: Saints. Gosse, From Shak., etc., p. 12.
Precision (III.): J. War. to present. Much in use.

I. Exact; clear cut in outline and in detail; referring more usually to the mental imagery, occasionally to the language and logical construction.

Precise ballance. T. NEWTON, Spenser Society, XLIII., p. 2.

Milton's figures have all the elegance and precision of a Greek statue. HAZLITT, Eng. Poets, p. 80.

Sometimes in painting, and sometimes in poetry, an object should not be quite precise. LANDOR, III., p. 444.

II. Occasionally the term denotes accuracy to fact.

The final end of all style is precision, veracity of utterance, truth to the thing to be presented. SYMONDS, Es., Sp. & Sug., p. 242.

Pregnant (XVI.): Camden to present.

I. In early criticism the term indicated certain capacities of the author, fertile device and prolific invention.

Our poets . . . are pregnant both in witty conceits and devices. CAMDEN, p. 337.

Peele's pregnant dexterity of wit and manifold dexterity of invention. 1589 NASH, in Literaria Centuria, II., p. 238.

II. In the present century the term denotes an allusive, suggestive, and perhaps impassioned method of writing, which fully calls out the sympathies and interests of the reader, stimulating in him further thought and feeling.

So pregnant with feeling and reflection. WILSON, V., p. 395.
Pregnant with important truths. ID., p. 366.
The style is what was called pregnant, leaving much to be filled up by the reader's reflection. HALLAM, Lit. Hist., III., p. 378.
Milton's . . . pregnant, allusive way. M. ARNOLD, Cel. Lit., p. 206.

Preposterous (XX.): Jef., Gosse.
Childish and preposterous. JEFFREY, I., p. 212.

Pretentious (XIX.) *b*: Ros. to present.
Pretense, an inflation of mind, and overstrained use . . . of temporary catch words. ROSSETTI, Lives, p. 390.

Pretty (V.): Camden to present.

The term denotes a highly elaborated form of elegance and ornament; conceits and images which please by their constructive ingenuity, but not by their force of meaning, fitness, or literary significance. With the suffix "ness" or "ish," the term is uniformly employed in an unfavorable sense; with the suffix "ly," in a favorable sense. The term "pretty" represents one of the very lowest qualities of literary composition.

Prettily handled. WEBBE, p. 55.
Crashaw's thoughts are . . . pretty, but oftentimes far-fetched. POPE, VI., p. 117.
Too much prettiness and too modern an air. J. WARTON, I., p. 11.
Walsh . . . seldom rises higher than to be pretty. S. JOHNSON, VII., p. 244.
A mere luxurious dreaming, where the beautiful very speedily degenerates into the pretty or picturesque. STEPHEN, I., p. 121.

Prim (IV.): Whip., Gosse.
A prim grace of construction. GOSSE, Hist. Eng. Lit., p. 265.

Prismatic: His style is prismatic. It unfolds the colours of the rainbow. HAZLITT, Age of El., p. 233.

PROBABILITY (VIII.).

The critics have often distinguished in theory between particular and general probability. Particular probability refers to single detached events, and is to be determined by observation and the laws of evidence. General probability is the determination of belief in the actual occurrence of any event from its general correspondence to other events which are well known. In actual criticism, particular probability does not perhaps occur. Until about the middle of the eighteenth century, the term uniformly indicated general probability, — a similarity to the usual course of historical events. *As general correspondence to past events.*

> It belongs to the same faculty of the mind to recognize both truth and the semblance of truth; and further mankind have a considerable aptitude toward what is true; wherefore an aptness in conjecturing probabilities belongs to him who has a similar aptness in regard to truth. ARISTOTLE, Rhet., p. 7.
> Poetry treats more of the general, history of the particular. The general tells us what might occur according to probability. ID., Poetics, p. 29.
> A play is still an imitation of nature; we know we are to be deceived, and we desire to be so; but no man ever was deceived but with a probability of truth. 1668. DRYDEN, XV., p. 360.
> Many things are probable of particular men, because they are true, which cannot be generally probable; and he that would be feigning persons should confine his fancy to general probability. RYMER, 1st Pt., p. 17.
> Poetry . . . should be probable . . . upon certain suppositions. S. JOHNSON, VII., p. 128.

Since the latter portion of the eighteenth century, it has usually been recognized that a close historical probability is not to be required in literary representation. The series of events portrayed must perhaps be capable of being conceived of as possible occurrences. Probability represents the his- *As general consistency of plot.*

torical sense of what has been, as acting within the limits of the æsthetic sense of what is and ought to be. The only essential for this literary or "dramatic" probability is a certain dream-like consistency of plot construction.

> There are degrees of probability proper even to the wildest fiction. 1814. SCOTT, Life of Swift, p. 315.
>
> In dramatic probability . . . the poet does not require us to be awake and believe; he solicits us only to yield ourselves to a dream. 1817. COLERIDGE, III., p. 564.
>
> Ben Jonson's plots are improbable by an excess of consistency. 1819. HAZLITT, Eng. Com. Writers, p. 51.
>
> The modern mind, so minutely self-scrutinizing, if it is to be affected at all by a sense of the supernatural, needs to be more finely touched than was possible in the older romantic presentation of it. The spectral object, so crude, so impossible, has become plausible as
>
>> The blot upon the brain,
>> That will show itself without,
>
> and is understood to be but a condition of one's own mind. 1865. PATER, Ap., p. 99.

Profound (XIII.) *b* : Swift to present.

> Moral profundity. M. ARNOLD, Cr. Es., 1st S., p. 111.

Profusion (XIX.) *b*: Cole. to present.

> Profusion of interesting detail. BAGEHOT, Lit. St., I., p. 120.

Progression (XVIII.): Want of progression, so that he cannot induce the story to move on at all. GOSSE, From Shak., etc., p. 129.

Prolix (XIX.) *b*: Gas. to present.

> A man may become prolix from the fulness or fervency of his mind; but prolixity produced by this finical minuteness of language ends by distressing one's nerves. STEPHEN, Hrs. in a Lib., I., p. 365.

PROPER (IV.).

During the first century and a half of English criticism, the term "proper" was occasionally used to denote merely propriety of words. This technical use of the term is derived from ancient rhetoric and criticism, yet its meaning was not so definite as it was in the ancient theory of the term. It tended in English criticism to become more inclusive, to indicate a correct use not so much of separate words as of language in general. *As propriety of words.*

> Words are: —
> 1. Proper, — fixed to things.
> 2. Metaphorical, — in places foreign to them.
> 3. Invented, — by ourselves. CICERO, Orators, p. 375.
>
> Words are proper when they signify that to which they first applied; metaphorical when they have one signification by nature, and another in the place in which they are used. QUINTILIAN, I., p. 53.
>
> Proper and apt words. 1568. ASCHAM, III., p. 211.
>
> For word and speech, Plautus is more plentiful, Terence more pure and proper. ID., p. 247.
>
> Their terms proper, their meter sweet. 1585. PUTTENHAM, p. 76.
>
> Scholastic terms, yet very proper. ID., p. 159.
>
> Improper words . . . antiquated by custom . . . incorrect English. 1670. DRYDEN, IV., p. 228.

Even in early English criticism, however, "proper" was often employed as a synonym for "propriety." Since the beginning of the eighteenth century, this has been the universal use of the term. *As propriety in general.*

> Proper for the subject. 1585. K. JAMES, p. 64.
> Proper to poets. 1586. WEBBE, p. 57.
> Nothing is truly sublime that is not just and proper. 1681. DRYDEN, VI., p. 407.

Prophetic (XVI.): Swinburne, Es. & St., p. 17.

PROPORTION (II.).

Previous to the present century, the term "proportion" drew its meaning chiefly from external nature and from moral conduct. It signified a general harmony and adaptation of the parts of a composition to one another, of the thoughts expressed, and of the language employed in its expression. This harmony and adaptation was sometimes said to be determined, in part at least, by "nature" regarded as an activity of the mind; but as employed in actual criticism, proportion was not so changeable a quantity as this dependence upon internal nature would cause it to be. Proportion was almost exclusively determined by applying to the literary work under discussion precepts, methods, and principles, derived from preceding literature, especially from the masterpieces of Greece and Rome. Proportion, thus externally considered, tended to become mechanical and conventional, and to oppose all growth and development in the form of literary expression.

As external symmetry.

> Metaphors must be constructed on principles of analogy (proportion), else they will be sure to appear in bad taste. ARISTOTLE, Rhet., p. 210.
> The world is made by symmetry and proportion, and is in that respect compared to music, and music to poetry. CAMPION, p. 231.
> Lydgate, noted for good proportion of his verse. WEBBE, p. 32.
> This lovely conformity or proportion or convenience between the sense and the sensible hath nature herself most carefully observed in all her own works, then also by kind graft it in the appetites of every creature. 1585. PUTTENHAM, p. 269.
> Of the indecencies of an heroic poem, the most remarkable are

those that show disproportion either between the persons and their actions, or between the manners of the poet and the poem. 1650. HOBBES, IV., p. 454.
Knavery is mere dissonance and disproportion. SHAFTESBURY, I., p. 164.
Harmony . . . symmetry and proportion are founded in nature, let men's fancy prove ever so barbarous, or their fashions ever so Gothic in their architecture, sculpture, or whatever other designing art. ID., p. 276.
All disproportion is unnatural. 1781. S. JOHNSON, VII., p. 156.

During the present century the term "proportion" has occupied a much more subordinate position in criticism than formerly. But during the latter half of the century it has received some little notice when given a psychological explanation. Proportion, considered as an inner sense, can never be said at any given time to have fully manifested itself in literature. Each literary work is in a manner a law unto itself. The term becomes more elastic and more capable of being adapted to the constant change of form and method of expression which has taken place in the development of literature. *As a sense of harmony.*

Proportion is a principle, not of architecture, but of existence . . . and in the fine arts it is impossible to move a single step, or to execute the smallest and simplest piece of work, without involving all those laws of proportion in their full complexity. 1853. RUSKIN, Lec. on Art and Painting, p. 110.
Heine himself . . . seems to me wanting in a refined perception of that inward propriety, which is only another name for poetic proportion. 1866. LOWELL, II., p. 170.
Possessing a sense of proportion based upon the highest analytic and synthetic powers,— a faculty that can harmonize the incongruous thoughts, scenes, and general details of a composite period. 1875. STEDMAN, Vict. Poets, p. 199.

As a literary critic, Carlyle was sometimes perverse; he missed proportions; now and then he would resolutely invert things, and hold them up to mockery in grotesque disarray. 1887. Dowden, Tr. & St., p. 183.

PROPRIETY (IV.).

Propriety denotes a general harmony among all the elements that enter into the composition of a work of literature. In so far as any harmony is capable of being determined analytically, it is necessary to have for the different elements entering into it a common basis, a common unit, so to speak, by a reference to which they are given their relative values. As propriety has been employed in actual criticism, this common basis of reference is scarcely ever given. Yet according to the variation in this basis of reference,— usually to be ascertained by inference,— the changes of meaning in the term "propriety" have taken place. The history of the term may be divided into four periods.

Until the latter portion of the eighteenth century, propriety represented the influence in literature of an

<small>As an instinctive conformity to well established principles, and to "nature."</small> instinct developed by culture, an instinct for regularity and probability, derived from the past, for temperance in statement and consistency, which spring largely from a sense of accuracy to present fact, and, perhaps, to a slight extent, for harmony and beauty, which may refer to the future. But the term usually indicated a conformity to well established principles in the literature of the past. From the study of this literature there was developed a cultured instinct by the activity

of which propriety was determined, in so far as propriety was synthetic, an immediate sense or feeling. Occasionally, however, the propriety or fitness of the literary elements was determined in a more or less analytic manner. There is found mentioned a propriety or fitness of language, of phrase, of sounds, of names of characters, of versification, of figures of speech, of fictions, of sentiments, of characters, of the nature of the composition itself,—all instances in which but one of the three factors necessary for the analytic determination of propriety is found within the composition that is being criticised. The other factors are to be derived by inference from the principles of earlier literature. The term "propriety" was in very great use during the seventeenth and eighteenth centuries, representing more than any other expression the conservative methods of criticism then dominant.

> Propriety consists neither in rapidity or conciseness, but in a mean betwixt both. ARISTOTLE, Rhet., p. 248.
> As to propriety, no direction seems possible to be given but this, that we adopt a character of style fuller, plainer, or middling, suited to the subject on which we are to speak. . . . To know what is becoming is an affair of judgment, to be able to do the becoming is the part of art and of nature. CICERO, Orators, p. 395.
> By displacing no word . . . the verse . . . be wrested against his natural propriety. 1586. WEBBE, p. 63.
> To the propriety of expression I refer that clearness of memory by which a poet when he hath once introduced any person whatsoever, speaking in his poem, maintaineth in him to the end the same character he gave him in the beginning. 1650. HOBBES, IV., p. 454.
> Tragedy . . . is an imitation of one entire, great, and probable

> action; not told, but represented; which, by moving in us fear and pity, is conducive to the purging of those two passions in our minds: . . . or tragedy describes or paints an action, which action must have all the proprieties above named. 1679. DRYDEN, VI., p. 260.
>
> Propriety of thought is that fancy which arises naturally from the subject, or which the poet adapts to it; propriety of words is the clothing of those thoughts with such expressions as are naturally proper to them. 1685. ID., VII., p. 228.
>
> A mixture of British and Grecian ideas may justly be deemed a blemish in the Pastorals of Pope; and propriety is certainly violated when he couples Pactolus with Thames, and Windsor with Hybla. 1756. J. WARTON, I., p. 4.

During the latter half of the eighteenth century the terms "propriety" and "beauty" were often used together. Propriety indicated a conformity of the different parts of a composition with one another, or with the nature of the composition itself, the conformity to be determined primarily by the sense of beauty within the mind; but also in part from well known images, customs, and principles derived from literature and experience.

As an instinctive sense of harmony within the composition itself.

> With what wildness of imagination, but yet with what propriety are the amusements of the fairies pointed out in the Midsummer Night's Dream; amusements proper for none but fairies. 1756. J. WARTON, I., p. 223.
>
> It has been the lot of many great names not to have been able to express themselves with beauty and propriety in the fetters of verse. ID., pp. 265, 266.
>
> In a work of so serious and severe a cast, strokes of levity, however poignant and witty, are ill-placed and disgusting, are violations of that propriety which Pope in general so strictly observes. ID., III., p. 112.
>
> What is false taste but a want of perception to discern propriety and distinguish beauty. 1761. GOLDSMITH, I., p. 324.

> Even in describing fantastic beings, there is a propriety to be observed, but surely nothing can be more revolting to common sense than this numbering of the moonbeams among the other implements of Queen Mab's harness. 1762. ID., p. 381.
>
> Pope had an intuitive perception of consonance and propriety. 1781. S. JOHNSON, VIII., p. 320.

During the first half of the present century the term fell wholly into disfavor. It represented a conformity to customs and principles, merely because those customs and principles were old and well established. It denoted a total want of originality and native power.

As conventionality.

> One would not surely be frightful when one's dead;
> And Betty, give this cheek a little red. (Dying words of Narcissa. Pope.)
> Was that right, to provide for coquetting in her coffin? Why, no, not strictly right; its impropriety cannot be denied, etc. 1848. DE QUINCEY, XI., p. 76.

During the latter portion of the present century the term has not been very much in use. It has had, however, three different meanings. The endeavor has been made to distinguish between an extrinsic and an intrinsic propriety. Extrinsic propriety has to do with the externals of literature, those things which may be derived from precept and custom, and may be reduced to rule and method.

As "extrinsic" harmony.

> The first demand we make upon whatever claims to be a work of art . . . is that it shall be in keeping. Now this propriety is of two kinds, either extrinsic or intrinsic. . . . Extrinsic propriety relates rather to the body than the soul of the work, such as fidelity to the facts of history . . . congruity of costume and the like. 1868. LOWELL, III., p. 69.

> The literary artist is of necessity a scholar. . . . His punctilious observance of the proprieties of his medium will diffuse through all he writes a general air of sensibility, of refined usage. 1888. PATER, Ap., pp. 8, 9.

Intrinsic propriety, on the other hand, may be said to represent the growing sense of beauty, which, how-ever, takes into account more than usual the results of past achievement, which finds more pleasure than the ordinary sense of beauty in regularity and method.

As "intrinsic" harmony.

> Intrinsic propriety consists of three elements: —
> 1. Co-ordination of character.
> 2. Consistency.
> 3. Propriety of costume . . . to satisfy the superhistoric sense. All these come within the scope of imaginative truth. LOWELL, III., p. 69.

Throughout the whole history of the term, and especially of late, it has occasionally been employed to indicate a conformity in literary representation to the moral sense of decency and decorum.

As moral decorum.

> The Anglo-Saxon novel is really not so prudish after all. . . . Sometimes a novel which has this shuffling air, this effect of truckling to propriety, etc. HOWELLS, Crit. & Fiction, p. 148.
> The propriety of the morals, the congruity of the sentiments. 1882. SAINTSBURY, Hist. Fr. Lit., p. 531.

Prosaic (XXII.) *b*: Bentley to present.
> Prosaic accuracy of detail. STEPHEN, L., p. 57.

Prosing: Jef. to present.
> Mystical and prosing. JEFFREY, I., p. 284.

Provincial (I.): Gold. to present.
> The provincial spirit exaggerates the value of its ideas for want of a high standard at hand by which to try them. M. ARNOLD, Cr. Es., 1st S., p. 66.

Prudish: The Anglo-Saxon novel is really not so prudish after all. HOWELLS, Crit. & Fiction, p. 148.
Prurient (XV.): Effeminate or prurient. SWINBURNE, Mis., p. 230.
Puerile (XII.): Mil. to present.
> By puerility we mean a pedantic habit of mind which by over-elaboration ends in frigidity. LONGINUS, p. 6.
> The circumstance in this line is puerile and little: —
>> And little eagles wave their wings in gold.
>> J. WARTON, II., p. 202.

Puerism (I.): Lessing's style is pure without puerism. CARLYLE, I., p. 40.
Puling: Puling classical affectation. JEFFREY, II., p. 248.
Pungent (XX.) *b*: Scott to present. Swinburne, Es. & St., p. 65.
Puny; Puny affectation. JEFFREY, II., p. 175.
PURITY (I.).

Until the latter portion of the eighteenth century purity of language usually indicated a scholastic refinement of the popular idiom. Whenever English critics referred to Latin and Greek authors, purity, perhaps, signified merely a choice of specific and appropriate expressions, and their arrangement according to the rules of composition; but whenever English literature was the subject of criticism, purity denoted further a selection and arrangement of words and phrases in conformity with the literary principles of the ancient masterpieces.

As refined language.

> Purity . . . the foundation of all style . . . consists of five things:
> 1. Connective particles.
> 2. Particular terms (as against Generalities).
> 3. Clearness (avoiding ambiguities).
> 4. Correct genders of nouns.
> 5. Correct numbers of words. ARISTOTLE, Rhet., pp. 219-222.
>
> Pureness of phrase . . . and propriety of words . . . in Terence. ASCHAM, p. 144 (Arber).

> For word and speech, Plautus is more plentiful, Terence more pure and proper. ID., III., p. 247.
> As simplicity is the distinguishing characteristic of Pastoral, Virgil hath been thought guilty of too courtly a style; his language is perfectly pure, and he often forgets he is among peasants. 1713. POPE, X., p. 508.
> Surrey, for his justness of thought, correctness of style, and purity of expression, may justly be pronounced the first English classical poet. 1778. T. WARTON, Hist. Eng. Poetry, p. 645.

During the present century two other uses of the term are to be noted. Purity often designates the well-established native idiom of the language, as opposed to innovations of all kinds, whether scholastic, foreign, or popular in their origin, whether referring to the selection of words alone, or to the phraseology also.

As idiomatic language.

> Spenser's language is less pure and idiomatic than Chaucer's. 1818. HAZLITT, Eng. Poets, p. 56.
> There is nothing so unclassical, nothing so impure in style, as pedantry. 1864. BAGEHOT, Lit. St., II., p. 360.

During the present century, however, purity has usually referred not to language directly, but to thought and conduct. The word "purity" has been appropriated to express the rising sense of morals in literature. Purity of language has received less attention in criticism during this century than formerly, and is usually expressed by less ambiguous terms than "purity."

As moral uprightness.

> A lyrical purity and passion. 1887. DOWDEN, Tr. & St., p. 167.
> Milton's power of style has for its great character elevation; and Milton's elevation clearly comes in the main from a moral quality in him,—his pureness. M. ARNOLD, Mixed Es., p. 202.

Puzzling (III.): Startling, unclassical, and puzzling. JEFFREY, I., p. 266.

QUAINT (IX.): Camden to present. Much in use.

I. Until within the first few decades of the present century, "quaintness" usually represented an obscure and antiquated oddity, the result of affectation and a lack of originality.

>There are, my friend, whose philosophic eyes
>Look through and trust the Ruler with his skies.

This is . . . quaint and obscure. J. WARTON, II., p. 327.
Tricks, quaintnesses, hieroglyphics, and enigmas. WORDSWORTH, II., p. 103.
Quaint and prosaic. JEFFREY, II., p. 348.
Quaint low humour. HAZLITT, El. Lit., p. 24.
Quaintness, coldness, and conceit. WILSON, V., p. 362.

II. Since the first few decades of the present century, and occasionally throughout its entire history, quaintness has usually represented a mystical and remote oddness, primitive simplicity, and naïveté, embodied in more or less primitive methods of expression.

A quaintness . . . something poetical. BENTLEY, I., p. 266.
Quaintness merging into grotesqueness. M. ARNOLD, Cel. Lit., p. 175.
A touch of naïveté, of old-world quaintness. ROBERTSON, Es., etc., p. 3.

Questionable (VIII.): Jeffrey, III., p. 102.
Quibbling (XI.): Shaftes. to present.
All humour had something of the quibble. The very language of the court was punning. SHAFTESBURY, I., p. 48.
Quick (XII.): Camden to present.
Quick with bright spontaneous feeling. DOWDEN, Shak., etc., p. 333.
Quiet (XIX.) a: Swin., Sted. Swinburne, Mis., p. 97.
Racy (XII.): Jef. to present.

The idiomatic and unconventional in expression; the native, sincere, and direct in thought; strength of local coloring, at the expense, perhaps, of artistic refinement.

    Racy humour. JEFFREY, I., p. 214.
    Strength of contrast, a raciness and a glow. LAMB, P. P. & Es., p. 261.
    Vigorous, rough and racy lines. WILSON, II., p. 285.
    A spirit and raciness very unlike these frigid conceits. HALLAM, III., p. 257.
    Racy words: bam, kick, whop, twaddle, fudge, hitch, etc. M. ARNOLD, Cel. Lit., p. 69.
    Metaphors and similes are racy of the soil in which they grow, as you taste, it is said, the lava in the vines on the slopes of Ætna. MATHEWS, Lit. St., p. 15.

Radiant: Low. to present.
    Radiant verses. LOWELL, Prose, IV., p. 313.

Raillery (XVII.): Dry. to present.
    The raillery is carried to the verge of railing, some will say ribaldry. J. WARTON, II., p. 250.

Rambling (XVIII.): Wil. to present.
    Desultory and rambling. WILSON, VI., p. 238.

Rancid (XIV.): Stale and rancid. SWINBURNE, Mis., p. 111.

Rancour (XIV.): Saints., Gosse. Saintsbury, Hist. Eng. Lit., II., p. 232.

Range (XIII.) *b*: Swin., Beers.

Rant (XIX.) *b*: Collier to present.
    Gasping, ranting, wheezing, broken-winded verse. SWINBURNE, Mis., p. 76.

RAPID (XVIII).

The term "rapid" began to become prominent in criticism about the middle of the eighteenth century, and its use has been constantly upon the increase to the present time. There has been some little variation as to the portion of the composition designated by the term, but there has perhaps been no change in its meaning. The term represents an intensity of mental interest, and a constant development in the elements which go to make up that interest,— a swift sequence of sounds and rhythms, of thoughts, of mental images, and of the incidents of plot construction. Ease in a composition is in a sense a prerequisite for rapidity. Rapidity is attained only by means of great energy and animation. Hence the term tends to characterize those features of a composition which most excite one's sympathy and interest,— to the mental imagery and to the development of the plot. It occasionally, however, refers to the literary work as a whole.

> Rapid and approach nearer to conversation. 1756. J. WARTON, II., p. 356.
> Dryden is sometimes vehement and rapid. S. JOHNSON, VIII., p. 324.
> Clarendon's narration is not, perhaps, sufficiently rapid, being stopped too frequently by particularities. 1751. ID., III., p. 83.
> Animation, fire, and rapidity. BLAIR, Rhet., p. 40.
> Demosthenes has a rapid harmony, exactly adjusted to the sense. 1742. D. HUME, I., p. 170.
> The rapidity, and yet the perspicuity of the thoughts. J. WARTON, II., p. 20.
> Of all Shakespeare's plays, Macbeth is the most rapid, Hamlet the slowest, in movement. 1810. COLERIDGE, IV., p. 133.
> In variety and rapidity of movement, the Alexander's Feast has all that can be required in this respect. 1818. HAZLITT, Eng. Poets, p. 108.

Rapture (XV.): Low. to present. Rossetti, Lives, p. 57.
Rash (XII.): Jeffrey, II., p. 375.
Rational (XX.): Jef. to present.
> Simplicity and rationality . . . of Voltaire. M. ARNOLD, Cel. Lit., p. 164.
> Pope was a . . . rationalist and formalist. T. ARNOLD, p. 418.

Rattling (X.): Rattling verses ... of Hudibras. GOSSE, Hist. Eng. Lit., p. 27.

Raving (XV.): Raving style admired in Germany. JEFFREY, I., p. 289.

Raw: Saintsbury, Es. in Eng. Lit., p. 257.

Reach (XIII.) *b*: Low. to present.

    Less depth and reach and force. SWINBURNE, Es. & St., p. 100.

Readable (XXII.) *a*: Swin., Gosse.

1. Somewhat interesting.

    Gosse, Seventeenth Cent. St., p. 179.

2. Not morally offensive and disgusting.

    No longer readable comedies of Mariage à la Mode. GOSSE, Hist. Eng. Lit., III., p. 43.

REALITY (VIII.).

The term "reality" began to be employed in criticism during the latter portion of the eighteenth century, and its use has been constantly upon the increase until the present time. "Reality," primarily a philosophical term, denotes in general the external world of appearances, or whatever seems to be such, or whatever fully explains these appearances. Three different meanings have been given to the term. In the first portion of the present century, occasionally later, reality indicated the essential reason or principle, which underlies appearances, that which renders their existence possible, and gives to them unity and significance.

As the fundamental principle of existence.

    Truth is correlate to being. Knowledge without a correspondent reality is no knowledge. 1817. COLERIDGE, III., p. 342.

    Poetry must dwell in reality, and become manifest to men in the forms among which they live and move. CARLYLE, I., p. 56.

    We create nine-tenths at least of what appears to exist externally; and such is somewhere about the proportion between reality and imagination. 1832. WILSON, VI., p. 109.

Literature is the record of man's attempt to make actual to thought a life approaching nearer to reality than the boasted actual life of the world. . . . If the phrase, realizing the ideal, were translated into the phrase, actualizing the real, much ambiguity might be avoided. 1845. WHIPPLE, Es. & Rev., p. 300.

In Keats and Guérin, in whom the faculty of naturalistic interpretation is overpoweringly predominant, the natural magic is perfect; when they speak of the world, they speak like Adam, naming by divine inspiration the creatures; their expression corresponds with the thing's essential reality. 1865. M. ARNOLD, Cr. Es., 1st S., p. 112.

Throughout its whole history the term "reality" has often been employed to denote an imaginative heightening of ordinary events and appearances, which, by holding the attention spellbound, seems itself to represent actual appearances, that have become externalized, as it were, and made a basis, perhaps, for future thought and action. *As imaginative fascination.*

Waller borrows too many of his sentiments and illustrations from the old mythology, for which it is vain to plead the example of ancient poets; the deities which they introduced so frequently were considered as realities, so far as to be received by the imagination, whatever sober reason might even then determine. 1781. S. JOHNSON, VII., p. 216.

Don Quixote . . . presents something more stately, more romantic, and at the same time more real to the imagination than any other hero upon record. 1819. HAZLITT, Eng. Com. Writers, p. 145.

Imagination has . . . in Milton's Satan . . . achieved its highest triumph, in imparting a character of reality and truth to its most daring creations. CHANNING, p. 446.

Vivid realism of the impossible. SWINBURNE, Es. & St., p. 120.

We have admitted that Beatrice Portinari was a real creature, but how real she was, and whether as real to the poet's memory as to his imagination may fairly be questioned. 1872. LOWELL, IV., p. 206.

But the term "reality" has been employed to denote the facts and events of actual life far more frequently than in the uses of the term just given. In this more common and general use of the term, two distinctions of meaning at least should be drawn. Until within the latter portion of the present century, the term usually denoted the facts and events of actual life, considered in so mechanical a fashion that every one would agree even as to the most minute details of the facts or events portrayed. Hence the subject-matter of literature was inevitably taken from those phases of actual life well known in ordinary experience, but new, perhaps, to literary treatment. The realistic method of literary treatment was usually assumed to be a full, detailed, and accurate account of the fact or event recorded,— selection in the details being permissible only for the purpose of avoiding incoherency and tediousness.

<small>As actuality, external, ordinary, unselected.</small>

> We are more affected by reading Shakespeare's description of Dover Cliff, than we would be with the reality; because in reading the description we refer to our own experience, and perceive with surprise the justness of the imitations.   1761.   GOLDSMITH, I., p. 339.
>
> They (formerly) loved, I will not say tediousness, but length and a train of circumstances in a narration. The vulgar do so still: it gives an air of reality to facts, it fixes the attention, raises and keeps in suspense their expectation, and supplies the defects of their little lifeless imagination.   1762.   GRAY, I., p. 392.
>
> The plot and character are natural without being too real to be pleasing.   1829.   NEWMAN, Es. on Aristotle, p. 16.
>
> Fiction has no business to exist unless it is more beautiful than reality.   1865.   M. ARNOLD, Cr. Es., 1st S., p. 392.   (Quoted.)
>
> Exaltation of the commonplace through the scientific spirit in realism.   HOWELLS, Crit. and Fiction, p. 16.

More recently it has usually been recognized that external facts and events can be conceived of only as they are brought into relation with some unifying principle which is not external. In literature, this unifying principle is some ethical motive or the action of the æsthetic instincts. Selection of details in composition has been recognized not only as a necessity, but often as constituting the chief means for a vivid representation of the actual fact. Also, the representation of the more uncommon features of actual life is not thought to be inconsistent with the realistic method of treatment. Hence the recent use of the term "reality" represents a broader conception of actual life than the early use of the term, a more discriminative selection of the details to be mentioned, and a wider limit to the subject-matter of literary representation.

As actuality motived and selected.

> A figure may be ideal and yet accurate, realistic and yet untrue, as a fact not thoroughly fathomed may be in effect a falsehood. There is a far stronger cross of the ideal in the realism of Æschylus or Shakespeare than runs through the work of the great modern writers. 1869. SWINBURNE, Es. & St., p. 220.
>
> A vigorous grasp of realities is rather a proof of a powerful than a defective imagination. 1874. STEPHEN, Hrs. in a Lib., p. 283.
>
> When we speak of Middlemarch as more realistic, and Daniel Deronda as more ideal, it is not meant that one is true to the facts of life and the other untrue; it is rather meant that in the one the facts are taken more in the gross, and in the other there is a passionate selection of those facts that are representative of the highest (and also of the lowest) things. DOWDEN, St. in Lit., p. 285.
>
> Thus every workman must be a realist in knowledge, an idealist for interpretation, and the antagonism between realists and ro-

mancers is a forced one. 1892. STEDMAN, Nat. of Poetry, p. 199.

That only is real for us which reappears before our solitude when, closing our eyes and letting our spirit ruminate upon itself, we evoke our personal mirage of the universe. — P. BOURGET, p. 190.

Reasonable (XX.): Low. to present.

Voltaire tells that Mr. Addison was the first Englishman who had written a reasonable tragedy. LOWELL, IV., p. 14.

Recondite: Swin. to present.

So recondite and exquisite as the choral parts of a Greek play. SWINBURNE, Es. & St., p. 162.

Recreation: Saintsbury, Es. in Eng. Lit., p. 268.

Redundant (XIX.) *b*: B. Jon. to present.

Redundancy of humours. SHAFTESBURY, I., p. 131.

Refinement (V.): Mil. to present.

I. Previous to the present century, "refinement" usually represented a cultured use of language, and an apt selection of the facts of history for literary composition.

Endeavor . . . by precepts and by rules to perpetuate that style and idiom . . . which have flourished in the purest periods of the language. . . . it gives gentility, elegance, refinement. MILTON, III., p. 496.

The ancients refined upon history. RYMER, 1st Pt., p. 16.

II. During the present century, refinement has usually represented certain mental characteristics: delicate sensibility, and chastened emotions and feelings.

Poetic imagery . . . must elevate, deepen, or refine the human passion. WORDSWORTH, II., p. 56.

Reflective (XX.) *b*: T. War. to present.

Reflective and self-sustained. WHIPPLE, Es. & Rev., p. 49.

REGULARITY (II.).

There has been considerable change in the favor with which the term "regularity" has been regarded in English criticism, but there has perhaps been no change in its meaning. It has been employed chiefly to characterize the general design or plot construction of a literary production, but it sometimes refers to the more subordinate features of a composition, especially to the versification. Regularity is determined less immediately than proportion by an inner sense, and it makes less assumption of law and fixed method than order. It denotes a more or less mechanical correspondence between the different parts of a composition, or between the parts of one composition and those of other compositions. Regularity was first opposed to variety, then to imagination. In the early portion of the present century the term fell almost wholly into disfavor, but more recently it has again come into active use in connection with the criticism of prose literature.

 Regularities: The unities of action, time, and place. RYMER, 1st Pt., p. 24.
 Regularity and roundness of design. ID., 2d Pt., p. 85.
 The genius of the English cannot bear too regular a play; we are given to variety. 1690. DRYDEN, VII., p. 313.
 Imagination, a licentious and vagrant faculty, unsusceptible of limitations, and impatient of restraint, has always endeavored to baffle the logician, to perplex the confines of distinction, and burst the inclosures of regularity. 1751. S. JOHNSON, III., p. 93.
 The work of a correct and regular writer is a garden accurately formed and diligently planted, varied with shades, and scented with flowers; the composition of Shakespeare is a forest, etc. 1765. S. JOHNSON, V., p. 127.
 The essence of verse is regularity, and its ornament is variety. 1781. ID., VII., p. 346.
 The true ground of the mistake lies in the confounding mechanical regularity with organic form. 1810. COLERIDGE, IV., p. 55.

The thoughts are vast and irregular; and the style halts and staggers under them. 1820. HAZLITT, Age of El., p. 44.
The needful qualities for a fit prose are regularity, uniformity, precision, balance. M. ARNOLD, Cr. Es., 2d S., p. 39.
Relief (IX.): Relief and variety. JEFFREY, II., p. 405.
Rememberable: A rememberable verse. LOWELL, Prose, II., p. 146.
Remote: Pope to present. S. Johnson, VII., p. 208.
Repartee (XVII.): Dry. to present.
Repartee is the soul of conversation. DRYDEN, III., p. 245.
Repartee . . . a chase of wit. ID., XV., p. 334.
Bon mots and repartees. J. WARTON, II., p. 144.
Repose (XIX.) *a*: Jef., Stephen.
Want of plainness, simplicity, and repose. JEFFREY, II., p. 471.
Repulsive (XXII.) *b*: Swin. to present. Dowden, Shak., etc., p. 82.
Reserve (XIX.) *b*: Jef. to present.
Reserve and gravity of the style. JEFFREY, I., p. 367.
Resonance (X.): Swin. Gosse, Hist. Eng. Lit., III., p. 237.
Restless (XIX.): Howells, Crit. and Fiction, p. 24.
Restrained (XIX.) *b*: Low. to present.
Restrained vigor. LOWELL, I., p. 296.
Revolting (XXII.) *b*: Jef., Gosse.
Revolting in its details. JEFFREY, III., p. 133.
Rhapsodical (XXI.): Campbell to present.
Poetical and rhapsodical. ROSSETTI, Pref. to Blake, p. cxiii.
Rhetorical (XIX.) *b*: Lodge to present.
Rhetoric . . . a sort of art is immediately thought of that is ostentatious and deceitful; the minute and trifling study of words alone; the pomp of expression; the studied fallacies of Rhetoric; ornament substituted in the room of use. BLAIR, Rhet., p. 10.
The prosing rhetoric of the French tragedy. BAGEHOT, II., p. 273.
Macaulay was a born rhetorician; but beyond the apparent rhetorical truth of things he never could penetrate. M. ARNOLD, Cr. Es., 1st S., p. 304.
Rhetorical, ornate, — and poetically quite false. ID., 2d S., p. 97.
RHYTHMICAL (X.).

The rhythmical, unlike the metrical, is not regarded as a quality which inheres objectively, as it were, in the composition considered as a completed product. The rhythmical refers wholly to the effect which the literary work produces upon the mind of the reader. It consists of such a succession of regular and irregular movements as shall to a certain extent gratify the expectation or anticipation aroused, but shall also by means of little surprises constantly give the expectation new material upon which inferences may be based.

> I would trace the origin of meter to the balance in the mind effected by that spontaneous effort which strives to hold in check the workings of passion. 1817. COLERIDGE, III., p. 415.
> Rhythmical and sweet. HALLAM, III., p. 335.
> Rhythmic emotion. LOWELL, III., p. 2.
> The language, alike of poetry and prose, attains a rhythmical power, independent of metrical combination, and dependent rather on some subtle adjustment of the elementary sounds of words themselves to the image or feeling they convey. 1874. PATER, Ap., p. 57.

Ribald (XIV.): J. War., Gosse. J. Warton, II., p. 250.
Rich (XI.) *b*: Dekker to present. Much in use in present century.
> Richness and sweetness of sound. COLERIDGE, III., p. 276.
> Rich in colour. SWINBURNE, A St. of B. Jonson, p. 65.
> Rich perfume. DOWDEN, Tr. & St., p. 207.

Ridiculous (XVII.): Pope to present.
> The only source of the true ridiculous . . . is affectation. FIELDING, J. Andrews, Pref., pp. 13, 14.

Rigmarole: Saintsbury, Eng. Lit., p. 319.
Ringing: Gosse, Brooke.
> Ringing hyperboles. GOSSE, Hist. Eng. Lit., p. 43.

Ripe: Swin., Gosse.
> Ripe and . . . free from all romantic influence. GOSSE, From Shak., etc., p. 94.

Robust (XII.): Cole. to present.
> Robustness is the great characteristic of Dryden's poetry. ROSSETTI, Lives, p. 106.

Romance (XXI.): Campbell to present.

Upon these three columns — chivalry, gallantry, and religion — repose the fictions of the middle ages, especially those usually designated as romances. HALLAM, Lit. Hist., 1., p. 135.

The impotent feelings of romance, so singularly characteristic of this century, may indeed gild, but never save, the remains of those mightier ages to which they are attached like climbing flowers. RUSKIN, Stones of Venice, I., p. 62.

Diffusion is in the nature of a romance. SWINBURNE, Es. & St., p. 122.

ROMANTIC (IX.).

The history of the term "romantic" may be divided into three periods. During the first period, which includes the last half of the eighteenth century, the term was employed in two more or less distinct ways. The romantic sometimes indicated the general spirit of romance and adventure. When given this meaning, the term was not very much in favor with the critics. The chivalric passion and the beautiful superstitions with which it was historically associated, could not fail, indeed, to elicit admiration. But it was necessary to ascribe to this chivalric passion very many improbable adventures, extravagant combinations of incidents, and inconceivable feats of daring, — all of them flagrant violations of "truth" and "nature."

As wild, chivalric passion and adventure.

> (Of Corneille's Plays.) It is observed how much that wild goose chase of Romance runs still in their head; some scenes of love must everywhere be shuffled in, though never so unseasonably. RYMER, 2d Pt., p. 62.
>
> Those intrigues and adventures to which the romantic taste has confined modern tragedy. T. TICKELL, Arber's Garner, VI., p. 520.

> He who would think the Faery Queen, Palamon and Arcite, The Tempest, or Comus, childish and romantic, might relish Pope. 1756. J. WARTON, II., p. 403.
>
> That for which Tasso is most liable to censure is a certain romantic vein which runs through many of the adventures and incidents of his poem. BLAIR, Rhet., p. 497.

Often, also, the romantic represented any unusually striking and beautiful mental image or view of natural scenery. When thus employed, the term was always regarded with favor by the critics. But the romantic scene or image was often merely the background and localized setting, so to speak, for the activity of the romantic passion, and hence the two meanings of the term blended imperceptibly into a single meaning.

As wild, picturesque scenery and imagery.

> The country of the Scotch warriors described in . . . Chevy Chase . . . has a fine romantic situation. 1710. ADDISON, II., p. 378.
>
> I cannot at present recollect any solitude so romantic. . . . The mind naturally loves to lose itself in one of these wildernesses, and to forget the hurry, the noise, and splendor of more polished life. 1756. J. WARTON, I., p. 349.
>
> Wild and romantic imagery. ID., II., p. 35.
>
> Beautifully romantic. ID., p. 65.

During the early portion of the present century the opposition between the terms "romantic" and "classical," which had hitherto been, for the most part, merely historical and casual, developed into a philosophical antithesis, in which the terms were intended to be really and essentially opposed and complementary to each other. The romantic became more refined and intellectual than it had

As energetic, passionate, and suggestive idealization.

formerly been. Chivalric passion was transformed into poetic passion; wild and picturesque imagery into suggestive imagery. The romantic represented the more pronounced idealizing tendencies in literature, a broader and yet broader view of human life, depth of conception and feeling, a fierce intellectual tension, from hovering ever on the borders of the incomprehensible, the mysterious, the infinite.

> In Shakespeare, the commonest matter-of-fact has a romantic grace about it. 1817. HAZLITT, Shak., p. 196.
> Romantic and enthusiastic. ID., p. 182.
> The great difference, then, which we find between the romantic and classical style, between ancient and modern poetry, is, that the one more frequently describes things as they are interesting in themselves, the other for the sake of the associations of ideas connected with them; that the one dwells more on the immediate impressions of objects on the senses, the other on the ideas which they suggest to the imagination. 1820. ID., Age of El., p. 246.
> Romantic beauty and high-wrought passion. ID., El. Lit., p. 126.
> Romantic, sweet, tender. ID., p. 169.
> The real and proper use of the word romantic is simply to characterize an improbable or unaccustomed degree of beauty, sublimity, or virtue. . . . True friendship is romantic, to the men of the world; true affection is romantic; true religion is romantic. 1853. RUSKIN, Lecture on A. & P., p. 62.

During the latter portion of the present century the "romantic" has been placed in opposition to the "realistic" no less than to the "classical." As *As suggestive, impassioned, and artistic idealization.* opposed to the "realistic," the "romantic" denotes an artistic selection and an impassioned treatment of the subject-matter of literature. As opposed to the classical, "romantic" has become for the most part a classifying term, being employed to designate two periods of English literature, — Shakespeare being the culmination of the first period, Wordsworth of the second.

> It is this warmth of circumstance, this profusion of interesting detail, which has caused the name romantic to be perseveringly applied to modern literature. 1856. BAGEHOT, Lit. St., I., p. 120.
>
> The side of Elliott's genius which is most remote from reality, which loved to be romantic, was his less true self, and in his romantic poems there is unquestionably a note of spuriousness. DOWDEN, St. in Lit., pp. 39, 40.
>
> The romantic movement was as universal then as the realistic movement is now, and as irresistible. It was the literary expression of monarchy and aristocracy, as realism is the literary expression of republicanism and democracy. HOWELLS, Mod. It. Poets, p. 133.
>
> At its best, romantic literature in every period attains classical quality, giving true measure of the very limited value of those well-worn critical distinctions. 1886. PATER, Ap., p. 161.

Rough (II.): Ascham to present.
> Lucretius is scabrous and rough in these . . . antique words. B. JONSON, Timber, p. 61.

Rough-hewn (II.): Bentley's vernacular style is rough-hewn. GOSSE, Hist. Eng. Lit., p. 104.

Rubbishy (XI.): Ros. Gosse, From Shak., etc., p. 139.

Rude (V.): Ascham to present.
> Rude and imperfect. BENTLEY, I., p. 324.
> Rude, inartificial majesty. S. JOHNSON, III., p. 83.

Rugged (V.): Collier to present.

I. Rough.
> After about half a century of forced thoughts and rugged meter, some advances toward nature and harmony had been made by Waller and Denham. S. JOHNSON, VII., pp. 307, 308.

II. Sturdy.
> Rugged simplicity . . . of Burns. CARLYLE, II., p. 11.

Rustic (V.): Sidney to present.
Rustic and awkward. . . . Rustic terms are unlikely to be compounded with accuracy. LANDOR, VIII., p. 407.
Saccâde: Saccâde, — its rapidity is jerky. M. ARNOLD, Celtic Lit., p. 194.
Sad (XIV.): Whip. to present.
Wordsworth has not the note of plangent sadness which strikes the ear in men as morally inferior to him as Rousseau, Keats, etc. MORLEY, St. in Lit., p. 41.
Sagacity (XX.) *b*: Jef., Mor.
Depth of sagacity. JEFFREY, II., p. 91.
Salient (XVI.): Low. to present.
Donne is full of salient verses. LOWELL, Prose, III., p. 35.
Salt (XVII.): Dry., Wil.
His wit is faint and his salt . . . almost insipid. DRYDEN, XIII., p. 88.
As for the saltness of sagacity and wit, Mr. Wordsworth looks down upon it as a profane thing. WILSON, V., p. 395.
Sameness (II.): Collier to present.
Between variety and sameness. HUNT, Im. & Fancy, p. 37.
Sanity (XX.) *b*: Noble sanity. DOWDEN, Tr. & St., p. 302.
Sappy: Weightiness of sappy words. NEWTON, Spenser Society, XLIII., p. 3.
Sarcasm (XVII.): Gold. to present.
Wit and humour stand on one side, irony and sarcasm on the other. LANDOR, IV., p. 282.
Sardonic: Sardonic persiflage. SAINTSBURY, Es. in Eng. Lit., p. 254.
Satire (XVII.): Dry. to present.

I. Previous to the present century the satirical usually represented raillery and sarcasm at the less favored conditions and the less refined achievements of life, viewed from the standpoint of the more cultured attainments and conditions.

Satire: a sharp, well-mannered way of laughing a folly out of countenance. 1693. DRYDEN, XIII., p. 112.
Satire is the poetry of a nation highly polished. T. WARTON, p. 950.

II. During the present century satire has indicated a more or less genial play of humor upon the incongruities of actual life, in view of an ideal, — the purpose or ideal being more persistent and definite than in the case of pure humor, and thus causing it to verge toward bitterness and malignity.

    Richter's satire is playful . . . never bitter, scornful, or malignant. DE QUINCEY, XI., p. 271.
    Whenever the satire of the noble grotesque fixes upon human nature, it does so with so much sorrow mingled amidst its indignation; in its highest forms there is an infinite tenderness, like that of the fool in Lear. RUSKIN, Stones of Venice, II., p. 194.

Savour: Swin., Mor. Swinburne, Es. & St., p. 71.
Scabrous (II.): B. Jon., Dry. B. Jonson, Timber, p. 61.
Scholastic (XV.): S. John., E. Brown.
    Scholastic . . . but not inelegant. S. JOHNSON, VII., p. 19.
    The pedantry . . . of Milton . . . (if it is to be so called), of the scholastic enthusiast, who is constantly referring to images of which his mind is full, is as graceful as it is natural. HAZLITT, Round Table, p. 47.
Scientific: "Zenith-height" is harsh to the ear and too scientific. GRAY, III., p. 74.
Scrupulous (XIX.) *b*: Scrupulous delicacy of taste. JEFFREY, I., p. 165.
Sculpturesque (XIX.) *b*:
    In the Greek drama one must conceive the presiding power to be Death; in the English, Life. What Death? What Life? That sort of death or of life locked up and frozen into everlasting slumber, which we see in sculpture; that sort of life, of tumult, of agitation, of tendency to something beyond, which we see in painting. The picturesque, in short, domineers over English tragedy; the sculpturesque or the statuesque over the Grecian. DE QUINCEY, X., p. 315.
Scurrilous (XIV.): Hal. Saintsbury, Hist. Eng. Lit., p. 246.
Seasonable (IV.): Rymer to present. RYMER, 2d Pt., p. 62.

Sedate (XIX.) *a*: Swin., Gosse.
  Grave and sedate. SWINBURNE, Mis., p. 105.
Seductive (XXII.) *b*: Jef., Saints.
  Seductive beauty. SAINTSBURY, Hist. Eng. Lit., II., p. 42.
Seemly (IV.): Put., Webbe.
  Seemely simplicity. WEBBE, p. 53.
Selection (XXIII): S. John. to present.

I. Until within the first few decades of the present century, selection denoted an intellectual choice, a more or less logical severity, leading to condensation and accuracy.

> Young's poetry . . . abounds in thought, but without much accuracy or selection. S. JOHNSON, VIII., p. 461.
> Crabbe's great selection and condensation of expression. JEFFREY, II., p. 276.

II. During the latter portion of the present century selection has indicated an instinctive and æsthetic appropriation of certain possible elements in the construction of literature, leading to its elevation and perhaps to its idealization.

> Your historian with absolutely truthful intention . . . must needs select, and in selecting assert something of his own humour, something that comes not of the world without, but of a vision within. PATER, Ap., p. 5.
> A passionate selection of those facts that are representative of the highest (and also of the lowest) things. DOWDEN, St. in Lit., p. 285.

Self-assertive (XII.): Ros., Swin. Rossetti, Lives, p. 105.
Self-control (XIX.) *b*: Dowden, Tr. & St., p. 229.
Self-retarding: A self-retarding movement. M. ARNOLD, Cel. Lit., p. 206.
Self-withdrawal: Rossetti, Lives, p. 157.
Senile (XII.): Whip., Stephen. Whipple, Am. Lit., p. 264.
Sensational (XV.): T. Arnold to present.

Melo-drama, or what is generally called sensational writing. STE-
PHEN, I., pp. 222, 223.

Sense (XX.): Dry. to present.
What rhyme adds to the sweetness, it takes away from the sense.
DRYDEN, XIV., p. 212.

Sensibility (XV.): Jef. to present.

Sensible (XX.) *a*: Ascham to present.
Sensibly, pithily, bitingly. NEWTON, Spenser Society, XLIII.,
p. 3.

Sensual (XIV.): Hunt to present.
A poet is innocently sensuous when his mind permeates and illumines the senses; when they, on the other hand, muddy the mind, he becomes sensual. LOWELL, IV., p. 317.
The sensual fervours of Swinburne's earlier poems. DOWDEN, Tr. & St., p. 225.
Passion rises above the sensuous, certainly above the merely sensual, or it has no staying power. STEDMAN, Nat. & El. of Poetry, p. 262.

Sensuous (XV.): Mil., Low. to present.
Poetry . . . simple, sensuous, and passionate. MILTON, Mis., III., p. 473.
A wild, convulsed sensuousness in the poetry of the Middle Ages, in which the things of nature begin to play a strange, delirious part. PATER, Ap., p. 218.

Sententious: Har. to present.
A pithey and sententious proposition. T. WILSON, Rhet., p. 121.
The moral sententiousness of . . . Timon of Athens. HAZLITT, El. Lit., p. 46.
Antithetical and sententious to affectation. HALLAM, II., p. 295.

SENTIMENT (VI.).

Until the middle of the eighteenth century sentiment denoted any reflection or opinion concerning facts, or upon questions which from their nature are incapable of definite solution and exact statement. The word "sentiments" was uniformly employed to indicate the thoughts expressed by

As thought in general.

the characters of a drama, or of any other literary production, — thoughts which revealed character, and served as indices for action; which thus gave in a sense the ethical purpose, of which the plot development was the tangible outcome.

> Sentiment, — That whereby they in speaking prove anything or set forth an opinion. ARISTOTLE, Poetics, p. 21.
> Sentiment, — To it appertains all the effect that should be produced by the language, — proving and refutation, producing emotion, . . . and exaggerated or reduced ideas. ID., p. 59.
> When objects of any kind are first presented to the eye or imagination, the sentiment which attends them is obscured and confused. 1742. D. HUME, I., p. 274.
> Sentiments and understanding are easily varied by education and example. ID., p. 164.
> Sentiment is only a return upon ourselves. Ideas relate to objects outside of us. Their number occupying the mind enfeebles the sentiment. 1759. GIBBON, IV. p. 78.

In the latter portion of the eighteenth century sentiment was associated less with the thought of a literary production than formerly, and more with the mental imagery. Sentiment was thought to consist not so much in definite expressions as in the general tone of the literary work. Sentiment represented the contemplative attitude of mind attendant upon a somewhat intense and a continued form of æsthetic feeling. Sentiment, abstracted and followed for its own sake, was called sentimentalism. Sentiment itself was usually associated with passion and imagination, and was more or less under the influence of an ethical purpose. The term represents, however, at least in the present century, a conservative tendency in literature.

As pensive feeling.

It may be said to blend and modify the immediate æsthetic effect by means of past æsthetic effects. It is always pensive; it may even become conventional.

> Wordsworth was the first man who impregnated all his descriptions of external nature with sentiment or passion. 1818. WILSON, V., p. 402.
> Richardson's nature is always the nature of sentiment and reflection, not of impulse or situation. 1819. HAZLITT, Eng. Com. Writers, p. 160.
> A certain intenseness in the sentiment. 1820. ID., Age of El., p. 177.
> They affect sentiment and passion, which, divested of imagination, are other names for caprice and appetite. 1821. SHELLEY, VII., p. 117.
> Sentiment is a complex thing, the issue of sensibility and imagination; and without imagination sentiment is impossible. 1850. WHIPPLE, Lit. and Life, p. 288.
> State truths of sentiment, and do not try to prove them. (From Joubert.) M. ARNOLD, Cr. Es., 1st S., p. 286.
> Sentiment is intellectualized emotion, emotion precipitated, as it were, in pretty crystals by the fancy. 1867. LOWELL, II., p. 252.
> Wordsworth had much conventional sentiment. 1874. PATER, Ap., p. 38.
> Sentiment may be regarded as the synthesis of thought and feeling. T. ARNOLD, Hist. of Eng. Lit., p. 556.
> M. Coppée's poetry ... possesses sentiment, but hardly passion. DOWDEN, St. in Lit., p. 421.

Sentimental (XV.): Gold. to present.

I. Occasionally the term has designated a kind or species of dramatic composition.

> Sentimental Comedy, — in which the virtues of private life are exhibited rather than the vices exposed; and the distresses rather than the faults of mankind make our interest in the piece. GOLDSMITH, I., p. 400.

II. Occasionally, also, the term represents a fulness or richness of sentiment, not necessarily to be regarded as a literary fault or blemish.

> Sentimental and expressive metaphor. T. WARTON, p. 661.
> Sentimental, — always ready to react against the despotism of fact. M. ARNOLD, Cel. Lit., p. 77.

III. Usually, however, — during the present century almost uniformly, — the sentimental has indicated an excess of sentiment, a failure thoroughly to assimilate or fathom the subject-matter of literature, to see and feel it in all its relations: and hence a lack of balance between the sensuous and the more rational powers of the mind; the rule of the sensuous, — of mere sensibility and feeling, — in matters where reason ought to hold sway; the narrowing of æsthetic feeling to the immediate impression, and the most elementary sense of contrast, thus basing it upon primitive sensation rather than regarding it as the culmination of all the normal activities of the mind.

> Unless seasoned and purified by humour, sensibility is apt to run wild; will readily corrupt into disease, falsehood, and, in one word, sentimentality. CARLYLE, I., p. 14.
> Carlyle's innate love of the picturesque . . . is only another form of the sentimentalism he so scoffs at. LOWELL, II., p. 92.
> A laudable subjectivity dwells in naturalness, — the lyrical force of genuine emotions, including those animated by the zeitgeist of one's own day. All other kinds degenerate into sentimentalism. STEDMAN, Nat. of Poetry, pp. 142, 143.

Serene (XIX.): Hume to present.
> Pathetic yet august serenity. DOWDEN, Shak., etc., p. 380.

Serious (XIV.): Put., Jef. to present.
> Chaucer lacks the high seriousness of the great classics. M. ARNOLD, Cr. Es., 2d S., p. 34.

Severe (XIX.) *b*; Dry. to present.

A HISTORY OF ENGLISH CRITICAL TERMS. 275

The term "severe" represents a union of strength and definiteness. The strength must be restrained and regulated; the definiteness manifests itself in the general conception or design of the literary work, in the use of language, in the mental imagery employed, in the logical construction, and in accuracy to the facts represented.

 Virgil and Horace, the severest writers of the severest age. DRYDEN, V., p. 116.
 Severity of thoughtfulness. GOLDSMITH, IV., p. 378.
 No Greek severity, no defined outline. BAGEHOT, I., p. 73.
 Keats entirely fails of Milton's nervous severity of phrase. LOWELL, IV., p. 86.
 Severity and purity of the style. T. ARNOLD, p. 382.
 The spirit of . . . Antony and Cleopatra . . . is essentially severe. That is to say, Shakespeare is faithful to the fact. DOWDEN, Shak., etc., p. 308.

Shallow: De Quin. to present. Swinburne, Es. & St., p. 170.
Shambling: Vicar of Wakefield . . . is shambling. GOSSE, Hist. Eng. Lit., p. 349.
Shapeless (II.): Wil. Swinburne, Es. & St., p. 86.
Sharp (XX.) *b*: Camden to present.
 Freshness and sharpness. JEFFREY, I., p. 392.
 Bright sharp strokes. SWINBURNE, Es. & St., p. 16.
 Sharp and delicate. GOSSE, From Shak. etc., p. 188.
Sharply-cut: Sharply-cut dialogue. GOSSE, Life of Congreve, p. 35.
Shining (V.): Dry., Jef.
 Exquisite and shining passages. JEFFREY, II., p. 92.
Short: Wil. to present.
 Sudden, short, and strong. WILSON, VIII., p. 17.
Showy (V.): Haz. to present.
 Showy, Asiatic redundancy. HAZLITT, Sp. of A., p. 204.
Shrewd (XX.) *b*: M. Arn. to present. Saintsbury, Hist. Fr. Lit., p. 195.
Shrill (X.): Shrill, monotonous treble . . . of Waller. GOSSE, From Shak., etc., p. 156.

Shuffling (XVIII.): Haz., Saints.
    Shuffling anapœst. SAINTSBURY, Hist. Eng. Lit., II., p. 61.
Sickly (XIV.): Swinburne, Mis., p. 82.
Significant (XVI.): Put. to present.
Silly (XX.): Jef. to present.
    Distinguished silliness. WILSON, VI., p. 126.
Simpering: This simpering style . . . of 1660–1700. GOSSE, From Shak., etc., p. 223.
Simpleness (XX.): Cole., Swin.
    A downwright simpleness under the affectation of simplicity. COLERIDGE, IV., p. 196.
Simplicité: The real quality . . . the French call simplicité, the semblance simplesse. M. ARNOLD, Cel. Lit., p. 289.
SIMPLICITY (III.).

The history of the term "simplicity" may be divided into four periods. Until the middle of the seventeenth century simplicity indicated a sincere directness of conception in the author, unelaborated methods of composition, and unity of effect in the reader.

As a unified conception and impression.

    Simple, naïve, sincere. 1585. PUTTENHAM, pp. 67, 68.
    (Of Spenser.) . . . In all seemely simplicity, of handling his matter and framing his words. 1586. WEBBE, p. 53.

From about the middle of the seventeenth to within the latter portion of the eighteenth century, simplicity indicated a formal unity of design and construction in the composition, brought about by a refined method of selecting and arranging both the language and the thought,—a method so refined that it concealed its own artifice. The Greek Parthenon, the sober coloring and severe outlines of classic architecture, gave the general image and idea which controlled the use of the term during this period. Sim-

As a constructed unity.

plicity was placed in opposition to the subtle and fine, to conceit and the quaintness of wit, to Gothic ornaments, epigrammatical conceits, turns, points, and quibbles, to the "artificial and the fanciful," to "affectation" and "extraneous ornament," and to the "distorted and unnatural."

> The simple manner, which, being the strictest imitation of nature, should of right be the completest in the distribution of its parts and symmetry of its whole, is yet so far from making any ostentation of method, that it conceals the artifice as much as possible; endeavoring only to express the effect of art under the appearance of the greatest ease and negligence. SHAFTESBURY, I., p. 202.
>
> Much less ought the low phrases and terms of art that are adapted to husbandry have any place in such a work as the Georgiac, which is not to appear in the natural simplicity and nakedness of its subject, but in the pleasantest dress that poetry can bestow on it. ADDISON, I., p. 158.
>
> The sentiments of Chevy Chase . . . are extremely natural and poetical, and full of the majestic simplicity which we admire in the greatest of the ancient poets. 1710. ID., II., p. 384.
>
> The great beauty of Homer's language consists in a noble simplicity, and yet his diction, contrary to what one would imagine consistent with simplicity, is at the same time very copious. 1708. POPE, VI., p. 13.
>
> Simplicity passes for dullness, when it is not accompanied with great elegance and propriety. 1742. D. HUME, I., p. 243.
>
> Poetry cannot dwell upon the minuter distinctions by which one species differs from another, without departing from that simplicity of grandeur which fills the imagination. 1750. S. JOHNSON, II., p. 178.

From near the middle of the eighteenth century until within the first few decades of the present century, simplicity in composition was thought to be derived entirely from the unity of literary impulse or incentive in the mind of the author. The

As a unity of artistic impulse.

literary expression of this unified incentive, when formally or intellectually considered, might seem to be quite intricate and complex; yet the emotional effect upon the reader was supposed to be always a counterpart of the original inspiration and conception in the mind of the author.

> Judge of the Faery Queen by the classic models, and you are shocked with its disorder: consider it with an eye to its Gothic original, and you find it regular. The unity and simplicity of the former are more complete: but the latter has that sort of unity and simplicity which results from its nature. 1762. HURD, IV., p. 279.
>
> Dryden . . . had so little sensibility of the power of effusions purely natural that he did not esteem them in others. Simplicity gave him no pleasure. 1781. S. JOHNSON, VII., p. 340.
>
> Cultivate simplicity; banish elaborateness; for simplicity springs spontaneous from the heart, and carries into daylight its own modest buds, and genuine, sweet, and clear flowers of expression. 1796. LAMB, Letters, I., p. 46.
>
> The unconscious simplicity of nature. 1820. HAZLITT, Age of El., p. 96.
>
> Rugged simplicity. 1828. CARLYLE, II., p. 11.

During the latter portion of the present century more attention has been given to the formal expression of the literary conception. The genuineness of the author's incentive has often been held in question. Simplicity borders closely upon "simpleness," "the ordinary," "commonness," "vulgarity," "baldness," and "poverty of language." Nothing is simple which essentially contradicts the facts of actual experience. Simplicity usually indicates an immediate perception or intuition, as it were, of truth and

As unity of conception and directness of statement.

reality, and its most direct and unelaborated expression in language, — occasionally it denotes also a unity of emotional effect.

> The characteristic of the classical literature is the simplicity with which the imagination appears in it. 1856. BAGEHOT, Lit. St., I., p. 118.
> The direct intelligence of simple reason. 1872. SWINBURNE, Es. & St., p. 28.
> Simple, natural, and honest. HOWELLS, Crit. & Fiction.
> Statuesquely simple. 1872. LOWELL, IV., p. 232.
> Kingsley . . . tried with too obvious an effort to be simple and unaffected. 1879. STEPHEN, Hrs. in a Lib., p. 408.
> This simplicity at first hand is a strange contrast to the sought out simplicity of Wordsworth. 1883. PATER, Ap., p. 222.
> The train of passion which the common movement of these various actions calls out in the sympathy of the reader is as simple as the plot itself is intricate. 1885. MOULTON, Shak. as a D. A., p. 208.

SINCERE (VII.).

The term "sincere" has been much in use during the present century. It is aimed chiefly at false ornament and over-refinement in style, and it represents a union, so to speak, of moral incentive and power of artistic expression. Art must be not only spontaneous, but it must be spontaneous with an inherent ethical purpose. Literature must represent life not only as it has been, but also as it is and will be: literature expresses ideals, which control action; literature is thus an expression and controlling influence of real life, and sincerity is the first prerequisite in its production.

> Simple, naïve, sincere. 1585. PUTTENHAM, pp. 64, 68.
> Pope was incapable of a sincere thought or a sincere emotion. 1851. DE QUINCEY, XI., p. 125.

The beauty of Milton's sonnets is their sincerity. 1819. Hazlitt, Table Talk, p. 242.
The sincerity and directness of the British taste. 1840. De Quincey, X., p. 141.
Lack of sincerity is always lack of truth. 1892. Stedman, Nat. of Poetry, p. 233.

Sinewy (XII.): B. Jon. to present.
There be some styles again that have not less blood, but less flesh and corpulence. These are bony and sinewey. B. Jonson, p. 66.

Sing-song (II.): Sing-song of Collins' generation. Lowell, IV., p. 4.

Singular (IX.): Jef. to present.
Singular though beautiful style. Jeffrey, II., p. 54.
The truth is that all genius implies originality, and sometimes uncontrollable singularity. De Quincey, XI., p. 351.

Sinuous (II.): Lamb, Swin. Lamb, Letters, II., p. 79.

Skill (V.) *b*: Camden to present.
Skill, variety, efficacy, and sweetness, the four material points required in a poet. Camden, p. 337.
That skill in the conduct of the scene ... which is the result of art. Hurd, I., p. 350.

Skipping (XVIII.): Light skipping verse. Saintsbury, Hist. Fr. Lit., p. 164.

Slack (XII): Slackness and deviations ... of Faery Queene. Saintsbury, Hist. Eng. Lit., II., p. 95.

Slangy (I.): Saintsbury, Hist. Eng. Lit., II., p. 48.

Slight: Homely, genial, and slight. Gosse, Life of Congreve, p. 140.

Slipper (XVIII.): Put., Brooke.
Sounds most flowing and slipper upon the tongue. Puttenham, p. 129.
Slippered wording. Brooke, Tennyson, p. 62.

Slipshod (XVIII.): Swin. to present. Saintsbury, Es. in Eng. Lit., p. 57.

Slovenly (XIX.): Gold. to present.
A slovenly sort of versification. Goldsmith, V., p. 160.

Slow (XVIII.): Put., B. Jon. to present.
Of all Shakespeare's plays, Macbeth is the most rapid, Hamlet the slowest in movement. Coleridge, IV., p. 133.

Sly: Jef. to present.
    Sly humour. SAINTSBURY, Es. in Eng. Lit., p. 329.
Smart (V.)*b*: Gold. to present.
    Skill and smartness. JEFFREY, I., p. 164.
Smiting: Smiting, clashing sound. BROOKE, Tennyson, p. 389.
Smooth (X.): Camden to present.
    In any smooth English verse of ten syllables, there is naturally a pause at the fourth, fifth, or sixth syllable. POPE, VI., p. 57.
    Massinger's verse is smooth rather than melodious; the thoughts are not born in music, but mechanically set to a tune. WHIPPLE, Lit. of Age of El., p. 183.
Sober (XIX.)*b*: Scott to present.
    Exactness and sobriety . . . of Virgil. SCOTT, Life of Dryden, p. 348.
Soft (X.): Dry. to present. In considerable use.
    Some passages are beautiful by being sublime; others by being soft. ADDISON, III., p. 283.
Solecism (I.): Dry. to present.
Solemn (XIV.): Put. to present.
    Solemnity and stateliness are Milton's chief characteristics. LANDOR, V., p. 561.
Solid (XIII.): T. War. to present. Swinburne, Es. & St., p. 308.
Sombre (XIV.): Car. to present.
    Sombre beauties. SWINBURNE, Es. & St., p. 303.
Sonorous (X.): Dry. to present.
    Sonorous, high, and pompous strain. SHAFTESBURY, I., p. 200.
Soul (XXII.)*b*: Wil., M. Arn.
    Your fact or observation is not literature until it is put in some sort of relation to the soul. BURROUGHS, Indoor Studies, p. 232.
    The union of soul with intellect. M. ARNOLD, Cr. Es., 1st S., p. 301.
    Soul as opposed to mind in style . . . soul securing colour, as mind secures form. PATER, Ap., etc., p. 23.
Sounding (X.): Dry. to present.
    The sounding strain. WILSON, VIII., p. 41.
Spacious (XI.): Low. to present.
    Spacious style . . . of Spenser. LOWELL, IV., p. 307.

The Ancient Mariner has . . . breadth and space. SWINBURNE, Es. & St. p. 264.

Sparkling: Haz. to present.
Sparkling archaisms. HAZLITT, Sp. of Age, p. 145.

Spasmodic (II.): Whip., Saints. Whipple, Es. & Rev., II., p. 19.

Spirit (XII.): Mil. to present. Much in use.

I. Tone; manner; atmosphere.

Style and spirit. HAZLITT, Age of El., p. 119.

II. Life; feeling; inner principle.

To give to universally received truths a pathos and a spirit, which shall readmit them into the soul like revelations of the moment. WORDSWORTH, II., p. 63.

Spiritual (XXII.) *b*: Words. to present.
So spiritualized as to be above their sympathies WILSON, VII., p. 297.
Style being a visible emblem of spiritual traits. STEDMAN, Vic. Poets, p. 481.

Splendid (XXII.) *b*: S. John. to present.
Addison's style is splendid without being gaudy. BLAIR, Rhet., p. 209.

Splendor (V.): S. John. to present.
Splendor of elegance. S. JOHNSON, VII., p. 452.

Spontaneous (VII.) : Cole. to present. Much in use.

The significance of the term is chiefly negative. The spontaneous is that which is not imitated or elaborated, which is not attained by means of conscious design or method. As to the positive significance of the term, during the first portion of the present century, the spontaneous was usually assumed to result only from impulse, feeling, and emotion; during the latter portion of the century, there has been recognized a spontaneity of intellect and even of taste.

Simplicity springs spontaneous from the heart, and carries into daylight its own modest buds, and genuine, sweet, and clear flowers of expression. LAMB, Letters, I., p. 46.

Taste, however responsive to cultivation, is inborn, — as spontaneous as insight. STEDMAN, Nat. of Poetry, p. 47.

Arnold's . . . intellectual processes are spontaneous. ID., Vic. Poets, p. 91.

Sportive (XVII.): Sid., Chau. to present. Dowden, Tr. & St., p. 278.

Sprightly (XVIII.): S. John. to present.
Sprightliness of poetry . . . clearness of prose. S. JOHNSON, VII., p. 63.

Springy: Rapid and springy. LOWELL, I., p. 294.

Spurious (VIII.); Ros. to present. Dowden, St. in Lit., p. 40.

Squalid: Whipple, Lit. of Age of El., p. 247.

Stable (XI.): Hal., Ros.
Stable or tangible sense. ROSSETTI, Pref. to Blake, p. cxxii.

Stagnant (XII.): Jef., Swin. Jeffrey, I., p. 415.

Staid (XI.): Staid and serious. DOWDEN, Tr. & St., p. 278.

Stale (IX.): Stale uncleanliness. SWINBURNE, Mis., p. 86.

Startling (IX.): Jeffrey, I., p. 266.

Stately (XI.): Sid. to present.

I. As graceful massiveness, dignity, and poise.

The stateliness of style removed from the rude skill of common ears. 1557. SURREY, in Lit Centuria, I., p. 246.

Gorboduc . . . is full of stately speeches and well-sounding phrases. SIDNEY, p. 47.

Stately march of hexameters. T. WARTON, p. 889.

II. As unwieldy massiveness, and dull rigidity.

A stiffness and stateliness and operoseness of style. BENTLEY, II., p. 84.

Cornelia is a model of stately dulness. SAINTSBURY, Hist. Eng. Lit., p. 74.

Statuesque (XIX.) *b*: Cole. to present. (See **Sculpturesque**.)
Ancient art was . . . statuesque, modern, picturesque. COLERIDGE, IV., p. 58.

Steady (XI.): Jef. to present. Jeffrey, I., p. 163.
Sterile (XVI.): Ros. to present.
    Art severed from a social faith becomes, sooner or later, sterile. DOWDEN, St. in Lit., p. 424.
Stiff (XVIII.): Rymer to present.
    Stiff and Gothic. RYMER, 2d Pt., p. 78.
Stilted (VII.): Gosse, From Shak. etc., p. 86.
Stinging (XXII.) *b*: Vigorous, stinging . . . lines. ROSSETTI, Lives, p. 186.
Stirring (XII.): T. Arn. to present. Stedman, Vic. Poets, p. 69.
Stormy (XII.): Stormy and impulsive poems. WHIPPLE, Es. & Rev., p. 294.
Straight: Ascham, Spenser.
    Straight, fast, and temperate style. ASCHAM, III., p. 204.
    Your artificial straightness of verse. SPENSER to Harvey, p. 36.
Straight-forward: Wil. to present. In considerable use.
    The straight-forward and strong simplicity of nature and truth. WILSON, VI., p. 120.
    Classic straightforwardness. SWINBURNE, A St. of B. J., p. 20.
Strained (XII.): Put. to present.
    Without strain or parade. ROSSETTI, Lives, p. 391.
Strange (IX.): Scott to present.
    Full of beauty and strangeness. DOWDEN, Tr. & St., p. 230.
STRENGTH (XII.): Dry. to present.

Strength in composition results from the use of simple monosyllabic words, representing images which are vivid and familiar rather than refined and rare; and from the most unelaborated methods of logical construction. The term has almost uniformly been associated with the Gothic, with feeling, and with passion rather than with the more intellectual characteristics of literature.

    Recent writers . . . elegant and glaring, Shakespeare . . strong and solemn. POPE, X., p. 549.
    A clear expression belongs to the understanding, a strong expression to the passions. BURKE, p. 180.

And glut thyself with what thy womb devours. (Milton.)
It is incredible how many disgusting images Milton indulges in. In his age, and a century earlier, it was called strength. LANDOR, IV., p. 515.

In the storm and stress period in Germany . . . beauty seemed synonymous with strength. CARLYLE, I., p. 58.

Strenuous (XII.): Swin. to present. Swinburne, Mis., p. 369.
Stress (XII.): Intensity . . . and . . . stress. DOWDEN, St. in Lit., p. 275.
Strict: Ruskin.
A strict and succinct style is that where you can take away nothing without loss. B. JONSON, Timber, p. 62.
Striking (IX.): S. John. to present. Hallam, Lit. Hist., I., p. 433.
Studied (VII.): J. War. to present.
Stumbling (XVIII.): Stumbling stanzas. SWINBURNE, Mis., p. 76.
Stupid (XX.) *b*: Gray to present. J. Wilson, VI., p. 284.
STYLE: Low. to present.

I. An ornament or external glitter designed to render the work striking and effective.

Style . . . an ornament adapted to vulgar tastes. ARISTOTLE, Rhet., p. 204.

II. A habit or method of writing acquired either by effort or without design.

Style is a constant and continual phrase or tenor of speaking and writing . . . such as he either keepeth by skill, or holdeth on by ignorance. PUTTENHAM, p. 162.

III. During the latter portion of the present century, "style" has become an active critical term. It represents the literary or artistic personality of the author, permeating the thought and expression of the literary work and thus rendering its general "tone" or "atmosphere" a direct reflection of the æsthetic sense of the writer.

Style . . . the establishment of a perfect mutual understanding between the worker and his material. LOWELL, III., p. 37.

Style . . . consists mainly in the absence of undue emphasis and exaggeration, in the clear uniform pitch which penetrates our interest and retains it. ID., p. 353.

That fine effluence of the whole artistic nature which can hardly be analyzed and which we term style. DOWDEN, St. in Lit., p. 192.

The common and erroneous idea of style as the dress of thought, and the true definition of it as the incarnation of thought. SAINTSBURY, Es. in Eng. Lit., pp. 335, 336.

Style is what a sentient being, when he tries to imitate, cannot help adding to the thing he renders. SYMONDS, Es., Sp. & Sug., p. 146.

Suavity (XXII.) *b*: Scott to present.

Suavity and grace. GOSSE, From Shak., etc., p. 186.

Subdued (XIX.) *b*: J. War. to present.

Subdued passion. POE, I., p. 304.

Subjective: Whip. to present.

Elizabethan style is . . . subjective rather than objective. STEDMAN, Vic. Poets, p. 47.

SUBLIME (XI.).

Until within the eighteenth century the sublime was thought to consist of bold figures of speech, a series

As bold figurative language.

of metaphors, which seemed in fancy to annihilate space and time, to bring things far apart together, and thus to violate "nature" and the well known experiences of actual life. With their attention centred upon the language of literature, the early critics considered the sublime as something either to be avoided or to be subordinated to more regulated methods of composition.

Nothing is truly sublime that is not just and proper. 1681. DRYDEN, VI., p. 407.

To write thus upon low subjects is really the true sublime of ridicule; it is the sublime of Don Quixote. 1726. POPE, VIII., p. 219.

Too true it is that while a plain and direct road is paved to their ὕψος or sublime, etc. ... The sublime of nature is the sky, the sun, moon, stars, etc. SWIFT, XIII., p. 32.

It is easy to imagine that, amidst the several styles and manners of discourse or writing, the easiest attained and earliest practised was the miraculous, the pompous, or what we generally call the sublime. SHAFTESBURY, I., p. 190.

The eighteenth century was a period of transition from this grammatical view of the "sublime" to the modern conception of the term. The term "sublime" referred chiefly to the thought of the composition. *As bold picturesque thought and imagery.* The thought must be impressive and striking; it must stir up in the mind of the reader a sort of passive excitation and surprise. In the philosophy of the eighteenth century, the sublime was traced to ideas of pain, themselves pleasurable, with an accompanying paralysis of energy. In actual criticism the sublime was almost synonymous with the pathetic, as the pathetic was then understood. (See "Pathetic.") The sublime represented a certain compass and vividness of thought, and sometimes of imagery, the outlines of which were often definitely marked, which did not usually reach out by suggestion toward the unknown and infinite, and which did not stand over, as it were, against the reader himself, and call out his reactive impulses. The sublime was a fascination and a pleasure, and the pleasure often sprang as much from the evident skill in execution as from the thought which was represented.

> Nor is it sufficient for an Epic poem to be filled with such thoughts as are natural, unless it abound also with such as are sublime. 1711. ADDISON, III., pp. 186, 187.
>
> Whatever is fitted in any sort to excite the ideas of pain and danger, that is to say, whatever is in any sort terrible, or is conversant about terrible objects, or operates in a manner analogous to terror, is a source of the sublime. 1756. BURKE, I., p. 74.
>
> Those feelings are delightful when we have an idea of pain and danger without being actually in such circumstances. ID., p. 84.
>
> The sublime and the pathetic are the two chief nerves of all genuine poesy. What is there transcendentally sublime or pathetic in Pope? 1756. J. WARTON, I., p. vi.
>
> > My fancy form'd thee of angelic kind,
> > Some emanation of the all-beauteous mind.
> > How oft when press'd to marriage have I said,
> > Curse on all laws but those which love has made. (Pope.)
>
> This is . . . poetical and even sublime. ID., p. 306.
>
> Paradise Lost sometimes descends to the elegant, but its characteristic quality is sublimity. S. JOHNSON, VII., p. 131.

During the present century — and to a certain extent during the latter portion of the century preceding — the term "sublime" has represented not vividness of immediate impression so much as suggestion of what lies beyond the immediate impression. There must be indefiniteness, obscurity, and mystery of some kind, and this must stir the deepest latencies of the intellectual powers. The thoughts and images represented must be directly related to the most central interests of human life; they must be imbued with passion; they must in some manner be typical of the highest and most intense activity of which the human mind is capable. Occasionally this is attained by the representation of little more

As supreme power, magnitude, and suggestion.

than mere physical power, but more usually by suggesting and calling forth the very highest ethical ideals and purposes.

> The sublime must come unsought, if it come at all; and be the natural offspring of a strong imagination. BLAIR, Rhet., p. 47.
> Greek art is beautiful . . . but Gothic art is sublime. 1810. COLERIDGE, IV., p. 235.
> It is the nature of thought to be indefinite; definiteness belongs to external imagery alone. Hence it is that the sense of sublimity arises, not from the sight of an outward object, but from the beholder's reflection upon it; not from sensuous impression, but from the imaginative reflex. ID., p. 146.
> The kind of sublimity with which the English have always been chiefly delighted, consists merely in an exhibition of the strength of the human energies . . . e. g. Coriolanus, Richard the Third, Satan in Paradise Lost, etc. 1810. WILSON, V., p. 393.
> The terrific is sublime only when it fixes you in the midst of all your energies, and not when it weakens, nauseates, and repels you. 1826. LANDOR, IV., p. 442.
> Sublimity is Hebrew by birth. 1832. COLERIDGE, VI., 406.
> Let it be remembered that of all powers which act upon man through his intellectual nature, the very rarest is that which we moderns call the sublime. The Grecians had apparently no word for it, unless it were that which they meant by τὸ σεμνὸν: for ὕψος was a comprehensive expression for all the qualities which gave a character of life or animation to the composition, — such, even, as were philosophically opposed to the sublime. In the Roman poetry, and especially in Lucan, at times also in Juvenal, there is an exhibition of a moral sublime, perfectly distinct from anything known to the Greek poetry. 1839. DE QUINCEY, X., p. 400.
> So long as a man continues artificial, the sublime is a conscious absurdity to him. 1871. LOWELL, IV., p. 32.

Subtle (V.) *b*; cf. (XX.) *b*: Put. to present.

Delicate discrimination, springing from an unerring sense of native affinities and relations and the most penetrative intellectual acumen.

In Gower's inventions . . . is small subtlety. PUTTENHAM, p. 76.
Subtlety . . . nicety of distinction. S. JOHNSON, VII., p. 16.
Subtle adjustment of the elementary sounds, of words themselves to the image or feeling they convey. PATER, Ap., p. 57.

Succinct (XX.) *b*: Cam. to present. (See **Strict**.)
Sudden (IX.): Jef. to present. Swinburne, Es. & St., p. 65.
Sufficient: Sufficient and strong. SWINBURNE, Es. & St., p. 126.
Sugared: Sidney.

Heliodorus in his sugared invention. SIDNEY, p. 11.

SUGGESTIVE (XVI.).

The term "suggestive" has been prominent throughout the criticism of the present century. It is often mentioned in connection with the imagination, whose activity it in part represents. The term refers primarily to the sentiment and imagery immediately represented in the literary production. What this sentiment and imagery is suggestive of is usually left to be determined from each one's own interest and experience. In general, however, the suggestive denotes such a portrayal of details as by means of the association of ideas shall give glimpses into the depths of human character, shall fill the mind with a sense of the illimitable nature of thought and feeling, and shall perhaps awaken half-slumbering longings and ideals.

> Suggestion doth assign and direct us to certain marks or places, which may excite our mind to return and produce such knowledge as it hath formerly collected, to the end we may make use thereof. 1605. BACON, Ad. of L., p. 156. (Oxford, 1891.)
>
> Painting gives the object itself. . . . Poetry suggests what exists out of it in any manner connected with it. But this last is the proper province of the imagination. 1818. HAZLITT, Eng. Poets, p. 14.
>
> The most striking characteristic of the poetry of Milton is the extreme remoteness of the associations by means of which it acts

on the reader. Its effect is produced not so much by what it expresses as by what it suggests. 1825. MACAULAY, I., p. 22.

The truth is, painting and sculpture are literally imitative arts, while poetry is metaphorically so. . . . I would rather call poetry a suggestive art. 1825. BRYANT, Prose, I., p. 5.

Descriptive poets . . . forget that it is by suggestion, not cumulation, that profound impressions are made upon the imagination. 1868. LOWELL, III., p. 42.

In Measure for Measure . . . we have a real example of that sort of writing which is sometimes described as suggestive, and which by the help of certain subtly calculated hints only brings into distinct shape the reader's own half-developed imaginings. 1874. PATER, Ap., p. 179.

Suitable (IV.): Walton to present.
Strokes of levity . . . unsuited to so grave and majestic a poem. J. WARTON, I., p. 391.

Sumptuous (V.): Imaginative and sumptuous. ROSSETTI, Lives, p. 31.

Sunny (XIV.) Swin., Gosse.
Bright and sunny. GOSSE, Hist. Eng. Lit., p. 46.

Superb (XXII.) *a*: Wil., Swin., Gosse. Swinburne, Mis., p. 44.

Superficial (XX.): Gib. to present.
Sidney Smith's mirth lies in the superficial relations of phenomena. BAGEHOT, Lit. St., p. 136.

Superfluous: Ascham to present.
When superfluousness of words is not occasioned by overflowing animal spirits . . . there is no worse sign for a poet. HUNT, Im. & Fancy, p. 41.

Supple (XVIII.): Jef. to present. Jeffrey, II., p. 60.

Supreme (XXII.): Swinburne, Es. & St., p. 72.

Sure (VIII.): Hal. to present.
Sure facility . . . of Waller. HALLAM, IV., p. 233.

Shakespeare himself, divine as are his gifts, has not, of the marks of the master, this one: perfect sureness of hand in his style. Alone of English poets . . . Milton has it; he is our one . . . first rate master in the grand style. M. ARNOLD, Mixed Essays, p. 300.

Surging (XVIII.): Free, surging, melodious. ROSSETTI, Life of Keats, p. 179.

Sustained (XIII.): Jef. to present.
    Sustained and continuous. HAZLITT, Eng. Poets, p. 16.
Sweeping (XIII.): J. Wil. to present.
SWEET (X.): Cam. to present. Much in use.

I. Often the term "sweet" denotes the pleasing and attractive in composition attained through delicacy and tranquil feeling, rather than by any manifestation of strength in the thought or emotion.

    Raleigh's Cynthia . . . a fine and sweet invention. HARVEY, Malone's Shakespeare, II., p. 579.
    The uttering sweetly and properly the conceits of the mind . . . is the end of speech. SIDNEY, p. 55.
    Sweet expressions of love. WALTON, Lives, p. 121.

II. More usually, however, sweetness has direct reference to the sound, to the musical properties of the composition. Sweetness represents that which in the sound charms and attracts, a certain smoothness, a gentle rhythm, and a harmony unbroken by jar or discord.

    Harmonious sweetness. DRYDEN, VII, p. 229.
    Pope's versification is tiresome from its excessive sweetness and uniformity. HAZLITT, Eng. Poets, p. 18.
    Sweetness . . . a smooth progression between variety and sameness, and a voluptuous sense of the continuous. HUNT, Im. & Fancy, p. 37.
    Sweet and manifold in cadence. SAINTSBURY, Hist. Fr. Lit., p. 63.

Swelling (X.): Sid. to present.
    Swelling style. DRYDEN, VI., p. 407.
Swift (XVIII.): Campion to present.
    The verse moves swiftly enough. BROOKE, Tennyson, p. 114.
Symbolical (XVI.): External appearances . . . symbols of internal sentiment. HAZLITT, Eng. Poets, p. 31.

Symmetry (II.): Campion to present.
  Symmetry more than sensation is the effect which has an attraction for his genius. MOULTON, Shak., etc.
Sympathy (XV.): Jef. to present.
  A strange mixture of satire and sympathy in all Crabbe's productions. JEFFREY, II., p. 354.
  Sympathetic humor. BURROUGHS, Birds and Poets, p. 61.
  In Burns . . . a sympathy so vivid and intimate as to pass continually into the domain of imagination. ROSSETTI, Lives, p. 200.
Symphonical (X.): Swinburne, Es. & St. p. 11.
Systematic (II.): Systematic as a country cemetery. LOWELL, IV., p. 274.
Tact (V.) *b*: Jef. to present.
Talent (V.) *b*: S. John. to present.
Tame (XII.): Jef. to present.
  Tameness and poorness of the serious style of Addison and Swift. JEFFREY, I., p. 167.
Tangible (III.): Ros. to present.
  No stable or tangible sense. ROSSETTI, Pref. to Blake, p. cxxii.
  The pathos is more direct and tangible. SWINBURNE, Es. & St., p. 26.
Tardy (XVIII.): Jef., How.
  Tardy, laborious, and obscure. JEFFREY, II., p. 43.
TASTE (XXII.) *b*.

The term "taste" has always represented to a certain extent both native sensibility and an instinct which _{As a desire} has been acquired and cultivated by the _{for the novel and striking.} study of literature already written. Until the middle of the eighteenth century there were two uses of the term "taste." Often the term was employed to characterize a crude preference for the more glaring and startling features of literature, a perverse relish for literary work which was not in accord with the principles of literature already well established. This was usually characterized as "false" taste.

> Style seems to be an ornament adapted to vulgar tastes. ARISTOTLE, Rhet., p. 204.
>
> A wrong artificial taste ... formed ... upon little fanciful authors and writers of epigram. 1710. ADDISON, II., p. 374.
>
> Those intrigues and adventures to which the romantic taste has confined modern tragedy. TICKELL, in Arber's Garner, VI., p. 520.

More often taste denoted the appreciation of literature in so far as it agreed with the most approved and most firmly established methods of literary composition. This was "true" taste, or merely taste without any qualifying adjective. Usually, however, both a "false" and a "true" taste were recognized and were kept distinct from each other.

As a cultivated sense of the proprieties.

> Metaphors must be constructed on principles of analogy (proportion), else they will be sure to appear in bad taste. ARISTOTLE, Rhet., p. 210.
>
> Taste is not to conform to the art, but the art to the taste. 1710. ADDISON, II., p. 292.
>
> A just taste cannot be obtained without the antecedent labour of criticism. SHAFTESBURY, III., pp. 114, 115.
>
> It is rare to meet with a man who has a just taste without a sound understanding. 1742. D. HUME, I., p. 278.
>
> Tastes unformed from the true relish of possibility, propriety, simplicity, and nature. 1756. J. WARTON, II., p. 21.
>
> Taste comes from two sources: —
>   1. Sensibility, — if lacking, one wants taste.
>   2. Judgment, — if lacking, one has bad taste. 1756. BURKE. p. 64.

During the present century there are also two uses of the term. Often it denotes the acquired feelings and instincts which prompt to a judgment of literature in accordance with literary principles already well established. *As conventional literary appreciation.* In this sense of the term, taste has almost uniformly been regarded as an inadequate test of the æsthetic value of a literary production. It is wholly conservative, and opposes all progressive literary tendencies.

> It is for the most part in our skill in manners, and in the observances of time and place, and of decency in general . . . that what is called taste . . . consists, and which is in reality no other than a more refined judgment. 1756. BURKE, I., p. 63.
>
> Every author, as far as he is great and at the same time original, has had the task of creating the taste by which he is to be enjoyed. 1802. WORDSWORTH, II., p. 125.
>
> Proportion and congruity . . . are subjects upon which taste may be trusted, since . . . the mind is then passive. ID., p. 127.
>
> Taste . . . is representative of our past conscious reasonings, insights, and conclusions. 1817. COLERIDGE, III., p. 428.
>
> Classical taste and sound reason. 1838–39. HALLAM, II., pp. 23, 24.
>
> Good taste is an excellent thing when it confines itself to its own rightful province of the proprieties. 1871. LOWELL, IV., p. 21.
>
> Taste . . . is in reality condensed experience. . . . But the judicial attitude of mind is itself a barrier to appreciation, as being opposed to that delicacy of receptiveness which is a first condition of sensibility to impressions of literature and art. MOULTON, Shakespeare as a Dramatic Artist pp. 6, 7.

More often, perhaps, taste has represented both cultivated instinct and native sensibility, — sensibility which is open to impressions from actual life as well as from literature, and which is susceptible to new forms of beauty as well as to those which are already familiar. *As a cultivated, developing appreciation of literature.* Used in this sense, taste is the exact measure of the extent and limits of literary art at any given stage of its development.

> A strong imagination, the parent of what we call true taste. 1751. HURD, I., p. 282.
>
> The principal ingredient in the composition of taste is a natural sensibility. 1761. GOLDSMITH, I., p. 324.
>
> One . . . must have sensibility before he feels those emotions with which taste receives the impressions of beauty. 1761. GOLDSMITH, I., p. 327.
>
> Virtue and taste are built upon the same foundation of sensibility. ID., p. 331.
>
> Could we teach taste or genius by rules, they would be no longer taste and genius. J. REYNOLDS, I., p. 56.
>
> Taste is nothing but sensibility to the different degrees and kinds of excellence in the works of art or nature. 1819. HAZLITT, Sk. & Es., pp. 158, 159.
>
> I would reverse the rule, and estimate every one's pretensions to taste by the degree of their sensibility to the highest and most varied excellence. 1819. ID., p. 164.
>
> Taste relates to that which . . . is calculated to give pleasure. Now to know what is calculated to give pleasure, the way is to inquire what does give pleasure: so that taste is, after all, much more a matter of fact and less of theory than might be imagined. ID., p. 170.
>
> Taste is a sense to discern and a heart to love and reverence all beauty, order, goodness. 1827. CARLYLE, I., p. 34.
>
> Taste: a . . . noble sense of harmony and high poetic propriety. 1867. SWINBURNE, Es. & St., p. 141.
>
> Into the mind sensitive to "form," a flood of random sounds, colours, incidents, is ever penetrating from the world without, to become, by sympathetic selection, a part of its very structure, and in turn, the visible vesture and expression of that other world it sees so steadily within, nay, already, with a partial conformity thereto, to be refined, enlarged, corrected at a hundred points; and it is just there, just at those doubtful points,

that the function of style, as tact or taste, intervenes. 1888. PATER, Ap., pp. 28, 29.

The truth is that taste, however responsive to cultivation, is inborn, as spontaneous as insight, and indeed with an insight of its own. 1892. STEDMAN, Nat. of Poetry, p. 47.

Tautology (XIX.) *b*: Bentley to present. Swinburne, Es. & St., p. 188.

Tawdry (V.): Haz. to present.

Frivolous and tawdry ornament. MACAULAY, IV., p. 380.

Technical: Gib. to present.

The diapason closing full in man. (Dryden.)
"Diapason" is too technical. S. JOHNSON, VII., p. 324.

Technique: Sir Thomas Browne . . . stood in need of technique, of a formed taste in literature, of a literary architecture. PATER, Ap., etc., p. 130.

Tedious (XXII.) *b*: Gos. to present.

Avoid prolixity and tediousness. GASCOIGNE, pp. 39, 40.
The tedious historic style. CAMPBELL, I., p. 14.
Scott was often tediously analytic. HOWELLS, Crit. & Fiction, p. 21.

Tedium: Bombast and tedium. SAINTSBURY, Hist. Eng. Lit., p. 69.

Telling: Low., Gosse.

Original and telling in construction. GOSSE, Seventeenth Cent. St., p. 294.

TEMPERATE (XIX.) *b*: Ascham, Jef. to present.

The direct significance of the term is chiefly negative. Temperance is the absence of excess in any form. But it almost invariably denotes a moderation of passion or feeling, and thus it becomes associated with the judicious, with propriety, with all the terms that might be classified under the conception of the classical.

Temperance is a measuring of affections according to the will of reason. T. WILSON, Rhet., p. 38.
Temperance and propriety of all the delineations of passion. JEFFREY, I., p. 394.

Virgil . . . is temperate, chaste, judicious. LANDOR, III., p. 473.
Temperance of tone . . . makes The Deserted Village classical. LOWELL, IV., p. 370.
Tender: Dry. to present.
A delicacy and tenderness. DE QUINCEY, III., p. 37.
Tenuity: Tenuity and caprice. ROSSETTI, Pref. to Blake, p. cxxxi.
Terrible (XII.): Scott to present.
The tragic and the terrible. DOWDEN, Shak., etc., p. 23.
Terse (XIX.) *b*: Dekker to present.
Weight and terseness of his maxims. JEFFREY, II., p. 349.
Theatrical: Swin., Dow.
Theatrical observance of effect. SWINBURNE, Es. & St., p. 57.
Thin: Whip. to present.
Light and thin. WHIPPLE, Es. & Rev., II., p. 57.
Thoughtful (XX.): Whip. to present. Swinburne, Mis., p. 241.
Thrilling (XXII.)*b*: Swin., Gosse. Swinburne, A St. of B. J., p. 59.
Tightness: Tightness of phrase. GOSSE, Hist. Eng. Lit., III., p. 286.
Timid (XIV.): Jef. to present. Jeffrey, I., p. 45.
Tinsel (V.): Tinsel and embroidery. JEFFREY, I., p. 412.
Tiresome (XXII.) *b*: T. War. to present.
Tiresome harmony. STEPHEN, I., p. 135.
Titanic: A Titanic or Cyclopean style. SWINBURNE, Mis., p. 98.
Tone (XIII.): Jef. to present.
Tone, not words, is what distinguishes the master. LOWELL, III., p. 41.
Topographical: Gosse, From Shak., etc., p. 89.
Tormented: Homer's plain thought is tormented, as the French would say. M. ARNOLD, Cel. Lit., p. 166.
Tortuous (II.): Haz. to present.
Tortuous, long-winded verbosities. CARLYLE, II., p. 82.
Tortured (II.): J. War., Gosse.
Tortured, fantastical, rhetorical. GOSSE, Hist. Eng. Lit., III., p. 77.
Touching (XVII.) *b*: Blair to present.
Sweet and touching. JEFFREY, II., p. 464.
Tough: B. Jonson's tough diction. WHIPPLE, Es. & Rev., II., p. 33.

TRAGIC (XVII.) *b*: K. James to present.

I. As a purely classifying term, tragedy gradually became widely distinguished from comedy, giving rise to an intermediate form of the drama between them, tragi-comedy. (See " Comedy.") As thus employed, the tragic had no immediate critical significance.

> Tragedy represents men better than they are, comedy worse. ARISTOTLE, Rhet., p. 9.

II. Recently, the word has come somewhat into use as an active critical term, representing that which is both striking and strongly pathetic, which, by arousing the imagination and sympathies of the reader, reveals the profundity and sublimity of human character.

> Dante . . . did not understand by the tragic style what we understand by it, but merely the style of grand and sublime poems, such as the Æneid. T. ARNOLD, Hist. Eng. Lit., p. 498.
>
> Humour . . . united with his tragic and imaginative powers, makes Shakespeare. SAINTSBURY, Hist. Eng. Lit., p. 78.

Trailing (XVIII.): Heavy and trailing. M. ARNOLD, Cel. Lit., p. 147.

Transcendental: Low. to present.

In theory, the transcendental is that which can be represented only indirectly by means of symbols or by suggestion; that which completely surpasses adequate explanation or definition. In actual criticism it is usually associated with the vague and obscure.

> To the transcendentalist . . . the origin and existence of Nature is greatly simplified; the old hostility of matter is at an end, for matter is itself annihilated. CARLYLE, II., p. 205.
>
> All poetry must to a great extent be transcendental. WHIPPLE, Es. & Rev., p. 229.

Transcendental subtlety of "No, Time, thou shalt not boast that I do change," etc. LOWELL, III., p. 61.

The word transcendental may be used in both a definite and a vague sense; in a definite sense as opposed to the empirical way of thinking. . . . The transcendentalist thinker believes that the mind contributes to its own stores ideas or forms of thought not derived from experience. DOWDEN, St. in Lit., p. 47.

Transitory (XI.): Words., Ros. Wordsworth, II., p. 63.
Translucent (III.): Simple and translucent. STEDMAN, Vic. Poets, p. 54.
Transparent (III.): T. War. to present. Swinburne, Es. & St., p. 154.
Tremulous: Swinburne, Es. & St., p. 68.
Trenchant (XX.) *b*: Trenchant concision of style. SWINBURNE, Mis., p. 319.
Trite (IX.): J. War. to present.
In a court poem all should be trite and on an approved model. HAZLITT, Sp. of Age, p. 141.
Triumphant: Swinburne, Mis., p. 119.
Trivial (XI.): Dry. to present.
Too trivial and common to excite any emotion whatever. BRYANT, Prose, I., p. 13.
Tropical (XIX.) *b*: In the Religio Medici . . . are many things delivered rhetorically, many expressions therein merely tropical. 1635. Sir T. BROWNE, Intr. to Religio Medici.
Trumpet-notes: Swinburne, Mis., p. 147.
Trumpet-tones (X.): Ros. Dowden, Shak., etc., p. 81.
TRUTH (VIII.).

Until the latter portion of the eighteenth century the term "truth" usually represented something external *As historical* to the mind, something more or less histori-*fact.* cal in its nature. In this general use of the term, two special meanings are to be distinguished. Often truth was associated with probability, or was placed in opposition to fable or fiction. When thus employed, the term signified that which had actually occurred in the past, historical events considered externally, rather than as to their moral and psychical significance.

> But now it may be alleged that if this imagining of matters be so fit for the imagination, then must the historian needs surpass, who bringeth you images of true matters, such as indeed were done, and not such as fantastically or falsely may be suggested to have been done. 1583. SIDNEY, p. 18. (Cook.)
> The great art of poets is either the adorning and beautifying of truth, or the inventing pleasing and probable fictions. DRYDEN, XV., p. 408.
> For as truth is the bound of historical, so the resemblance of truth is the utmost limit of poetical liberty. 1650. HOBBES, IV., pp. 451, 452.
> We can always feel more than we can imagine, and . . . the most artful fiction must give way to truth. 1753. S. JOHNSON, IV., p. 79.
> Shakespeare's plots are generally borrowed from novels. . . . The mind which has feasted on the luxurious wonders of fiction, has no taste for the insipidity of truth. 1765. ID., V., p. 125.
> The portrait . . . has unrivalled force and beauty, with historic truth. 1820. HAZLITT, Age of El., p. 129.

Occasionally, however, even to the present, truth has denoted not something historical, but whatever exists at any given time, and can be considered as an actually ascertained fact. But external truth as an ascertained fact, and truth as a historical fact are almost identical with each other. The external fact, in order to be ascertained, must represent a completed experience, and has thus become historical. Hence it is often impossible to distinguish this use of the term "truth" from the preceding use.

As current fact.

> Natural, just, and true. RYMER, 2d Pt., p. 79.
> Poetry is the art of uniting pleasure with truth, by calling imagi-

nation to the help of reason. 1781. S. Johnson, VII., p. 125.

I cannot agree that this exactness of detail produces heaviness; on the contrary, it gives an appearance of truth. 1819. Hazlitt, Eng. Com. Writers, p. 159.

I confess that I do not care to judge any work of the imagination without first of all applying this test, Is it true? Howells, Crit. & Fiction, p. 99.

Since the latter portion of the eighteenth century truth has usually indicated some capacity or power of the mind. In the early portion of the present century truth very often represented the intuitive perception of beauty, the æsthetic apprehension of more essential relations in the ordinary events of experience than ordinary experience itself affords.

As æsthetic principle.

All beauty is truth. Shaftesbury, I., pp. 110, 111.
Not historically true, but poetically beautiful. 1756. J. Warton, I., p. 36.
In those species of poetry that address themselves to the heart, and would obtain their end, not through the imagination, but through the passions, there the liberty of transgressing nature is infinitely restrained; and poetical truth is, under these circumstances, almost as severe a thing as historical. 1762. Hurd, IV., p. 325.
What the imagination seizes as beauty must be truth, whether it existed before or not. 1817. Keats, Letters, pp. 41, 42.
To the genuine artist, truth, nature, and beauty are almost different names for the same thing. 1817. Hazlitt, Round Table, p. 106.
(Of Wordsworth.) The force, the originality, the absolute truth and identity with which he feels some things makes him indifferent to so many others. 1825. Id., Sp. of Age, p. 163.

During the present century truth has also denoted the ethical principles of conduct, the instincts and impulses which lead to right action. It is usually assumed, and often asserted, that æsthetic truth and moral truth are fundamentally one and the same; that the ethical impulse to do and the æsthetic impulse to create are, to a certain extent at least, identical with each other. The tendency to thus identify æsthetic with moral truth has been more pronounced during the latter portion of the century than during the earlier portion.

As moral principle.

> To give to universally received truths a pathos and spirit, which shall readmit them into the soul like revelations of the moment. 1811. WORDSWORTH, II., p. 63.
> Rescues admitted truths from the neglect caused by the very circumstance of their universal admission. 1825. COLERIDGE, I., p. 117.
> Moral truths which find an echo in our bosoms. 1825. BRYANT, I., p. 12.
> The poetry of Burns ... has, beyond all that ever was written, this greatest of all merits, intense, life-pervading, and life-breathing truth. 1841. WILSON, VII., p. 3.
> It is astonishing how large a harvest of new truths would be reaped simply through the accident of a man's feeling, or being made to feel more deeply than other men. 1845. DE QUINCEY, XI., p. 315.
> Truth to nature can be reached ideally, never historically; it must be a study from the life, and not from the scholiasts. 1866. LOWELL, Prose, II., p. 128.
> Your historian with absolutely truthful intention ... must needs select, and in selecting assert something of his own humour, something that comes not of the world without but of a vision within. 1888. PATER, Ap., p. 5.
> All beauty is in the long run only finesse of truth. ID., p. 6.
> There is no beauty worthy of the name without truth. J. A. SYMONDS, Es., Sp., & Sug., p. 104.

Tumid (XIX.) *b*: T. War. to present.
> Ridiculously tumid. S. JOHNSON, VIII., p. 210.

Tuneful (X.): Swin. to present. Saintsbury, Es. in Eng. Lit., p. 219.
Tuneless (X.): Swinburne, Mis., p. 224.
Turbid (II.): Lan. to present. Swinburne, Es. & St., p. 65.
Turgid (X.): S. John. to present.
 There is nothing turgid in his dignity. S. JOHNSON, III., pp. 83, 84.
Turn: Words. to present.
 Dramatic turn of plot. WORDSWORTH, III., p. 303.
Ugly (XXII.) *b*: Ugliness and coarseness. GOSSE, From Shak., etc., p. 178.
Uncertain (III.): S. John. to present. Saintsbury, Es. in Eng. Lit., p. 287.
Unconscious (VII.): Jef. to present.
 Composed, calm, unconscious. JEFFREY, I., p. 225.

UNDERSTANDING (XX.).

The word has perhaps never been employed as an active critical term. It has, however, exercised a considerable schematizing influence over active critical terms, being considered as an ally, and in a sense as the source of taste, of proportion, and of external propriety. It has been placed in opposition occasionally to reason, and always to the imagination. The word has not been in much favor with the critics during the present century.

> It is rare to meet with a man who has a just taste without a sound understanding. HUME, I., p. 278.
> Whenever the wisdom of our Creator intended that we should be affected with anything . . . he endued it with powers and properties that prevent the understanding, and even the will; which, seizing upon the senses and imagination, captivate the soul before the understanding is ready either to join with them or to oppose them. BURKE.
> Enthusiasm sublimates the understanding into the imagination. LOWELL, Lat. Lit. Es., I., p. 196.

Unearthly: Mac., Whip.
  Wild, weird, unearthly. WHIPPLE, Am. Lit., p. 87.
Unexpected (IX.): J. War. to present.
  Wit discloses . . . some unexpected resemblance or connection. HUNT, Wit and Humour, p. 8.
Ungainly (II.): Mor. Saintsbury, Hist. Eng. Lit., II., p. 155.
Unhewn (II.): Rough and unhewn plots. SWINBURNE, Es. & St., p. 283.
Unicity (XIII.): Saintsbury, Hist. Eng. Lit., p. 291.
Uniform (II.): Dry. to present.
  There is no uniformity in the design of Spenser. DRYDEN, XIII., p. 17.
  The uniformity of cadence may conspire with the lusciousness of style to produce a sense of satiety in the reader. HALLAM, II., p. 196.
  The needful qualities for a fit prose are regularity, uniformity, precision, balance. M. ARNOLD, Cr. Es., 2d S., p. 39.
Unique (IX.): Jef. to present.
  Swift is unique and inimitable. JEFFREY, I., p. 168.
UNITY (XIII.).

Previous to the present century the term "unity" was employed in criticism chiefly to denote certain formal rules and methods of plot construc- *As continuity of scenic* tion. The action represented must be based *effect.* upon a single story or fable; the scene of the action must not be changed; and the time included in the representation must be confined as nearly as possible to a single day of twenty-four hours. These rules, however, were always put upon the defensive in English criticism. The best dramatists did not conform to them. This use of the term had more influence in theoretical discussion than it had in actual criticism.

  Unity: requires emphasis of the general plot. DRYDEN, XIII., p. 109.

> The old Scotch ballad Child Maurice is divine. Aristotle's best rules are observed in it in a manner that shews the author never had heard of Aristotle. It begins in the fifth act of the play. You may read it two thirds through without guessing what it is about; and yet when you come to the end, it is impossible not to understand the whole story. 1758. GRAY, II., p. 316.
>
> The Faery Queen . . . has that sort of unity and simplicity which results from its nature. 1762. HURD, IV., p. 279.
>
> The unity of action . . . is often found in Gothic fables. ID., p. 308.
>
> The unity of action: The soul seeks it in all fiction and in all truth. 1831. WILSON, VIII., p. 397.
>
> The "Unities" inapplicable to modern subjective literature. ID., pp. 402-4.

Occasionally during the latter portion of the eighteenth century, and during all of the present century, As continuity of thought and feeling. the term "unity" has represented an activity in the mind either of the author or of the reader; if in the mind of the author, the unifying principle is the imagination; if in the mind of the reader, the unity is one of mental impression, of emotional effect. But whether referring to the active creation of literature, or to its more passive appreciation, unity is never regarded as depending upon formal regularity within the composition itself. Unity represents an imaginative blending of the different parts of a composition with one another,—a continuity of thought and feeling.

> Instead of unity of action, I much prefer the words homogeneity, proportionateness, and totality of interest. 1810. COLERIDGE, IV., p. 110.
>
> Lamb . . . had more sympathy with imagination where it gathers into the intense focus of passionate phrase, than with that higher form of it where it is the faculty that shapes, gives unity of design, and balanced gravitation of parts. 1868. LOWELL, III., p. 30.

In these later plays, unity is present through the virtue of one living force, which animates the whole. The unity is not merely structural but vital. DOWDEN, Shak., p. 60.

That a play should impress itself upon our minds as a unity is only another way of saying that it is a work of art: it is a different thing when this impression of unity seems to be analysable, and can be wholly or partially formulated in words. 1885. MOULTON, Shak. as a Dramatic Artist, p. 276.

Just there in that vivid single impression left on the mind when all is over, not in any mechanical limitation of time and place, is the secret of the "unities"—the true imaginative unity—of the drama. 1889. PATER, Ap., p. 212.

Unshackled: Free and unshackled movement. SAINTSBURY, Hist. Eng. Lit., p. 301.

Unwieldy (XVIII.): J. Wil. to present.
Clumsy and unwieldy. WILSON, VI., p. 123.

Upright: Swinburne.
Manful, straightforward, and upright. SWINBURNE, A St. of B. J., p. 107.

Urbanity (V.): Dry. to present.
Urbanity ... a style of speaking which exhibits in the choice of words, in tone, and in manner, a certain taste of the city, and a tincture of erudition derived from conversation with the learned; something, in a word, of which rusticity is the reverse. QUINTILIAN, VI., p. 433.

His urbanity, that is, his good manners, are to be commended. DRYDEN, XIII., p. 88.

Dr. Newman's works are stamped throughout with a literary quality very rare in this country, urbanity ... the tone of the city, of the centre, the tone which always aims at a spiritual and intellectual effect, and not excluding the use of banter, never disjoins banter itself from politeness, from felicity. M. ARNOLD, Cr. Es., 1st S., pp. 60, 67.

Vacuity: Hal., Swin. Swinburne, Chapman, p. 92.

Vague (III.): Words. to present.
Vague, wordy. GOSSE, Seventeenth Cent. St., p. 8.

Vain (XIV.): A vain and verbose eloquence. SWINBURNE, Es. & St., p. 270.

Vapid (XII.): Mor., Gosse.
Full of vapid conceits. GOSSE, Life of Congreve, pp. 64, 65.
Vaporous: Shelley's poetry is often vaporous and unreal. DOWDEN, Tr. & St., p. 102.

VARIETY (IX.).

The term "variety" was much used by the critics previous to the present century. Variety was usually regarded as forming no real contradiction to order and regularity in literature. It represented, so to speak, a regulated method of apparently violating regularity, a means of avoiding complete uniformity and monotony. Nature was usually employed to illustrate the relations between variety and regularity, but nothing could be more methodic and orderly than nature as it was conceived of during the seventeenth and eighteenth centuries. There is found mentioned variety of language, of versification, of illustration, of figures of speech, of images, of sentiments, and of plot construction; but whether referring to any part of the composition, or whether referring to it as a whole, variety, it was usually asserted or assumed, was enclosed and controlled by an encompassing regularity.

As methodic irregularity.

> The order of the spheres ... variety of the seasons. 1579. GOSSON (Arber), p. 26.
> The recreations of his youth were poetry, in which he was so happy, as if nature and all her varieties had been made only to exercise his sharp wit and high fancy. 1640. WALTON, Lives, p. 53.
> Stanyhurst ... revived by his ragged quill such carterly variety:
>> Then did he make heaven's vault to rebound,
>> With rounce robble bobble,
>> Of ruffe raffe roaring,
>> With thick thwack thurly bouncing.
>>   1590. NASH, Lit. Cen., II., p. 241.

> Variety, as it is too often managed, is too often subject to breed distraction. 1679. DRYDEN, VI., pp. 133, 134.
> The genius of the English cannot bear too regular a play; we are given to variety. 1690. ID., VII., p. 313.
> In the end of the sentence, chiefest regard is to be had; because the fall of the sentence is most marked, and therefore, lest it fall out to be harsh and unpleasant both to the mind and ear, there must be most variety and change. . . . Now this change must not be above six syllables from the end, and that must be set down in feet of two syllables. HOBBES, VI., p. 520.
> Triplets and Alexandrines, inserted by caprice, are interruptions of that constancy to which science aspires. And though the variety which they produce may very justly be desired, yet, to make our poetry exact, there ought to be some stated mode of admitting them. 1781. S. JOHNSON, VII., p. 347.

Occasionally, however, variety referred not so much to a quality of the composition as to a tendency of the mind. When thus employed, variety represented the overflow of native mental power and energy in literary composition, the assertion of the instinctive sense of form and method as against the rules and methods already established. This tendency toward change was sometimes characterized as "Gothic conceit," sometimes as "the exuberance of genius;" but so long as this change was expressed chiefly by means of the term "variety," it was not regarded with much favor in criticism.

As irregularity.

> And seek for that variety in his own ideas which the objects of sense cannot afford him. 1750. S. JOHNSON, II., p. 30.
> There is nothing more prejudicial to the grandeur of buildings than to abound in angles; a fault obvious in many; and owing to an inordinate thirst for variety, which, whenever it prevails, is sure to leave very little true taste. 1756. BURKE, I., p. 103.
> Shakespeare, to enrich his scene with that variety which his exuberant genius so largely supplied. 1749. HURD, I., p. 69.

The great source of pleasure is variety. Uniformity must tire at last though it be uniformity of excellence. We love to expect; and when expectation is disappointed or gratified, we want to be again expecting. 1781. S. Johnson, VII., p. 151.

Varnished (V.): Whip. to present.
Rhetorical varnish. Whipple, Es. & Rev., II., p. 76.

Vast (XI.): Haz. to present.
The thoughts are vast and irregular. Hazlitt, Age of El., p. 44.

Vaulting (XVIII.): Dowden.

Vehemence (XII.): T. Wil. to present.
Vehemence of words full often helps the matter forward. T. Wilson, Rhet., p. 140.
The affection arousing the mind excites a large stock of spirit and vehemence. Hume, I., p. 262.
More vehemence than truth, more heat than light. M. Arnold, Cr. Es., 1st S., p. 270.

Veracity (VIII.): Emerson, to present.
Veracity, the truthfulness to fact. Dowden, St. in Lit., p. 277.

Verbiage (XIX.) *b*: Poe to present.
Prolixity and verbiage. Saintsbury, Hist. Fr. Lit., p. 146.

Verbose (XIX.) *b*: Put. to present.
Long-winded verbosities. Carlyle, II., p. 82.

Verisimilitude (VIII.): Scott to present. (See **Truth**.)
Swift possessed the art of verisimilitude. 1814. Scott, Life of Swift, p. 457.
Verisimilitude or interest. Jeffrey, I., p. 211.
Historical verisimilitude. Dowden, Shak., etc., p. 262.

Vernacular (I.): Haz. to present.
Spenser . . . a deliberate estrangement from the vernacular, which is of itself a fault. Saintsbury, Hist. Eng. Lit., p. 93.

Versatile: Jef. to present.
Spontaneous versatility of genius. Swinburne, Mis., p. 32.

Verve (XII.): Dry. to present.
Verve, as the French call it. Dryden, XIV., p. 206.
Natural verve and imagination. Saintsbury, Hist. Fr. Lit., p. 212.
Much descriptive verve. Gosse, Seventeenth Cent. St.

Vicious (XIV.): Words. to present.
Flaccid, crude, and vicious. Gosse, From Shak., etc., p. 218.

VIGOUR (XII.).

The term "vigour" has been frequently employed throughout all English criticism, yet there are no definitely marked periods in its history. As applying to the language of a composition, vigour requires that it be simple and offer no difficulties to the ready comprehension of the thought, and that the sound, "tone colour," and nature of the words chosen be such as to be suggestive of movement and power. *As effectiveness of language.*

> The French set up purity for the standard of their language; a masculine vigour is that of ours. 1696. DRYDEN, XIV., p. 209.
>> This vault of air, this congregated ball,
>> Self-centred sun and stars, that rise and fall.
>
> This is vigorous. 1756. J. WARTON, II., p. 327.
> Simplicity, ease, and vigour. MACAULAY, IV., p. 80.
> Simple, vigorous, clear. LANDOR, III., p. 441.

As applying to the thought of a composition, vigour represents a strength of conception and vividness of portrayal which is the result of moral sincerity, of enthusiasm, of imagination, of passion, of some mental power other than mere intellect. *As power of thought.*

> The songs of Comus are vigorous and full of imagery. 1781. S. JOHNSON, VII., p. 124.
> The following quatrain is vigorous and animated: —
>> The ghosts of traitors from the bridge descend,
>> With bold fanatic spectres to rejoice, etc.
>>> ID., p. 321.
>
> Vigour and originality. COLERIDGE, III., p. 589.
> Fertility and vigour. ID., IV., p. 190.
> There was no freshness and no variety, and in the absence of variety and freshness that of vigour was necessarily implied. 1882. SAINTSBURY, Hist. Fr. Lit., p. 33.

Vigour reveals the tragedy of life. To one who exists languidly from day to day . . . the cross and passion of any human heart cannot be intelligible. . . . The heart must be all alive and sensitive before the imagination can conceive. DOWDEN, Shak., pp. 25, 26.

Vile (XIV.): Vile in taste. SWINBURNE, Mis., p. 92.
Violent (XII.): Pope to present. Pope, VII., p. 401.
Virile (XII.): Sted. to present.
Virile barytone quality. STEDMAN, Vic. Poets, p. 111.
Visionary (VIII.): Haz. to present. Hazlitt, El. Lit., p. 119.
Vital (VII.): Low. to present. Swinburne, Es. & St., p. 126.
Vivacious (XII.): S. John. to present.
Vivid (III.): Blair to present.
Spenser's descriptions are exceedingly vivid . . . not picturesque . . . but composed of a wondrous series of images, as in our dreams. COLERIDGE, IV., p. 249.
Vociferous: Stilted but not vociferous. GOSSE, From Shak., etc., p. 86.
Volatile (XVIII.): Lan., Gosse.
Volatile and sparkling. GOSSE, Hist. Eng. Lit., p. 67.
Volcanic: Volcanic style. SAINTSBURY, Hist. Fr. Lit., p. 575.
Voluble (XIX.) *b*; Campion to present.
Volubility and levity. S. JOHNSON, II., p. 447.
Volume (XIII.) *b*: Howells to present. M. Arnold, Cel. Lit., p. 292.
Voluptuous (XIV.): Camp. to present.
A voluptuous sense of the continuous. HUNT, Im. & Fancy, p. 37.

VULGAR (V.): Har. to present.

I. A lack of refinement, delicacy, and purity in the use of language, and in the expression of thought and emotion.

Gallicism or vulgarity. HALLAM, III., p. 374.
The vulgarity which is dead to form. PATER, Ap., p. 264.

II. Obscenity; an utter want of purity in the expression of feeling and emotion.

It is not fastidiousness, but manliness and good feeling, which are outraged by such vulgarities. DE QUINCEY, XI., p. 340.

Vulgarism (I.): Gold. to present. Landor, IV., p. 62.

Wandering (XVIII.): Jef. to present.
Interminable wanderings. JEFFREY, II., p. 373.

Wanton: Webbe, Add. to present.
Ovid in his most wanton books of love. WEBBE, p. 44.
There is a wantonness of diablerie in this incident. DOWDEN, Shak., etc., p. 186.

Warmth (XVIII.): Dry. to present.
Warmth of circumstance. BAGEHOT, I., p. 120.

Waspish (XIV.): Waspish sentiments. GOSSE, Life of Congreve, p. 28.

Wasteful: Jeffrey, II., p. 456.

Weak (XII.): Ascham to present.
The abuse of strength is harshness and heaviness; the reverse of it is weakness. HUNT, Im. & Fancy, p. 34.

Weighty (XI.): T. Wil. to present.
Milton condenses weight into heaviness. HUNT, Im. & Fancy, p. 47.

Weird: Poe to present. Gosse, Seventeenth Cent. St., p. 48.

Well-considered (XIX.) *b*: Gosse, Seventeenth Cent. St., p. 279.

Well-languaged: Well-languaged Daniel. WHIPPLE, El. Lit., p. 362.

Well-sounding (X.): Sidney, p. 47.

Whimsical (XIX.): Camp. to present. Gosse, Hist. Eng. Lit., III., p. 27.

Wholesome (XIV.): Lamb to present. Lowell, III., p. 270.

Width (XIII.) *b*: Swin., Saints. Swinburne, Es. & St., p. 161.

Wild (XIX.): Dry. to present. J. Warton. I., p. 8.

Wilful (XIX.): Jef. to present. Rossetti, Lives, p. 361.

Wire-drawn: Lengthy and wire-drawn. GOSSE, Hist. Eng. Lit., III., p. 250.

Wise (XX.) *a*: Sted. Swinburne, Es. & St., p. 19.

WIT (XXIII.).

Previous to the present century four general shades of meaning may be distinguished in the use of the term "wit." Wit, as indicating the general knowing power of the mind, did not come

As justness of thought.

into use as a critical term. But wit, as representing that portion of the knowing power which results in propriety of composition, is a common use of the term until the latter portion of the eighteenth century. Wit represented a sort of instinctive judgment which was wholly controlled by the sense of propriety and cultivated taste.

> Wit is a propriety of thoughts and words; or in other terms thoughts and words elegantly adapted to the subject. 1674. DRYDEN, V., p. 124.
>
> True wit may be defined as a justness of thought and a facility of expression. 1704. POPE, VI., p. 16.
>
> In the better notion of wit considered as propriety, surely method is necessary for perspicuity and harmony of parts. 1707. ID., p. 34.
>
> Wit seems to be one of those undetermined sounds to which we affix scarce any precise idea. It is something more than judgment, genius, taste, talent, penetration, grace, delicacy, and yet it partakes somewhat of each. It may be properly defined ingenious reason. 1759. GOLDSMITH, II., p. 356.
>
> Wit,—that which is at once natural and new, that which not obvious, is upon its first production acknowledged to be just. 1781. S. JOHNSON, VII., p. 15.
>
> It is apparent that wit has two meanings; and that what is wanted, though called wit, is, truly, judgment. 1781. ID., VIII., p. 241.

Until the latter portion of the eighteenth century the term "wit" was often employed as a more or less complete synonym for the imagination, as the imagination was then understood. Wit was the fundamental detection of resemblances, and the consequent power of making new combinations of thoughts and images. It was regarded as a mental

As fancy and imagination.

process rather than as a literary product. It was always native, often wayward, but when inspired with a purpose indicative of great power.

> The poet . . . lifted up with the vigor of his own invention doth grow in effect into another nature . . . freely ranging within the zodiac of his own wit. 1583. SIDNEY, p. 7.
> Wit is the faculty of imagination in the writer. 1666. DRYDEN, IX., pp. 95, 96.
> Jonson is the more correct poet, but Shakespeare is the greater wit. 1668. ID., XV., p. 347.
> Wit lies most in the assemblage of ideas, and putting those together with quickness and variety. (Quoted from Locke.) 1710. ADDISON, II., p. 357.
> Wit and passion are entirely incompatible. When the affections are moved, there is no place for the imagination. 1742. HUME, I., p. 242.
> No man can say Shakespeare ever had a fit subject for his wit, and did not then raise himself high above the rest of poets. 1765. S. JOHNSON, V., p. 153.
> It is no more to be required that wit should always be blazing than that the sun should always stand at noon. . . . Milton, when he has expatiated in the sky, may be allowed sometimes to revisit earth. 1781. ID., VII., p. 138.

During the eighteenth century the imagination in literature was chiefly confined to the production of ornaments and conceits. Wit, likewise, came *As an ornamented conceit.* to be regarded, at its worst, as something which falsified truth and violated simplicity for the sake of glitter and polish: at its best it was a play of fancy, which softened the rigid outlines of historical fact.

> Conceit is to nature what paint is to beauty. . . . There is a certain majesty in simplicity, which is far above all the quaintness of wit. 1706. POPE, VI., p. 51.

> Some to conceit alone their taste confine,
> And glitt'ring thoughts struck out at every line;
> Pleased with a work where nothing's just or fit,
> One glaring chaos and wild heap of wit.
> 1711. ID., II., p. 50.
>
> The mind, in perusing a work overstocked with wit, is fatigued and disgusted with the constant endeavor to shine and surprise. 1742. HUME, I., p. 241.
>
> Wit should be used with caution in works of dignity, as it is only at best an ornament. 1759. GOLDSMITH, II., p. 357.

As the comical.
The fourth use of the term "wit" is the one which, with some slight variation, has continued throughout the present century. Wit was distinguished from the judging power of the mind even in the beginning of English criticism. Wit furnished the materials for judgment; it was more instinctive; it was "sharpness of conceit" or of fancy, which always produced some combination of ideas or images more or less surprising to the judgment. When the surprise was very great, and the combination was seen at once to be merely the work of fancy, a sense of the comical was produced, which was called wit or humor. Hence wit, when denoting the comical, includes not only the primary activity of wit in revealing unexpected analogies and contrasts, but also the immediate reaction of the judgment against the momentary surprise and deception, occasioned by the apparent analogies and contrasts.

> His wit shall be new set on work; his judgment for right choice truly tried. ASCHAM, III., p. 169.
>
> Wit and acuteness of fancy. 1668. DRYDEN, XV., p. 351.
>
> Wit in the stricter sense, that is, sharpness of conceit. . . . Jon-

son was not free from the lowest and most grovelling kind of wit, which we call clenches. 1670. ID., IV., p. 237.

If wit be pleasantry, Ovid has it to excess. 1693. ID., XII., p. 62.

There is in Othello some burlesque, some humour and ramble of comical wit. RYMER, 2d Pt., p. 146.

We have seen in our time the decline and ruin of a false sort of wit. . . . All humour had something of the quibble. SHAFTESBURY, I., p. 48.

During the present century wit has been more closely defined both in its own nature and in its ethical relations. Wit, as such, has uniformly been considered as a spontaneous, and chiefly, if not wholly, intellectual process. When wit as such is merely used in the interest of some ethical purpose, it becomes satire. When the unexpected contrast or similarity surprises, and is reacted against, not so much by a fixed habit of judgment derived from the past, as by ideals which are projected into the future, then wit passes over into humor.

As the unsympathetic sense of the incongruous.

> Wit consists in presenting thoughts or images in an unusual connection with each other for the purpose of exciting pleasure by the surprise. This connection may be real; and there is in fact a scientific wit. . . . But usually the connection is only apparent and transitory, and may be by thoughts (Butler), by words (Voltaire), by images (Shakespeare); the latter usually called fancy. 1810. COLERIDGE, IV., p. 75.
>
> In such periods as that of Charles II., wit succeeds to humour; we laugh from self-complacency and triumph, instead of pleasure. 1821. SHELLEY, VII., p. 117.
>
> Whilst wit is a purely intellectual thing, into every act of the humorous mood there is an influx of the moral nature. 1821. DE QUINCEY, XI., p. 270.
>
> Horne Tooke . . . was a wit, and a formidable one: yet it may

be questioned whether his wit was anything more than an excess of his logical faculty: it did not consist in the play of fancy, but in close and cutting combinations of the understanding. 1825. HAZLITT, Sp. of Age, p. 80.

Humour is wit appertaining to character, and indulges in breadth of drollery rather than in play and brilliancy of point. 1826. LANDOR, IV., pp. 270, 271.

Voltaire's wit ranks essentially among the lowest species even of ridicule. It is at all times mere logical pleasantry; a gaiety of the head, not of the heart; there is scarcely a twinkle of humour in the whole of his numberless sallies. 1829. CARLYLE, II., p. 167.

The living spirit of wit, its poetic and imaginative power . . . never had a medium of expression comparable to the verse of Byron. 1869. SWINBURNE, Es. & St., p. 306.

The proper antithesis to humour is satire; wit is common to both. 1872. MINTO, Man. of Eng. Lit., p. 23.

Milton has flashes of wit, though not many; his indignation of itself sometimes makes him really sarcastic. But humorous he is never. SAINTSBURY, Hist. Eng. Lit., p. 324.

Witticism (XVII.): Dry. to present.
I have heard, says a critic, of anchovies dissolved in sauce; but never of an angel in hallelujahs. A mighty witticism (if you will pardon a new word). DRYDEN, V., p. 122.

Wooden (VII.): Conventional and wooden. SAINTSBURY, Es. in Eng. Lit., p. 347.

Wordy (XIX.) *b*: Jef. to present. Jeffrey, II., p. 404.

Yonkerly: Your Latin farewell is a goodly, brave, yonkerly piece of work. HARVEY, Letters, p. 24.

Youthfulness: Saintsbury, Hist. Fr. Lit., p. 208.

Zest (XV.): Stedman, Vic. Poets, p. 111.

APPENDIX.

THE HISTORICAL GROUPING OF THE TERMS.

IT will be recognized by even the most casual student of the history of criticism that certain general features of literary composition have at some times been emphasized more than at other times. Thus, speaking broadly, during the first century of English criticism the attention of the critics was occupied chiefly with the language and mechanical construction of literary composition, and also with a vague æsthetic sense of proportion and decorum; during the next century, with the thought or sentiment of literature, and also with a conservative æsthetic sense of fitness or propriety; then, for nearly a century, with the imagery of a composition, and also with a vigorous æsthetic sensibility and passion; and finally, for more than half a century, with the reality of a composition, its correspondence to actual life, and also with a refined æsthetic and artistic sensibility and feeling.

These conceptions or principles of literature and criticism, and such as these, as they have risen into prominence, have exerted an organizing influence over the entire critical vocabulary. Any critical term or principle which occupies for any length of time the foreground of attention compels other critical terms or principles to come into some sort of relation to it. By methods explained in the Introduction, by synonymous use, by contrast and by inclusion, critical terms thus historically organize themselves. *E. g.*: —

> Superseding Shakespeare's *wild* beauties and Milton's *ruggedness* by establishing the reign of *classic elegance, polish,* and *correctness.* (Quoted from "Extract Book.") T. Arnold, Man. of El. Lit., p. 306.

The following lists are intended to gather up the results of this historical grouping of terms, — a grouping which was controlled more or less by the immediate feeling for some concrete portion of literature rather than by an abstract theory of how the terms ought to be grouped. The lists are the result of much painstaking comparison as to the actual use of critical terms. The organizing conception for most of the groups is very evident in criticism. For historical reasons, however, many groups have been divided which could otherwise have been classified together. It has also been impossible to classify with any degree of accuracy many sporadic and figurative terms, whose critical significance has not as yet been definitely determined by their actual application to literature.

The first column of each list is composed of positive terms, those which represent some positive literary quality or characteristic; the second and third columns are composed of negative terms, those which deny the presence of the positive literary quality or characteristic. Some positive terms may have two negatives, one of "deficiency" and one of "excess." The terms denoting a deficiency of some literary quality are placed in the second column, those denoting an excess in the third column. The negative terms are usually to be considered, not so much as the direct opposite to any one positive term, as to the general conception represented by all the positive terms.

I. PURITY. CORRECTNESS. GRAMMATICAL.

Positive.	Deficient.	Excess.
Chaste.	Archaic.	Purism.
Clean.	Barbarism.	
Correct.	Colloquial.	
English.	Corrupt.	
Grammatical.	Gallic.	
Idiomatic.	Germanisms.	
Marble-pure.	Hebraism.	
Mot-propre.	Ink-horn.	
Pure.	Latinism.	
Vernacular.	Licentious.	
	Obsolete.	
	Provincial.	
	Slangy.	
	Solecism.	
	Vulgarism.	

Roger Ascham's "Scholemaster," written in 1557, was an innovation in more ways than one. It marks the beginning in England of pedagogical discussion, of a scholarly prose literature, and of criticism. The criticism which it contains is incidental to the pedagogical discussion of certain Latin authors, who are recommended for study. The prose style in which it is written gives constant evidence of the Latin influence; the separate words only are English; the Latin order and idiom are paramount. In fact, more than half a century after the publication of Ascham's "Scholemaster," Bacon, utterly distrusting the native tongue as a means of scholarly expression, wrote his Novum Organum in Latin. This overpowering influence of Latin scholarship in composition gradually gave way to the English idiom. But the process was a slow one. The native idiom was crude and unrefined, and the improvement of the language of literary composition was perhaps the most fundamental problem with which English criticism had to deal during the first century of its development.

II. ORDER. PROPORTION. REGULARITY.

Positive.	Deficient.		Excess.
Antithetical.	Amorphous.	Intricate.	Mannered.
Balanced.	Arabesque.	Invertebrate.	Monotony.
Consecutive.	Blundering.	Involved.	Sameness.
Equal.	Changeful.	Jagged.	Sing-song.
Even.	Chaotic.	Motley.	Uniformity.
Form.	Clumsy.	Perplexed.	
Methodic.	Complicated.	Rough.	
Order.	Confused.	Rough-hewn.	
Periodic.	Contorted.	Roundabout.	
Poised.	Convolution.	Scabrous.	
Proportion.	Crabbed.	Shapeless.	
Regular.	Crooked.	Sinuous.	
Symmetry.	Cumbrous.	Spasmodic.	
Systematic.	Distorted.	Straggling.	
	Eccentric.	Tortuous.	
	Erratic.	Tortured.	
	Fantastic.	Turbid.	
	Fitful.	Ungainly.	
	Inchoate.	Unhewn.	
	Insouciance.		

This list of terms refers to the methodic arrangement of the parts of a literary production, of the sounds, syllables, words, phrases, sentences, and occasionally of the plot or fable,—this methodic arrangement to take place perhaps to a certain extent in accordance with the native sense of harmony in the mind, but more usually in accordance with certain given rules of composition. Incidentally, the terms may indicate a sufficient logical arrangement of the argument or thought to avoid confusion or contradiction. Method in composition grew very largely out of the attempt to purify the language, and to elevate it by analogy with Greek and Roman literature; and hence most of the terms of the present list were in great favor during the first two centuries of English criticism.

III. PERSPICUITY. CLEARNESS. SIMPLICITY.

Positive.		*Deficient.*	
Clarity.	Pellucid.	Abstruse.	Inexplicable.
Clear.	Perspicacity.	Ambiguous.	Misty.
Clear-cut.	Perspicuous.	Cloudy.	Mystical.
Definable.	Photographic.	Complex.	Obscure.
Definite.	Pictorial.	Covert.	Opaque.
Distinct.	Plain.	Dark.	Puzzling.
Exact.	Precision.	Difficult.	Turbid.
Explicit.	Simple.	Dim.	Uncertain.
Graphic.	Tangible.	Hard.	Vague.
Intelligible.	Translucent.	Indefinable.	
Lucid.	Transparent.		
Luminous.	Vivid.		
Obvious.			

The terms of this list represent the general requirement that the language of a composition shall be so arranged that the reader may most readily and vividly comprehend the thought expressed. The terms designate a general result, which is produced by a complex multiplicity of means, and the history of the different terms is to be traced by indicating the general change which has taken place in the means by which this general result is thought to be best brought about. For this ready comprehension of the thought, the early English critics laid chief stress upon the choice of words and the grammatical construction of sentences. From about the middle of the seventeenth century to the middle of the eighteenth century, the logical arrangement of the sentences was considered as the chief means for attaining this ready comprehension of the thought. During the latter half of the eighteenth and the early portion of the present century, the chief emphasis was laid upon the distinctness and vividness of the mental imagery employed. But during the greater portion of the present century it has been very frequently recognized that the thought can be readily comprehended only in so far as it is truthful to the facts represented, as it corresponds to reality. Most of the terms of the list given above have been very perceptibly affected by this general change of view as to the method by which the thought could be most efficiently expressed in language.

IV. PROPRIETY.

Positive.		Deficient.	Excess.
Adaptation.	Fitness.	Anachronism.	Ceremonious.
Appropriate.	Happy.	Ancient.	Conventional.
Apt.	Keeping (in).	Antiquated.	Fastidious.
Becoming.	Meetely.	Barbarous.	Formality.
Choice.	Modern.	Effete.	Prudery.
Chosen.	Proper.	Far-fetched.	Prim.
Concinnity.	Propriety.	Ill-placed.	Mannerism.
Congruous.	Pertinent.	Incongruous.	Over-castigated.
Consentaneity.	Seasonable.	License.	Over-mannered.
Decent.	Seemly.	Pseudo-antique.	
Decorum.	Suitable.	Unseemly.	
Fashionable.	Well-chosen.		
Felicity.			

APPENDIX. 325

The general conception of this list of terms is the harmonious adaptation of the various characteristics of a composition to one another, — of the subject chosen, the language employed, the figures of speech, the sentiments, the characters, — especially their moral deportment, — all these to be in conformity with the nature of the audience addressed, and with the personal character of the author himself. In tracing the history of the different terms of the list, the chief interest arises from the change which has taken place in the means by which the fitness or adaptation of the different parts of a composition is determined; a secondary interest arises from the variation as regards the part of the composition to which the term especially refers. The terms were in greatest use during the seventeenth and eighteenth centuries.

V. ORNAMENT. ELEGANCE. COLOR.

Positive.		Deficient.	Excess.
(a.) Adorned.	Jaunty.	Bare.	Aniline.
Artifice.	Lambent.	Base.	Arabesque.
Bright.	Many-colored.	Blunt.	Dazzling.
Brilliant.	Monumental.	Coarse.	Elaborate.
Brocaded.	Neat.	Crude.	Embroidery.
Chiselled.	Nicety.	Dead-colored.	Finery.
Color.	Nobby.	Gross.	Finical.
Costly.	Ornament.	Homely.	Flamboyant.
Courteous.	Ornate.	Horse-play.	Flashy.
Courtly.	Point	Mean.	Floribund.
Decorative.	Polished.	Pale.	Florid.
Elegance.	Polite.	Pallid.	Flowery.
Embellished.	Quality.	Rude.	Frippery.
Figured.	Refinement.	Rugged.	Gaudy.
Finish.	Shining.	Rustic.	Glaring.
Gentleman-like.	Splendor.	Sombre.	Gorgeous.
Gentlemanly.	Urbanity.	Vulgar.	High-colored.
Glitter.	Varnished.		Meretricious.
Glossy.			Over-jewelled.

	Positive.		Deficient.	Excess.
(b.)	*Skill*, etc.			Over-shining.
	Ability.	Execution.	Abortive.	Painted.
	Accomplished.	Expert.		Parade.
	Adroit.	Skill.		Plebeian.
	Alacrity.	Smart.		Pretty.
	Artful.	Subtle.		Showy.
	Capacity.	Tact.		Sumptuous.
	Clever.	Talent.		Tawdry.
	Cunning.	Technique.		Tinsel.
	Dextrous.			

The terms of this list indicate in general such a selection of facts and such a method of expressing them as shall give evidence of brilliant fancy and cultured feeling. The facts selected must be capable of entering, as it were, into good society; they must not offend by their crudeness; they must conform to good usage. The language must be slightly heightened above what is necessary for a plain statement of the facts, but still it must not be heightened so much as to become "extravagant," "florid," or "rhetorical." The positive and active use of these terms in English criticism is confined chiefly to the seventeenth and eighteenth centuries.

VI. ANCIENT TECHNICAL TERMS.

Character.	*Ethos.*
Elocution.	Manners.
Eloquence.	Sentiment.

Many of the technical terms of the ancient critical vocabulary became active naturalized expressions in English criticism. A few terms, however, occurring usually in dramatic criticism, failed to assimilate, so to speak, with the vocabulary of English criticism. They have scarcely ever been employed as active critical terms, nor do they exercise much schematizing influence upon other terms. Still they have helped to shape the general lines of discussion in English criticism, even to the present time, and a brief account of the changes of meaning which have taken place in the use of these words is imperative.

VII. NATURE. NATURAL. SINCERE.

Positive.		Deficient.	
Artless.	Naïveté.	Affected.	Falsetto.
Effortless.	Native.	Artificial.	Far-sought.
Genuine.	Natural.	Bastard.	Forced.
Home-bred.	Nature.	Bookish.	Labored.
Home-spun.	Organic.	Cant.	Literary.
Honest.	Sincere.	Conceited.	Mechanical.
Ingenuous.	Spontaneous.	Conscious.	Morbid.
Instinctive.	Unconscious.	Dilettantesque.	Pedantic.
Living.	Vital.	Dissembled.	Stilted.
Naïve.		Excrementitious.	Studied.
		Exotic.	Wooden.
		Factitious.	

Whatever is not consciously elaborated is included in a more or less vague manner by the general conception of this list of terms. They represent the "twilight of the mind," the "fringe" of conscious life, that which seems to be given to man, to come unsought from without and from within. Hence these terms indicate, on the one hand, the most simple and primary native powers of the mind brought into play in the production of literature; on the other hand, they denote accuracy to the most simple and primary apprehension of external facts.

VIII. PROBABILITY. TRUTH. REALITY.

Positive.		Deficient.	
(a.) Accurate.	Historic.	Caricature.	False.
Actual.	Inevitable.	Deceit.	Fictitious.
Authentic.	Life-like.	Delusive.	Figurative.
Exact.	Plausible.	Disputable.	Heightened.
Faithful.	Possibility.	Exaggerated.	Histrionic.
Fidelity.	Probability.	Excessive.	Hyperbolical.

Positive.		Deficient.	
Real.	Truth-like.	Hypocrisy.	Questionable.
Realism.	Undeniable.	Incredible.	Spurious.
Reality.	Veracity.	Mendacious.	Visionary.
Sure.	Verisimilitude.	Metaphorical.	
Truth.		Paradoxical.	
(b.) Circumstantial.		Abstract.	
Concrete.		Generality.	
Detailed.			
Minute.			
Particular.			

The terms of this list denote whatever in actual life can be accepted as fact, whatever can be most depended upon, and is most permanent in the interests of any individual or of any number of individuals. "Fact" in criticism consists in whatever is considered as most essential for literary representation. Before the present century, when the dominant type of literature was the epic, fact was thought to be attained by accuracy to historical events. In the present century, when poetry is chiefly lyrical, fact is supposed to be represented by the thoughts and feelings with which lyrical poetry deals.

IX. VARIETY. NOVELTY. GOTHIC. ROMANTIC.

Positive.		Deficient.	Excess.
Bizarre.	Relief.	Common.	Monstrous.
Curious.	Romantic.	Commonplace.	
Distinction.	Singular.	Hackneyed.	
Extraordinary.	Startling.	Magazinish.	
Fresh.	Strange.	Old-fashioned.	
Gothic.	Striking.	Ordinary.	
Grotesque.	Sudden.	Stale.	
New.	Unexpected.	Trite.	
Novelty.	Unique.		
Odd.	Variety.		
Quaint.	Weird.		
Rare.	Wonderful.		

APPENDIX. 329

The early critics found it necessary to insist upon regularity in composition in order to counteract the native tendency of English writers toward variety and novelty. This sense of variety, of constant change, of the developing movement in literature, was strong in the beginning of English criticism, and it has grown stronger and stronger until the present time. It is this conception of constant change and development, viewed as to its most general manifestation both in the mind and in the composition, that is represented by the present list of terms.

X. HARMONY. RHYTHMICAL. MUSICAL.

Positive.		Deficient.
Alliteration.	Metrical.	Cacophonous.
Ambling.	Modulation.	Clang.
Antiphonal.	Monochordic.	Clangour.
Assonant.	Musical.	Clashing.
Barytone.	Numbers.	Discord.
Cadence.	Numerous.	Dissonance.
Canorous.	Organ-like.	Harsh.
Clarion-versed.	Resonance.	Hurtling.
Dactylic.	Rhythmical.	Jarring.
Euphonious.	Rolling.	Jingle.
Flute-like.	Smooth.	Jumping.
Harmony.	Soft.	Rattling.
Hymnal.	Sonorous.	Rumbling.
Intonation.	Sounding.	Shrill.
Lilting.	Spondaic.	Tuneless.
Limpid.	Sweet.	Turgid.
Liquid.	Swelling.	Wheezing.
Measured.	Symphonical.	
Mellifluous.	Trumpet-tone.	
Melody.	Tuneful.	
Melting.	Well-sounding.	

The terms of this list represent the simple principles of music which are made use of in the composition of literature,— the sense of rhythm and of harmony in sound. Previous to the present century the terms were referred for explanation chiefly to the composition itself; during the present century, to the mind of the author or reader.

XII. VIGOUR. ENERGY. FORCE.

Positive.	*Deficient.*	*Excess.*
Aggressive.	Abortive.	Audacity.
Ambitious.	Anti-climax.	Cut-and-thrust.
Animated.	Childish.	Ebullient.
Bold.	Effeminate.	Ferocious.
Cogent.	Effortless.	Fierce.
Daring.	Emasculate.	Fiery.
Emphatic.	Exhausted.	Furious.
Energy.	Feeble.	Impetuous.
Fearless.	Feminine.	Impulsive.
Fire.	Flaccid.	Intense.
Force.	Flat.	Intrepidity.
Full-blooded.	Inanity.	Rash.
Full-bodied.	Indolence.	Savage.
Hearty.	Infantile.	Stormy.
Life.	Insipid.	Strained.
Lively.	Jejune.	Terrible.
Lusty.	Languid.	Terrific.
Masculine.	Lax.	Tumultuous.
Momentum.	Meagre.	Vehement.
Muscular.	Mincing.	Violent.
Nervous.	Nerveless.	
Persistent.	Operoseness.	
Positive.	Otiose.	
Potent.	Paucity.	
Power.	Penury.	
Quick.	Platitude.	
Racy.	Poor.	
Resilient.	Poverty.	
Robust.	Puerile.	

Positive.	Deficient.
Sedulous.	Senile.
Self-assertive.	Slack.
Sinewy.	Stagnant.
Speed.	Tame.
Spirit.	Torpid.
Stirring.	Vapid.
Strength.	Weak.
Strenuous.	Weary.
Stress.	
Verve.	
Vigour	
Virile.	
Vivacious.	

The terms of this list were very prominent in English criticism from about the middle of the eighteenth century until within the early portion of the present century. Although the words do not have much history, which is peculiar to them as critical terms, their constant and frequent mention would seem to indicate that they must represent some fundamental artistic impulse or literary instinct of the mind.

XI. MAJESTY. DIGNITY. SUBLIMITY.

Positive.		Deficient.
(a.) August.	Heroic.	Babyish.
Cyclopean.	High.	Bathos.
Dense.	Immense.	Childish.
Dignity.	Imperial.	Drivelling.
Elevation.	Imposing.	Ephemeral.
Exalted.	Impressive.	Evanescent.
Firm.	Large.	Flippant.
Gigantic.	Lofty.	Frivolous.
Grand.	Magnificent.	Fugitive.
Grandeur.	Majestic.	Little.

Positive.		Deficient.
Massive.	Staid.	Niaiserie.
Might.	Stately.	Paltry.
Noble.	Steady.	Petty.
Oceanic.	Stolid.	Quibbling.
Ponderous.	Sublime.	Rubbishy.
Spacious.	Vast.	Transient.
Stable.	Weighty.	Transitory.
(b.) Abundance.	Copy.	Trifling.
Affluent.	Exuberance.	Trivial.
Ample.	Fulness.	
Amplitude.	Opulent.	
Copious.	Rich.	

There are few English critics who do not make their sense of power one of the chief means by which to test the merits of literary work. The subject must be so vividly conceived of by the author, and portrayed so effectively, that it shall seem to the reader to be a moving portion of real life. Thus, as to the drama, English taste required, not declamation concerning action, but action itself; in regard to descriptive poetry, it delights not in the immediate object so much as in the distant prospect, suggestive always of movement; and in poetry dealing with the states of the mind, it demands that the shades of character portrayed, however subtle they may be, shall be immediately related to the central interests of human life and human destiny. Now, energy may be represented as active at the time, or it may be represented, so to speak, as resisting itself, as self-contained, as displaying a vast capability of power without any immediate exercise of that power. These divisions of energy, which in philosophy and physics are known as dynamic and latent energy, are perhaps enough applicable to criticism to justify the classification of the terms denoting energy into two separate groups.

XIII. UNITY.

Positive.

Coherence.	Linked.
Compact.	Motive.
Complete.	Solid.
Connected.	Sustained.
Consistency.	Tone.
Continuity.	Unicity.
Fused.	Unity.
Homogeneous.	

Body.	Profound.
Breadth.	Range.
Compass.	Reach.
Comprehensive.	Scope.
Depth.	Sweeping.
Expansive.	Thorough.
Extensive.	Volume.
Grasp.	Width.

Deficient.

Abrupt.	Diverse.
Broken.	Eclectic.
Composite.	Excursive.
Digressive.	Indigested.
Disconnected.	Loose-jointed.
Discursive.	Loose-hung.
Disjointed.	Sketchy.

Limited.
Narrow.
Restricted.

The terms of this list are closely related on the one hand to the general conception of regularity, and on the other hand to those mental activities by means of which the unity of a literary production is apprehended and held in mind during the process of composition. In so far as the terms refer to regularity, they represent literary principles or features which are capable of exact definition, of being reduced to method and rule. In so far as the terms refer to mental activities, they are not capable of such exact definition. The general change of meaning in the terms has been from the standpoint of regularity to that of the psychical activities.

XIV. MORAL

Positive.		Deficient.	
Amenity.	Grave.	Acerbity.	Immoral.
Amiable.	Grim.	Acrid.	Indignant.
Candor.	Healthful.	Acrimony.	Insolence.
Catholic.	Human.	Asservity.	Levity.
Cheerful.	Innocence.	Bawdry.	Low.
Congenial.	Joyous.	Biting.	Obscene.
Conscientious.	Liberal.	Bitter.	Querulous.
Cordial.	Manly.	Carping.	Rancid.
Devout.	Melancholy.	Caustic.	Rancour.
Disinterested.	Moral.	Corrupt.	Ribald.
Earnest.	Pensive.	Cynical.	Sensual.
Ethical.	Plaintive.	Debased.	Servile.
Frank.	Sad.	Distrustful.	Sickly.
Gay.	Serious.	Egotistic.	Scurrilous.
Generous.	Solemn.	Far-grasping.	Vain.
Genial.	Sombre.	Fawning.	Vicious.
Gloomy.	Sunny.	Filthy.	Vile.
Good-tempered.	Timid.	Foul.	Voluptuous.
Gracious.	Tolerant.	Fulsome	Waspish.
Grateful.	Wholesome.	Ignoble	

There are very few critical terms which do not possess more or less ethical significance. The present list is composed of those terms the ethical significance of which is most immediate and direct. Literature, it is universally agreed, must not be immoral; but as to the manner in which it is to conduce to morality, there is no such universal agreement. Hence the unity of the present list is to be found in the negative rather than in the positive terms. It was near the beginning of the present century that morality and literature were first fundamentally identified with each other. This fact gives the historical setting for this list of terms.

XV. PASSION. IMPASSIONED. FEELING.

Positive.	*Deficient.*	*Excess.*
Affectionate.	Arctic.	Adolescent.
Amorous.	Austere.	Feverish.
Ardent.	Cold.	Flame.
Ardor.	Cold-blooded.	Frantic.
Ecstasy.	Dry.	Frenzy.
Emotion.	Frigid.	Hectic.
Enthusiastic.	Indifferent.	Hysterical.
Erotic.	Marble-cold.	Lachrymose.
Feeling.	Neutral.	Lascivious.
Fervent.	Scholastic.	Mawkish.
Fervors.		Namby-pamby.
Gusto.		Pothery.
Heat.		Prurient.
Impassioned.		Rabid.
Inspired.		Raving.
Passion.		Sensational.
Rapture.		Sensuous.
Sensibility.		Sentimental.
Sympathy.		
Warmth.		
Zest.		

The terms of this list are closely related to those denoting strength, morality, and æsthetic feeling. Æsthetic ideals continually become moral purposes, and from strength and persistency of impulse to realize these ideals and purposes there results passion or emotion, as it has usually been employed in criticism. In so far as the impulse receives emphasis, emotion or passion tends to become mere appetite. In so far as the ideal is emphasized, emotion becomes poetical, refined, artistic.

XVI. PICTURESQUE SUGGESTION.

Positive.		Deficient.
Allusive.	Pithey.	Arid.
Conspicuous.	Plentiful.	Bald.
Expressive.	Pregnant.	Barren.
Fecundity.	Prolific.	Naked.
Fertile.	Prophetic.	Sterile.
Fruitful.	Salient.	
Interpretative.	Significant.	
Latent.	Suggestive.	
Memorable.	Symbolical.	
Picturesque.		

The terms of this list represent in general the use of the association of ideas in the mind as the chief means of producing literary effects. The mind of the reader is filled more with a sense of what he does not directly see than of what he does. The author feels the depth and sincerity of human life, and with one masterly touch he strikes a chord which echoes far and wide within the realm of unexpressed memories, ideals, and longings. The immediate image becomes in a sense a symbol for the remote, the far-off, the mysterious. This reaching out of human thought toward the unlimited, the infinite, has been marked during the whole of the present century,— especially was it prominent during the early portion of the century.

XVII. PATHOS. HUMOR.

Positive.		Deficient.
Amusing.	Buffoonery.	Droll.
Archness.	Burlesque.	Dry.
Bon-mot.	Clench.	Dry-stick.

Positive.

Comical.	Repartee.
Cunning.	Ridiculous.
Cynical.	Salt.
Diverting.	Sarcastic.
Farcical.	Satire.
Humor.	Sportive.
Incongruous.	Witticism.
Irony.	
Ludicrous.	Affecting.
Mirth.	Moving.
Pleasantry.	Pathetic.
Poignant.	Touching.
Raillery.	Tragic.

The contrast between actual conditions and ideal possibilities gives rise to a feeling or "passion," which, during the present century, has been called pathos and humor, — pathos being relatively the more passive, humor the more active phase of the same sympathetic activity of the mind. Both terms, however, have an extended history, and were formerly used with meanings and relations quite other than those which they now possess. The terms of this list have their apparent unity in the simple feeling of the incongruous; they have their real unity in the idealizing tendencies, by means of which this feeling of the incongruous is rendered possible.

XVIII. EASY. RAPID. DIRECT.

Positive.		*Deficient.*	
Action.	Brisk.	Circuitous.	Constricted.
Airy.	Buoyant.	Club-footed.	Crabbed.
Blithe.	Crisp.	Constrained.	Creeping.

338 A HISTORY OF ENGLISH CRITICAL TERMS.

Positive.		Deficient.	
Currant.	Plastic.	Desultory.	Rambling.
Direct.	Playful.	Dragging.	Shuffling.
Ductile.	Pliant.	Embarrassed.	Slip-shod.
Ease.	Progression.	Flagging.	Slow.
Elastic.	Racy.	Floundering.	Sprawling.
Facility.	Rapid.	Halting.	Stiff.
Flexible.	Skipping.	Heavy.	Stumbling.
Flow.	Slipper.	Hobbling.	Tardy.
Fluent.	Sportive.	Lame.	Trailing.
Fluid.	Sprightly.	Limping.	Unwieldy.
Free.	Straight-forward.	Lumbering.	Wandering.
Leaping.	Supple.	Pedestrian.	
Light.	Surging.		
Lithe.	Swift.		
Motion.	Trippingly.		
Movement.	Vaulting.		
Nimble.	Volatile.		
Pert.			

The requirement of perspicuity and clearness in style, when joined with that of strength, or at least of movement, forms the general conception for the list of terms given above. Clearness as such, the mere desire of rendering the thought of a composition intelligible to others, may lead to loquacity and wordiness. The general conception of the present list of terms, however, assumes that the reader is, as it were, within the literary work itself; not waiting to be impressed by it, but actively participating in its movement, and demanding only that this movement shall not be unnecessarily retarded, whether from combinations of sound, from logical arrangement, from the flow of mental imagery, or from plot development.

XIX. CLASSICAL TEMPERANCE

Positive.		Deficient.	
Calm.	Abstinence.	Adventurous.	Effusive.
Equable.	Adequate.	Awkward.	Elliptical.
Equanimity.	Careful.	Blundering.	Extravagant.
Gentle.	Cautious.	Capricious.	Fustian.
Mild.	Chaste.	Careless.	Garrulity.
Placid.	Chastised.	Clownish.	Grandiloquent.
Quiet.	Classical.	Flighty.	Grandiose.
Repose.	Composed.	Hasty.	Grandity.
Sedate.	Guarded.	Hurried.	Gush.
Serene.	Moderation.	Inconstant.	Gusty.
Tranquil.	Modest.	Loud.	High-flown.
	Reserved.	Negligent.	Inflated.
	Restrained.	Restless.	Long-winded.
	Scrupulous.	Slovenly.	Loquacity.
	Sculpturesque.	Whimsical.	Luxuriant.
	Self-control.	Wild.	Magniloquence.
	Severe.	Wilful.	Noisy.
	Sober.		Oriental.
	Statuesque.		Ostentatious.
	Subdued.		Pomp.
	Temperate.		Pretentious.
	Well-considered.		Profuse.
			Prolix.
			Rant.
	Brevity.	Amplified.	Redundant.
	Compression.	Asiatic.	Rhetorical.
	Concentrated.	Bluster.	Superfluous.
	Concise.	Boisterous.	Tautological.
	Condensed.	Bombast.	Tropical.
	Laconic.	Brazen.	Tumid.
	Terse.	Declamatory.	Verbiage.
		Diffuse.	Verbose.
		Dilatation.	Voluble.
		Dilation.	Wordy.
		Dilution.	

The general conception of temperance or moderation in composition which this group of terms represents is intimately related to purity, regularity, clearness, and propriety. The most casual glance at the association of terms in the quotations given under the different terms of this list will make this fact evident. On the other hand, the general conception of temperance is connected in a scarcely less intimate manner with energy, power, and strength of style in a composition. The requirement is that this power in some manner be restrained. If the restraint is externally imposed, as it were, either immediately or mediately from custom and precedent, then temperance tends toward the proprieties. If the restraint is in a sense self-imposed, then temperance becomes dignity and grandeur.

XX. JUDICIOUS. INTELLECTUAL.

Positive.		Deficient.
Critical.	Reasonable.	Folly.
Good-sense.	Sense.	Foolish.
Instructive.	Sensible.	Nonsense.
Judicious.	Understanding.	Preposterous.
Just.	Wise.	Silly.
Rational.		Simpleness.
		Superficial.
Academic.	Logical.	Unmeaning.
Analytic.	Meditative.	
Brooding.	Philosophical.	Absurd.
Contemplative.	Reflective.	
Erudite.	Studious.	
Intellectual.	Thoughtful.	
Learned.		

Positive.		Deficient.
Acumen.	Pungent.	Dull.
Acute.	Sagacity.	Obtuse.
Cutting.	Sanity.	Stupid.
Discriminative.	Sharp.	
Edge.	Shrewd.	
Incisive.	Succinct.	
Keen.	Subtle.	
Penetrative.	Trenchant.	
Piercing.		

The use of intellectual and more or less logical terms in criticism was especially pronounced during the greater portion of the eighteenth century and during the latter portion of the present century. There is an important difference, however, in the nature of the intellectual terms employed during these two periods. In the eighteenth century the intellectual activities represented in criticism were chiefly deliberative,— such terms as "judicious" and "understanding" being in great favor. During the present century the intellectual terms which have been most employed in criticism represent native and unelaborated activities or capacities of the mind,— terms which either characterize the general mental temperament of the author as reflected in his work, or represent his native intellectual acuteness and penetration.

XXI. CLASSIFYING TERMS.

Allegorical.	Idyllic.
Bucolic.	Invective.
Choral.	Lyrical.
Comedy.	Narrative.
Didactic.	Panegyrical.
Dramatic.	Pastoral.
Elegiac.	Picaresque.
Epic.	Rhapsodical.
Farce.	Romance.

This list is composed of those terms which originally denoted certain forms or divisions of literature without any reference whatever to the critical significance of the different literary forms or divisions thus designated. But for reasons given in the Introduction it was impossible for these terms to preserve their critical neutrality. They have been used chiefly during the present century, and the numerous theoretical discussions relative to the "species" or divisions of literature have given these terms far more critical significance than they formerly possessed.

XXII. ÆSTHETIC TERMS.

I.—Mere Approval.

Positive.		Deficient.
Absolute.	Immortal.	Defective.
Admirable.	Impeccable.	Futile.
Adorable.	Inavertible.	
Brave.	Incomparable.	
Choice.	Inimitable.	
Commendable.	Marvelous.	
Competence.	Masterly.	
Conclusive.	Meritorious.	
Consummate.	Miraculous.	
Creditable.	Model.	
Distinguished.	Peerless.	
Effective.	Perfect.	
Eminent.	Readable.	
Excellent.	Sovereign.	
Exhaustive.	Speckless.	
Faultless.	Superb.	
Final.	Supreme.	
Flawless.	Typical.	
Great.	Unsurpassed.	

II.—ÆSTHETIC TERMS PROPER.

Positive.		Negative.
Aerial.	Fragrant.	Balderdash.
Æsthetic.	Graceful.	Brutish.
Affinity.	Handsome.	Cloying.
Agreeable.	Heavenly.	Detestable.
Airy.	Ineffable.	Doggerel.
Art.	Interesting.	Dreary.
Artistic.	Irresistible.	Empty.
Attractive.	Lovely.	Gibberish.
Beauty.	Luscious.	Gruesome.
Charm.	Magical.	Hideous.
Cogency.	Magnetic.	Horrible.
Comely.	Palpable.	Horrid.
Convincing.	Persuasive.	Impalpable.
Dainty.	Pleading.	Nauseous.
Delicate.	Pleasing.	Offensive.
Delicious.	Poetical.	Oppressive.
Delightful.	Redolent.	Philistinism.
Divine.	Seductive.	Prosaic.
Enchanting.	Soul.	Repulsive.
Engaging.	Spiritual.	Revolting.
Entertaining.	Splendid.	Tedious.
Ethereal.	Stimulating.	Tiresome.
Exquisite.	Stinging.	Ugly.
Facetious.	Suavity.	
Fascinating.	Taste.	
Fine.	Thrilling.	
Flavor.		

The terms which have been hitherto classified represent active qualities or principles, which tend to differentiate literature into its component parts, and to give to each part a more or less distinct valuation. The terms of the present list, on the contrary, tend to express the unified artistic effect which the literary work produces upon the mind of the reader. They indicate a complete acceptance of the literary work, or else they denote a complete rejection of it. No qualitative distinctions are set up. The æsthetic term as predicate, and the literary work as subject, are by definition coextensive and identical. In actual criticism, however, this identity is often by no means complete; and this variation, together with the changing limits of literary art itself, give the two points of view from which the history of the different terms may be traced.

XXIII. ELEMENTARY ARTISTIC TERMS.

Architectonics.	Imagination.
Conceit.	Imitation.
Constructive.	Ingenious.
Creative.	Insight.
Design.	Invention.
Device.	Mimetic.
Fancy.	Original.
Fantasy.	Selection.
Genius.	Wit.
Ideality.	

All critical terms, in so far as they are critical, except, perhaps, those of the preceding list, refer more or less directly to the active process of construction in composition, to the mental capacities by which any given form of literature is rendered possible. Many of these terms, however, do not refer to processes that are elementary. Thus, humor and pathos presuppose the exercise of the ideal making power of the mind. Many critical terms, also, such as "proportion" and "simplicity," are usually thought of as characterizing the literary work when considered as a completed product. Hence they tend to become more or less subject to fixed rules, by the application of which it is supposed the qualities of literature designated by the terms can always be attained. In this manner the process ceases to be elementary.

It is not claimed that the list of terms given above is a complete one, or even a representative one. After all the critical terms had been classified, as far as possible, according to their historical rise and development, certain terms remained, which represent some of the more primary activities of the mind that are brought into exercise in the production of literature. These terms constitute the present list, and in a sense they indicate the evolution of the fundamental artistic processes which has taken place during the different periods of English criticism.

www.ingramcontent.com/pod-product-compliance
Lightning Source LLC
Chambersburg PA
CBHW032355230426
43672CB00007B/708